Remaking the Godly Marriage

Remaking the Godly Marriage

Gender Negotiation in Evangelical Families

John P. Bartkowski

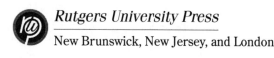

Rutgers University Press

New Brunswick, New Jersey, and London

Library of Congress Cataloging-in-Publication Data

Bartkowski, John P., 1966–
    Remaking the Godly marriage : gender negotiation in evangelical
families / John P. Bartkowski.
        p. cm.
    Includes bibliographical references and index.
    ISBN 0-8135-2918-2 (alk. paper)—ISBN 0-8135-2919-0 (pbk. : alk.
paper)
        1. Evangelicalism—United States—Case studies.   2. Sex role—
Religious aspects—Christianity—Case studies.   3. Family—Religious
aspects—Christianity—Case studies.   4. United States—Church
history—20th century—Case studies.   I. Title.

BR1642.U5 B37 2001
261 .8′343′0973—dc21

                                                                    00-045750

British Cataloging-in-Publication data for this book is available from the
British Library

Chapter 2 has previously been published in *The History of the Family,*
vol.3 (1998) under the title "Changing of the Gods: The Gender and
Family Discourse of American Evangelicalism in Historical Perspective."
Reprinted with permission of Elsevier Science.

A version of chapter 4 has appeared in *Journal of the Scientific Study of
Religion,* 36 (1997). With permission of the Society of the Scientific Study
of Religion.

Chapter 5 has previously been published in *Gender Issues* 17, 4 (1999)
under the title "One Step Forward, One Step Backward: Progressive
Traditionalism and the Negotiation of Domestic Labor within Evangelical
Families." Reprinted with permission of Transaction Publishers.

Manufactured in the United States of America

For Nicci

Contents

Preface

The account of evangelical gender and family relations rendered here is very different from the one I originally set out to write. When I embarked on this research, I had hoped to evaluate the gender beliefs and practices of evangelical spouses in light of the prescriptions found in best-selling conservative Protestant gender and family manuals. I had planned to combine analyses of primary and secondary survey data with ethnographic and in-depth interview data drawn from pastors and members at a growing evangelical church in a Texas metropolitan area. The project I envisioned would have given equal weight and equal space to these different methodologies in the hope of providing a well-rounded picture of evangelical spousal relations.

After spending a considerable amount of time analyzing the media culture of evangelicalism (specifically, conservative Protestant family advice manuals), I became increasingly aware of the utter inadequacy of the picture yielded by studying evangelical gender discourse as a seamless subcultural phenomenon collectively seeking to distance itself from secular American culture. As the following account reveals, there is a remarkable degree of heterogeneity within this religious subculture—so much diversity that the applicability to American evangelicalism of the singular term "subculture" could justifiably be challenged.

Ideological diversity and dramatic rhetorical shifts are clearly evidenced in the advice offered to evangelical couples via family manuals available in the thousands of Christian bookstores that now dot the American landscape.

The complexity of elite evangelical gender discourse has been given short shrift in previous research on conservative Protestant gender and family relations, much of which has focused instead on gender contradictions in the everyday lives of evangelical women. Inasmuch as confession is good for the soul, I must admit that the researcher who began this investigation was unprepared for the intensity, breadth, and practical significance of the family debates raging among elite evangelical Protestants. In light of the extensive attention that evangelical women have received thus far from scholars such as Judith Stacey, Susan Rose, Marie Griffith, and Brenda Brasher, I was far more prepared for the complexity and contradiction that emerged in everyday gender relations as I was conducting fieldwork at a prominent evangelical congregation in Texas.

Given the recent publication of such research on evangelical women, one might reasonably ask, "Why yet another book on gender within evangelical Protestantism?" First, as noted, the nuances and recent historical shifts marking elite evangelical gender and family discourse have virtually escaped sustained scholarly attention. Because I believe that language is a crucial site for cultural production and change, as well as a medium for shaping social experience, I devote three chapters of this book to discussing these debates and their evolution over the past three decades.

Second, this study departs from previous investigations in the way it conceptualizes and analyzes gender. I contend that an enriched understanding of gender negotiations among evangelical couples is more readily attained if we examine the social experiences of evangelical husbands and wives in tandem. This analytical approach reveals that evangelical men and women are both complicit in the ongoing production and negotiation of gender. I therefore seek to complement excellent ethnographic studies of evangelical women's experiences by exploring the collective negotiation of gender among conservative Protestant husbands and wives within the context of their marital relationships. While previous research on evangelical women did not go so far as to assume that evangelical men are mere conduits for the exercise of patriarchal power, a focus on evangelical women alone can inadvertently lend credibility to the erroneous assumption that men's participation in conservative religions is understandable, uninteresting, and unproblematic.

More recently, a small but growing body of scholarship has begun to examine in-depth interview data about gender ideals and practices culled from conservative Protestant men and women (Gallagher and Smith 1999; Smith 2000). While I applaud the insights gained by such path-breaking work, it is noteworthy that the male and female interview subjects in these studies are stand-alone respondents who are not married to one another. Such studies broaden our understanding of individual men's and women's experiences within evangelicalism. However, data of this sort do not permit an analysis of gender processes as they are negotiated within the context of an ongoing marital relationship and the broader milieu of shared congregational networks. Such is my task here.

Apart from these empirical and methodological considerations, this study seeks to bring new theoretical insights to bear on the topic at hand. To this end, I examine three configurations of gender—cathexis, power, labor—within evangelical family discourse and couples' households (cf. Connell 1987, 1995). Because gender and family relations within American evangelicalism remain highly contested, this study does not offer a finished account of its subject matter. Consequently, the question of women's place within the teaching structure of the Parkview Evangelical Free Church remains unresolved here—largely because such issues are not resolved within the congregation about which this story is told.

The account I offer is situated in the standpoint and experiences I brought to this research project. As a non-evangelical sociologist, I was initially somewhat intimidated by this foray into the field. It had been quite some time since I had darkened the doorstep of any church. Moreover, my parochial Catholic upbringing discouraged the drawing of fine-grained distinctions among the plethora of Protestant denominations, and my several years of graduate study left me with what might best be termed an intellectual familiarity with conservative Protestantism. Yet, as time passed, I became increasingly comfortable within this congregation and often found myself pondering, in a highly personal fashion, my subjects' commentary on family life. Indeed, my own family life was being tested at the time in the crucible of graduate school commitments and the dissertation grind.

In light of these factors, my churchgoing and emergent contacts in the field were inviting me to confront several uneasy questions: Was I being considerate of my own spouse's needs and honoring her wishes when disagreements arose within our relationship? Was my desire to obtain a doctorate in sociology and gain a professional foothold in a precarious academic job market interfering with my ability to cultivate a meaningful relationship with my young son? How could I become more aware of the impact my decisions (feminist in ideology, sometimes autocratic in practice) had on the other members in my family? In short, I found many thought-provoking themes in the sermons, Sunday school discussions, and Bible studies in which I was not only an observer but a participant of sorts. I pay my subjects the highest compliment, I think, in expressing my gratitude for the ways in which they broadened the moral horizons of a graduate researcher who was struggling to make sense of ethical issues—their issues and mine—on a number of different levels.

To the degree that this study was personally transformative, I similarly hope the portrait rendered here will call into question stereotypes of religious conservatives that still hold sway among many non-evangelicals. Preconceptions linking conservative Protestantism with authoritarianism were expressed to me during and even after this study by some of my closest colleagues and friends. Such individuals—whose commitment to the equalization of social opportunities for men and women I share—will find their assumptions about evangelical family life scrutinized here in a respectful yet critical fashion. Inasmuch as one of the unique contributions of sociological research is to call into question taken-for-granted assumptions about outgroups with whom we are personally unfamiliar, I hope that this study will challenge social researchers and non-evangelical laypersons to reexamine some of the preconceptions they may harbor about conservative Protestant family life. While that goal is perhaps a bit too ambitious, this study also aims to address significant contours of evangelical family life that have not attracted the attention they are due.

Acknowledgments

Although the refrain that no research project is ever a solo venture has prefaced many academic books, there is more than a grain of truth in this notion. Those who have contributed to this project in one way or another are many, and I beg the indulgence of anyone who has done so and is not mentioned here. To begin, I am most thankful to the women and men at the Parkview Evangelical Free Church in Texas who shared with me their insights and experiences and welcomed me to their Sunday services as well as their homes so that I could tell the story I recount here.

Second only to my respondents, I also wish to thank my spouse, Nicci, and my children, Stephen and Christine, for their patience with me as I conducted this research, wrote up this study, and sought to publish this monograph. My on-site research at the church kept me away from home for many Sunday mornings and early afternoons, and my interviews with spouses from the church occupied many weeknights that would otherwise have been spent with my own family. I still find it ironic that a study focused on the dynamics of other peoples' family lives impacted the lives of my family members so dramatically—hopefully for the better. My parents, who believe quite strongly in the merits of an educated mind, deserve my thanks as well. For the better part of my life, they have provided me with the material and personal resources to realize my intellectual aspirations.

I am also thankful to many groups and individuals at the University of Texas. The University provided financial support for this project during the

1995–1996 academic year in the form of a Continuing University Fellowship. I am also indebted to many faculty members within the department of sociology there. My mentor, Christopher Ellison, struck the perfect balance between providing intellectual and practical guidance where needed even as he encouraged my independent scholarly growth. Christine Williams has also offered many noteworthy contributions to this project. Her keen insights have impacted my understanding of gender and sociological theory. The one-on-one intellectual exchanges in which she and I have engaged over the last several years never failed to stimulate new insights for me.

Robert Fernea, Norval Glenn, and Debra Umberson also deserve thanks for their valuable input to this research project and for their patience with its many permutations. In seminar and throughout the research process, they have guided my scholarly growth and provided thoughtful feedback on my work. I also extend my thanks to Elizabeth Fernea, whose own scholarly research on Muslim gender and family relations speaks directly to many of the issues with which I wrestle in the pages that follow.

Among other colleagues who have read and remarked insightfully on portions of this manuscript are Kristin Anderson, Penny Edgell Becker, Edith Elwood, Pamela Klassen, Carolyn Pevey, and Lois Smith. I am most thankful for Jay Demerath's careful review and insightful commentary on the entire manuscript prior to publication. The patience and keen editorial eyes of David Myers and Brigitte Goldstein at Rutgers University Press have also contributed immensely to this volume. My thanks also to various colleagues for their feedback, conversational bits of wisdom, and supportive comments concerning this study: Nancy Ammerman, Ronald Angel, Don Bradley, Joanna Bradley, Alejandro Cervantes-Carson, Robert Cushing, Kirsten Dellinger, Leslie Dunlap, Louis E. Fisher, Patti Giuffre, Jeff Jackson, Daniel Mears, John Mulder, Robert Orrange, Ronnelle Paulsen, Frank Richardson, Daniel Rigney, Adam Shapiro, Darren Sherkat, Gideon Sjoberg, and William Swatos.

The Probe Center at the University of Texas made available some of the primary source materials I analyze in part 2 of this project, as did the Stitt Library at the Austin Presbyterian Theological Seminary. The Louisville Institute provided a fellowship for the 1996–1997 academic year to support this research. I am grateful for their financial support and for the interdisciplinary conference convened by the Institute in January 1997. This project is very much a product of the Institute's financial generosity and their willingness to bring together such a diverse group of social researchers for the thought-provoking forum that took place on that memorable January weekend. The Society for the Scientific Study of Religion provided a research grant that defrayed some of the expenses incurred by this research. Although I claim full responsibility for the analyses and interpretations that follow, I hope that the contributions of these many groups and individuals are recognizable in this work. They are certainly apparent to me.

Remaking the Godly Marriage

. . . men and women love in as many ways as there are men and women.
—Nancy Chodorow (1994)

Each of us speaks with many voices, like a tribal shaman in whom the ancestor ghosts are all talking at once; when we speak, we are not sure who is talking or what is being said, and our acts of power in communication are not wholly our own.
—J.G.A. Pocock (1984)

After all, what would be the value of the passion for knowledge if it resulted only in a certain knowingness . . . and not, in one way or another . . . the knower's straying afield from himself? There are times in life when the question of knowing if one can think differently than one thinks, and perceive differently than one sees, is absolutely necessary if one is to go on thinking and reflecting at all.
—Michel Foucault (1985)

Part I

Introduction and Background

One

Evangelical Family Life and America's Culture Wars

In recent decades, social researchers of various stripes have investigated the contours of the contemporary battle over the family. Many scholars have argued that this dispute pits feminists and proponents of democratic family relations against antifeminist religious conservatives who are committed to the preservation of patriarchal authority and gender distinctions in the home (Berger and Berger 1983; Conover and Gray 1983; Durham 1985; Eisenstein 1982; Hardacre 1993; Hunter 1991; Klatch 1988; Lakoff 1996; Lienesch 1993). Much of this scholarship asserts that the most outspoken and formidable purveyors of the traditional family are conservative (or evangelical) Protestants.[1]

Among the most prominent scholars in this now sizable research literature is James Davison Hunter (1991) who contends that social debates over the American family are the most contested front on which the contemporary culture wars are being waged. Following the lead of feminist (Cohen and Katzenstein 1988; Thorne and Yalom 1982) and neoconservative (Berger and Berger 1983) scholars who preceded him, Hunter's book, *Culture Wars: The Struggle to Define America,* demonstrates that debates over spousal relationships not only hinge on the state of the American family;

these acrimonious debates are also informed by assumptions about appropriate gender relations and, at a more fundamental level, divergent forms of moral authority—tacit assumptions about what is good and bad, right and wrong.

In Hunter's view, the culture wars over the family are waged between proponents of *progressivism* and defenders of *orthodoxy.* Whereas progressivists are said to be committed to subjectivist, rationalist, and historically contingent definitions of moral propriety (for example, personal experience or empirical inquiry), their orthodox counterparts are thought to adhere to fixed and transcendent visions of social morality (namely, tradition and sacred scripture). Moreover, Hunter contends that progressivists are committed to a family model that privileges structural diversity such as the legitimacy of both heterosexual and same-sex domestic partnerships, as well as the liberation of oppressed family members—specifically, women and children—from restrictive role expectations. By contrast, proponents of orthodoxy are purportedly beholden to the exclusive legitimacy of the traditional family, made up of sharp gender distinctions and predicated largely on the principles of hierarchy and authority.

Following up on this insight, Hunter argues that religious values are among the most significant and influential bases of moral authority in cultural warfare over the family. Hunter (1991: 184–185) takes pains to point out that various groups on both sides of this cultural divide invoke religious ideals as justification for their ideological positions. Nevertheless, religious ideologies seem to emanate most unabashedly from the stalwarts of orthodoxy. And among this group of cultural conservatives, evangelical Protestants are portrayed as the most vocal defenders of orthodox convictions (see Hunter 1991: 44, 82, 102–103) and the most strident guardians of traditional family values (181–182).[2]

Yet to what extent do leading evangelicals share common ground on such hot-button issues as a patriarchal family structure or the participation of wives and mothers in the labor force? And to what degree do the practices of evangelical husbands and wives conform to the traditionalist rhetoric of highly visible evangelical organizations such as Focus on the Family or Concerned Women for America? Research that has explored these questions offers conflicting answers.

The Case for Evangelical Traditionalism

A longstanding body of survey research does suggest that traditionalist gender ideologies are alive and well among many evangelicals. Using a local community sample of Oklahoma City residents, Grasmick and colleagues demonstrated that conservative Protestants are considerably more likely than their non-evangelical counterparts to support a patriarchal family structure in which the husband/father is construed as the ultimate decision-making authority in the family (Grasmick, Wilcox, and Bird 1990). Moreover, a sizable number of national-level studies have revealed that evangelical Protestants are much more likely to favor circumscribing a woman's family role to include only traditional domestic pursuits and household responsibilities (Hertel and Hughes 1987; Peek, Lowe, and Williams 1991). Finally, evangelical organizations such as Focus on the Family and Concerned Women for America are among the most highly organized, well-financed, and vocal pro-family groups in the United States (see various selections in Green et al. 1996).

It is hardly surprising that these organizations and their evangelical constituents have attracted considerable criticism from feminists, social scientists, and popular commentators who embrace a more egalitarian vision of the family (Brown 1994; Connell 1995: 39, 45, 177, 226–227; Epstein 1988: 42, 75, 239; Faludi 1991; French 1993; Scanzoni 1983. See Bartkowski 1995; McNamara 1985b; Smith 2000 for reviews). Noted anthropologist Karen McCarthy Brown (1994: 175–176), for example, characterizes fundamentalism as a "religion of the stressed and the disoriented" that appeals to those who "reject the modern world"; she charges that religious conservatives are preoccupied with "clarity, certitude, and control," and predicts unapologetically that "fundamentalism will always involve the control of women." Scholars and academics do not have a monopoly on such damning portrayals of religious conservatives. Media commentators frequently offer unflattering depictions of the ostensibly simplistic, authoritarian character of fundamentalism. *The Nation,* the leading Left periodical in the United States, regularly impugns fundamentalism as a religious and political orientation that is rigid and autocratic.[3] From this vantage point, fundamentalists are preoccupied with "a bright-line demarcation of boundaries [that are] not to be transgressed. . . . [F]undamentalisms are at heart authoritarian, and worse, encourage the brainlessness of the obedient foot soldier" (P. Williams 1997).

Progressivist Tendencies within
American Evangelicalism

In apparent contrast to the research findings and pejorative portrayals presented above, mounting evidence indicates that gender relations in conservative Protestant families are more nuanced and complex than they might appear at first blush. Carefully crafted survey analyses have recently demonstrated that the gender attitudes of religious conservatives exhibit a considerable degree of heterogeneity (Davis and Robinson 1996; Gay, Ellison, and Powers 1996; Smith 2000; Wilcox 1987, 1989). Religious conservatives, it would seem, are not of one mind concerning the most hotly debated family issues in American society. Other studies have highlighted the emergence of a feminist consciousness among evangelical women, particularly for those who draw distinctions between their orthodox religious sensibilities and their progressive politics (Wilcox 1989). Moreover, longitudinal studies suggest a convergence over time between the gender role attitudes of conservative Protestants and their non-evangelical counterparts (Blanche and Newton 1995), which may be due partly to the liberalization of gender convictions among younger evangelicals (Hunter 1987). Finally, there is some evidence that structural changes in evangelical households, such as increasing numbers of employed wives, might serve as a liberalizing factor in conservative Protestant family life (see Bartkowski and Xu 2000; Wilcox and Jelen 1991; Ellison and Bartkowski 2001).

Apart from these survey-based studies, qualitative inquiries have underscored the complexity of conservative Protestant family life. Textual analyses have hinted that gender and family relations are in fact the subject of some debate among leading conservative Protestants (Bartkowski 1997, 1999, 2000; Bendroth 1984, 1993; Fowler 1986; Quebedeaux 1974; Stacey and Gerard 1990). Even more compelling is the substantial body of ethnographic and interview data that highlight the negotiated character of evangelical gender and family relations (Ammerman 1987; Brasher 1998; Gallagher and Smith 1999; Griffith 1997; Ingersoll 1995; Manning 1999; McNamara 1985a; Pevey, Williams, and Ellison 1996; Rose 1987; Smith 2000; Stacey 1990; Stacey and Gerard 1990). Recent ethnographic inquiries (Brasher 1998; Griffith 1997) have fixed their attention on evangelical women in an effort to discern why women would affiliate with a religious subculture that prima facie seems to undermine their collective interests. These studies have revealed that conservative religious women are, in many cases, empowered by their affiliation with evangelical and fundamentalist religious institutions. In contrast to critics who portray evangelical women as simpleminded dupes of patriarchy, these studies have demonstrated that conservative religious women often exercise an unanticipated degree of authority in their homes and play active roles in their religious communities.

Such studies raise two crucial questions about evangelical gender relations that have yet to receive sustained attention. First, what are the contours of the gender and family debates that have emerged among evangelical elites over the past several decades? Although previous studies have hinted at such disputes, the significance, parameters, and sources of these internecine conflicts have escaped detailed analysis. In light of this suggestive research, how serious are the debates over gender and the family that are manifested within contemporary evangelicalism? What are the values that underlie this debate? Have the parameters of these internecine disputes been altered by the emergence of new evangelical social movements such as biblical feminism and the Promise Keepers?

Second, if in fact leading evangelicals advance competing visions of godly family life, how do conservative religious spouses make sense of their own family relationships and gender identities? Does the contested character of gender and family discourse within evangelicalism have any discernible impact on everyday practices in conservative Protestant homes?

Although previous ethnographic studies have investigated gender negotiation within American evangelicalism, these inquiries typically have not sought to explore such gender dynamics through the lens of recent historical shifts in elite conservative Protestant discourse. Moreover, previous ethnographic inquiries have focused almost exclusively on the self-perceptions and life experiences of evangelical women. Although such studies have illuminated women's motivations for affiliating so readily with conservative Protestant churches, evangelical men's complicity in producing gender within this religious subculture has been grossly undertheorized and largely uninvestigated. Yet if gender is jointly produced by both men and women—if men, like women, negotiate gender and bargain with patriarchy—it is imperative that scholars of evangelicalism now shift their attention to couple dynamics that mark gender relations between conservative Protestant husbands and wives. This study attempts to illuminate these pressing issues with a focused comparison of the advice in best-selling evangelical family manuals and the domestic experiences of married conservative Protestant husbands and wives. My inquiry suggests that social scientists often gloss over important points of dispute and nuance concerning evangelical married life. Ultimately, the argument made here seeks to clarify the contours of conservative religious debate over American families as we enter the twenty-first century.

Theoretical Considerations

I draw on several strands of social theory to render this account of evangelical gender and family relations.

Family Adaptive Strategies: Opportunity, Constraint, and Change in Domestic Life

Scholars guided by a family adaptive strategies analytical framework recognize that domestic relationships are negotiated as an amalgam of force and choice (see Moen and Wethington 1992 for a review of the relevant literature). On the one hand, the notion of family adaptive strategies "emphasizes the ways that larger social structural forces [e.g., gender norms, economic opportunities, ethnicity] constrain the repertoire of available adaptations" for households confronted with the exigencies of everyday domestic life—wage earning, decision making, housework, dependent care (Moen and Wethington 1992: 234). Based on this insight, I recognize the formative influence that elite evangelical discourse and congregational family ministry programs exert on the relationships of evangelical husbands and wives. Gender expectations within the context of a Christian marriage are highly salient to the husbands and wives I interviewed. These expectations are not formulated in isolation by individuals, but rather emanate from social and cultural sources—including the family discourses[4] articulated by elite evangelical advice authors.

On the other hand, the family adaptive strategies literature also recognizes the agency—i.e., "the role of choice, within the confines of structural constraints"—in family life. "Strategies, then, are the actions families devise for coping with, if not overcoming, the challenges of living, and for achieving their goals in the face of structural barriers" (Moen and Wethington 1992: 234). This stream of literature recognizes that family members sometimes comply with, and other times resist or reject, normative expectations concerning family life. So, although the everyday domestic practices of spouses featured here conform in some respects to elite portrayals of the godly Christian husband or wife, these couples' actions also commonly amend or subvert such ideologies.

Finally, the literature on family adaptive strategies seeks to understand domestic life and family members' practices in their historical context. This "life course approach points to the importance of historical time, life stage, and context in delimiting both family problems and the possible strategies to deal with them" (Moen and Wethington 1992: 234). Transformations in evangelical gender discourses over the past several decades have changed the parameters for gender negotiation among conservative Protestant couples. Moreover, despite Parkview families' shared middle-class status, couples at different stages of their domestic life course draw on diverse resources from the evangelical cultural repertoire to solve the particular exigencies facing them. Consistent with the analytical approach in family adaptive strategies scholarship, I seek to reveal the intersection of macro and micro social forces in the lives of these couples and aim to highlight the interplay between general patterns and particular life circumstances.

Multiple Configurations of Gender: Cathexis, Power, and Labor

My analysis of gender among evangelical couples is centered around a multidimensional definition of this construct. Following Connell (1987, 1995), I argue that gender is structured and negotiated through three key social configurations: cathexis, power, and labor. *Cathexis* highlights the way gender is produced through emotional ties, sexual desire, and experiences of embodiment—often hinging on the question of gender difference (i.e., are men and women inherently different from one another?). It is within the configuration of cathexis that issues of gender identity, emotional attachment, and sexuality surface most visibly.

Power entails the production and negotiation of asymmetrical gender relations. Social hierarchies that confer gender-specific privileges produce such asymmetries, which are then negotiated via the interplay of domination and resistance. Within the home, gender can be produced through a husband's attempt to exercise authority as the head of the household—e.g., via his self-designation as the family's leader or through the practice of autocratic decision making. However, because power is diffuse and domination is contestable, such patriarchal aims may meet with resistance or noncompliance from other family members. Power often operates subtly and invisibly (Bartkowski 1999; Komter 1989) in everyday family life through noncoercive, quotidian, and sometimes unconscious forms of influence. Sociological examinations of family power seek to link the household member's influence tactics to his or her position within a family system and also situate domestic asymmetries within a broader social context (see Blain 1994; Blumberg and Coleman 1989; Komter 1989; Kranichfeld 1987; see also Scanzoni and Marsiglio 1993). Disparities in family power often interface with extradomestic inequalities in resource distribution (e.g., the wage gap between men and women) or organizational networks (e.g., affiliation with a church headed by an all-male pastorship). With these considerations in mind, this configuration of gender calls attention to issues of authority, influence, and resistance.

Labor consists of the interface between gender and the allocation of practical responsibilities within social settings. Gender can be produced by dichotomous divisions of labor within the family as well as within gender-segregated occupations. The normative equation of wifeliness with homemaking and service to other family members, complemented by prescriptions for husband-providership, is but one example of the ways in which labor can be gendered within the domestic realm. A contrasting point on this continuum of gender entails task sharing within intimate partnerships. Task allocation is central to this configuration of gender.

Within contemporary evangelicalism, these gender configurations are produced in a multitude of social domains—gender discourses promulgated by evangelical elites; the organizational ideals and practices of local conservative Protestant religious congregations; and the beliefs, values, and social practices manifested in everyday domestic interactions. Taken together, parts 2 and 3 of this study chart the interplay among elite evangelical gender discourse, congregational practices, and the subjective dimensions of everyday life for conservative Protestant spouses situated squarely within this religious subculture. Throughout, I examine the production of evangelical family relations across these social domains while focusing my attention on the three configurations of gender—cathexis, power, labor—outlined above.

The Tandem Negotiation of Gender in Intimate Relationships

Although cathexis, power, and labor lend structure to social expectations and interactions, current scholarship also emphasizes the many ways in which individuals and groups negotiate gender—that is, how people both reinforce and contest gender norms through social practices. Because it is produced collectively through everyday social interaction, gender is best understood as an accomplishment (West and Fenstermaker 1993, 1995), a performance (Butler 1990; Denzin 1993), and a social practice or project (Connell 1987, 1995; Griffith 1997). Consequently, sociologists speak of "doing gender" (West and Zimmerman 1987) to emphasize how gender functions not only as a noun linked to cultural idealizations about men and women, but as an action-oriented verb invested in and produced through ongoing social practices. Contemporary gender scholars recognize the importance of bodily practices and experiences of embodiment to the negotiation of gender (Bartkowski 2000; Butler 1990; Connell 1995; Davis 1995, 1997). Recent research underscores how men's and women's bodies are a key site at which gender relations are reproduced, contested, and at times subverted.

Nevertheless, sociologists of gender complement a focus on micro-level social interactions (identity negotiation, bodily practice) with an analysis of the gendered organizations within which such encounters are situated (Acker 1990, 1992a, 1992b; Connell 1987, 1990; Lorber 1994; Williams 1995). Organizations are quite capable of doing gender by adopting practices that promote occupational segregation, or by applying negative sanctions to members who do not conform to gender-specific standards. However, it is important to recognize that even highly structured relations of gender within an organization may be negotiated. Organizational norms are often internally contradictory, and such structural fissures can facilitate creative acts of resistance. Moreover, because different organizations are often governed by distinctive normative standards, groups and individuals may transpose rival gender ideologies and practices from other social venues to bring about small-scale, and sometimes even large-scale, social change.

In my view, gender processes within marital relationships are most clearly illuminated when examined as tandem negotiations between husbands, wives, and the social milieu (e.g., kin relations, friendships, congregational networks) within which they are situated. It is my contention that a more holistic rendering of evangelical gender relations emerges when we explore how evangelical wives and husbands—sometimes in unison and quite often at odds—wrestle with the exigencies of everyday family life. Evangelical men, like women within this religious subculture, grapple with questions of gender identity, family power, and household labor—often in gender-specific ways that are intimately connected to their partners' desires, life circumstances, and gender negotiations.

The Rules and Tools of Religious Involvement: Structure, Culture, and Congregational Life

Finally, I draw on research within the sociology of religion that explores both cultural and structural dynamics of congregational and religious life (e.g., Ammerman 1997; Becker 1997, 1999; Kniss 1997; Smith 1998). Like other institutions, religious congregations are social organizations composed of persons charged with performing particular responsibilities who often function within the parameters of rule-governed roles. Such institutionalized responsibilities—sometimes tacit and sometimes openly codified—are often hierarchically arranged and gendered. Yet scholars now generally recognize that this structural view of religion, by itself, overemphasizes the static and rule-governed character of religious involvement. When religious involvement is viewed as a cultural resource, the dynamic and nuanced character of religious affiliation—quite constraining in some instances, powerfully enabling in others—can be more fully appreciated. From this viewpoint, individuals and families affiliated with a religious group have various tools within their cultural repertoire—religious ideologies, ritual practices, congregational networks—that they can use to make sense of their social experiences and produce a congregational identity distinctive from the world within which the believer and the faith community are situated.

Consistent with this attunement to cultural negotiation within congregations, a great wealth of recent studies reveal that religious communities are not homogeneous, seamless organizations; rather, congregations often become sites for social conflicts of various sorts (Ammerman 1997; Becker 1997; Feher 1997; Kniss 1997; Stocks 1997). Points of conflict may emerge within congregations whose members embrace divergent ideologies (e.g., feminist versus traditionalist); contention may arise between congregational factions who ascribe divergent meanings to a commonly valued religious symbol (e.g., sacred scripture); and conflict may mark religious communities whose faithful disagree about how to define their collective identity vis-à-vis their surrounding environment.

As the recent work of Becker (1997, 1999) reveals, religious communities often respond to the eruption of conflict by seeking to strike a balance between two competing forms of moral logic—an ethic of caring (based on the principles of forgiveness, love, and compassion) and an ethic of judgment (based on the principles of authority, truth-seeking, and justice) (see also Bartkowski and Regis 2001; Bartkowski and Wilcox 2000; Bartkowski, Wilcox, and Ellison 2000). Becker's research on congregational conflict reveals that the competence of religious leaders is often evaluated in terms of their ability to solve moral dilemmas by striking a balance between compassion and authority. These forms of moral logic are also invoked collectively as congregations negotiate their sense of distinctiveness from a surrounding milieu—as they find a niche that is "in but not of the world." Consistent with the research described above, this study explores how religious ideologies, congregational practices, familial ties, and everyday experiences provide evangelical couples with an array of tools they can use to fashion meaningful gender identities within their homes.

Study Overview

Before proceeding to address these issues in greater detail, an overview of this study and its most significant findings is in order. Chapter 2 sets the stage for my analysis of contemporary evangelical gender and family relations by recounting their history. Focusing on the relationship between cultural contradictions and social change, this chapter begins by demonstrating that eighteenth-century American evangelicalism began as a populist religious movement with largely egalitarian leanings. The sectarian—and culturally critical—character of early evangelicalism gradually eroded during the nineteenth century as this religious movement grew to become the predominant brand of American Protestantism in the Victorian era. The dominance of Victorian evangelicalism was eventually challenged during the late nineteenth and early twentieth centuries by first-wave feminism and the post-Victorian New Woman. These developments soon gave rise to the first wave of fundamentalist Protestantism. Theological schisms and ideological rifts developed—and persist to this day—among evangelicals with the rise and fall of first-wave fundamentalism.

Part 2 (chapters 3–5) proceeds to examine elite evangelical debates about gender and family relations from the late 1960s to the present. These three chapters are based on an in-depth analysis of popular evangelical advice manuals written by a wide range of conservative Protestant authors—from unabashed defenders of traditional family values to biblical feminists, with various permutations emerging amidst them.

Chapter 3 compares competing definitions of masculinity, femininity, and sexuality within contemporary evangelicalism and proceeds to review the biblical legitimations used to support these respective orientations. In short, a large group of evangelical essentialists (i.e., advocates of innate gender difference) argue that men are rational, inherently aggressive, and driven by instrumental achievement (e.g., labor force pursuits). These same authors contend that women are innately more responsive (i.e., other-centered) and oriented toward relational, humanitarian concerns. This coterie of essentialist advice authors is marked by important internal divisions. On the one hand, radical essentialists argue that inborn gender differences are largely immutable and decry efforts perceived as gender blending. On the other hand, moderate essentialists acknowledge the importance of innate gender differences but exhort their readers (particularly their male audience) to augment such inborn predispositions by cultivating desirable cross-gender traits.

Yet a third group of popular evangelical advice authors reject any form of essentialist rhetoric and instead champion gender sameness—the overwhelming similarity of men and women. Consequently, leading biblical feminists and a growing coterie of equality-minded evangelicals argue forcefully that God intends for all human beings to manifest the most admirable traits associated with masculinity and femininity. These various groups of advice authors are quick to point to biblical passages that seem to legitimate their respective definitions of gender and sexuality, thereby demonstrating that the Bible is a polysemous text capable of generating multiple contradictory readings.

Chapter 4 moves on to consider discourses of family power promulgated by these best-selling evangelical authors. This chapter contrasts dominant conservative Protestant defenses of wifely submission with oppositional evangelical support for mutual submission. Radical essentialists typically argue that God has ordained husbands as the ultimate decision makers in the family. This commitment to a patriarchal family structure rests on essentialist conceptualizations of masculine aggression and feminine responsiveness as well as select scriptural interpretations about husband-headship and wifely submission. By contrast, advocates of mutual submission—including biblical feminists and moderate essentialists—enjoin husbands and wives alike to sacrifice (i.e., submit) their personal interests and predilections jointly in the context of the marital relationship. Among the more interesting developments in this discourse of family power is the recent emergence of a group of new-guard defenders of the patriarchal family (such as leading Promise Keepers) who encourage men to become servant-leaders or servant-heads that take the "lead" in ministering to the needs of other family members rather than selfishly protecting their own interests.

Chapter 5, the last in this section, examines the divergent discourses of domestic labor that have emerged within contemporary evangelicalism. Many of the authors who argue for radical essentialism and wifely submission support dichotomous domestic responsibilities for husbands and wives. These authors charge wives with the lion's share of domestic tasks and childcare duties and argue that financial provision is a husband's responsibility. By contrast, advocates of gender sameness and moderate essentialists seek to orient their readers toward more fluid household roles in which financial provision, household tasks, and parental responsibilities are not divided on the basis of sex. Once again, this debate over household responsibilities not only turns on the foregoing conceptualizations of gender and family power, but also stems from hotly disputed biblical interpretations concerning these very issues.

Part 3 (chapters 6–8) examines the negotiation of these gender discourses within evangelical families. The introductory portion of part 3 briefly describes the congregation in which the participant-observation portion of this study was conducted—the Parkview Evangelical Free Church. Participant-observation and interview data are then examined in light of the three points of discursive debate reviewed in part 2. Beginning with definitions of masculinity, femininity, and sexuality (chapter 6), pastors and teachers at Parkview frequently employ essentialist rather than gender-sameness rhetoric; however, given their desire to keep from alienating those members (particularly women) whose personalities do not fit categorical gender distinctions such as masculine initiation versus feminine responsiveness, they typically present this rhetoric in a much more nuanced and conditional way than is depicted in the advice manuals. Unambiguous and categorical gender distinctions are inconsistent with the self-perceptions and lived experiences of many of Parkview's most committed members. Consequently, many Parkview spouses accept some aspects of gender difference while rejecting other essentialist tenets. Even where generic ideas about gender difference hold sway, spouses take care to highlight the many exceptions to such generalizations.

Gender beliefs and practices concerning family power (wifely submission versus mutual submission), the subject of chapter 7, reveal such nuances in even bolder relief. Among both the pastors and the members of this church, there is a measure of disagreement over exactly who is supposed to submit to whom within the marital relationship. Some family ministers and spouses argue that wives are indeed responsible for submitting to the authority of their husbands; others invoke the principle of mutual submission. Interestingly, all parties' definitions of submission in the home are so replete with ambiguity and exceptions that it is virtually impossible to distinguish any definitive position on this issue. More so than any other dimension of gender relations, this area of marital and identity negotiation is saturated with tension and contradiction.

Chapter 8 investigates ideals and practices concerning domestic labor—i.e., financial provision, housework, and dependent-care responsibilities—within four families from this church. The pastorship at Parkview does not explicitly prescribe the allocation of gender responsibilities within the home. And with a decidedly mixed membership of dual-earner and husband-breadwinner families, this organizational strategy is wise indeed. Using a case study approach, chapter 8 examines how spouses in four different types of families manage the tensions associated with wage-earning, housework, and child care. Each of these families is situated at a different point in its domestic life course. My analysis highlights how the ideological commitments of spouses often conflict with their practical family circumstances and explores the myriad ways in which husbands and wives confront—and sometimes overcome—the daily challenges associated with managing domestic labor. The conclusion begins with a restatement of the volume's major themes and then specifies its most noteworthy implications.

Two

Evangelical Families in Historical Perspective

Although contemporary conservative Protestantism has a rich cultural history and represents an admixture of various religious traditions—Baptist, Anabaptist, Pentecostal, and others (Hunter 1983:chap. 3)—many of the most salient theological commitments of contemporary evangelicals can be traced to the New England Baptist sects of the early eighteenth century. In stark contrast to the more established Puritan and Anglican communities of New England, these Baptist sects stressed a more individualistic view of salvation and, correspondingly, an emotionally intense and personally intimate relationship with God. Early Baptists also downplayed the importance of a formal ecclesiastical church structure, and as a result attracted large numbers of converts via religious revivals during the eighteenth and nineteenth centuries.[1] Established Puritan churches, by contrast, evinced a more rational conceptualization of God and subscribed to the doctrine of predestination. Consequently, Puritans tended to stress education and intellectual development, and were inclined to privilege God's absolute sovereignty in human history over individual volition. These same Puritan churches reinforced distinct social roles for the sexes.

17

The Egalitarian Impulse in Pre-Revolutionary Evangelicalism

In bold contrast to the highly gendered tenor of Puritan religion, historical evidence suggests that early Baptist evangelicalism—with its focus on the individual believer's direct relationship with God and its employment of an ecstatic worship style—posed a direct challenge to secular and non-evangelical mechanisms of social stratification (Juster 1994). Among the social hierarchies that were challenged by early Baptist worship gatherings were gender inequalities. In her study of Revolutionary-era New England evangelicalism, historian Susan Juster (1994: 19) describes the egalitarian dynamics of early "back-country" Baptist gatherings in which "no social distinctions were recognized, in defiance of Anglican gentry culture. Rich and poor, men and women, black and white all communed together in the presence of the Lord, often without a minister. . . . [T]he most radical feature of revival religion [was] its insistence that a church—any church—could not define the boundaries of the sacred community. Only the immediate presence of the Spirit of God, however fleeting, signified community."

Colonial evangelicalism is best understood as a liminal religion of the heart (Juster 1994:19–21). Liminality, a product of ecstatic religious fervor, enables worshipers to free themselves temporarily from social conventions and to experience genuine community ("communitas") devoid of socially reinforced distinctions. While early Baptist liminality was a transitory state of radical egalitarianism, the effects of these experiences were nevertheless manifested in an "assault on the principle of hierarchy" (Juster 1994:25). The liminal character of early evangelicalism provided women with symbolic and ecclesiastical benefits not available to their Puritan and Anglican counterparts. When evangelical churches coalesced from makeshift worship gatherings, female members enjoyed access to governance positions and often preached at church meetings. This "significant widening of women's sphere of authority within the church" (Juster 1994: 44) drew strident criticism from orthodox Anglican and Puritan ministers, many of whom argued for the continued silence of women at religious gatherings (see Juster 1994:30–31).

Yet despite such evidence of gender egalitarianism, these early Baptist sects did not wholly reject the patriarchal gender norms of their milieu. Remarkably consistent with the broader societal dichotomization of private and public spheres, revivalists tended to view their religion as feminine (i.e., highly personal) in character (Juster 1994:21, 44, 51). The feminization of early revivalism was due in part to the preponderance of women in evangelical communities. But it also derived from the prevailing belief that women—not unlike the orgiastic religion to which they flocked—were inherently disorderly and sensuous.

Simultaneous accommodation to and resistance against societal norms produced significant gender contradictions within early evangelicalism (Juster 1994:20–21, 44–45). Like femininity, evangelical liminality was at once prized and feared. The very same liminality that liberated believers from social conventions was thought to hold the potential to produce chaos among these sectarians. Moreover, revivalism reinforced societal constructions of femininity as an emotional phenomenon, even as its ungendered organizational structure challenged the pervasive view that women were inherently inept leaders. "However awkward such a feminine posture would become in later years, in the mid–eighteenth century evangelical religion did not shun the more female aspects of its piety just as it did not bar women from exercising their full rights as members of the body politic" (Juster 1994:45).

From the Margins to the Mainstream, 1775–1875: The American Revolution, Victorianism, and the Hegemony of Evangelical Religion

Amid the emergent gender contradictions of early and mid-eighteenth-century evangelicalism, a broader sociopolitical revolt began to coalesce. As the colonies began fighting for their independence from Britain, evangelicals—part of a hitherto marginalized subculture—confronted an important decision about the nature and future of revival religion in the colonies.

Faced with the choice of maintaining their otherworldly stance or joining with their colonial brethren in common cause against Britain, the evangelical leadership chose rebellion [against England]. In so doing they compromised the very essence of the evangelical community. . . . [The] surest way for dissenters to engage the Standing Order on their own terrain was to reorganize their polity along the model of the patriarchal household. Where renunciation was required, it was evangelical women who paid the price, while evangelical men reaped the civil benefits that came with patriotic service. (Juster 1994: 109)

In this way, the Revolutionary era witnessed the first step toward the taming of early evangelicalism's egalitarian character (Juster 1994: chap. 4). In the scramble for political power and influence that characterized the Revolutionary period, previously independent New England Baptist churches formed translocal associations and founded educational institutions.

To partake more fully in the patriotic fervor of the Revolution, to win new converts, and to ensure their very existence in the face of competing religious traditions, evangelical communities transformed the gender conceptualizations that held sway during the early and mid–eighteenth century, radically restructuring them and aligning them with patriarchal ideals.[2] Although evangelical churches had previously concerned themselves with winning individual souls, it was now the family—in all of its post-Revolutionary patriarchal splendor—that became elevated in status in the eyes of evangelical leadership. "Family government" in the form of a specific "chain of duties" among husbands and wives, parents and children, masters and servants, rose to prominence in evangelical discourse during this time. Evangelicals' commitment to highly ordered family relations was linked inextricably with both the well-being of the church community at large and the fate of individual believers' souls. "Fifty years earlier, the main enemies had been Satan and the corruption of one's own heart; now disorderly domestic relations threatened the welfare of the church" (Juster 1994: 114). Following closely from this reconstruction of gender relations in early evangelical families, post-Revolutionary debates arose about the legitimacy of women speaking at Baptist gatherings.

This pattern of convergence between evangelical values and patriarchal Victorian ideals continued well into the nineteenth century (Fishburn 1981; Friedman 1985; McDannell 1986; McLoughlin 1968: 17–19). Even lay-oriented nineteenth-century Southern Baptist churches in which women were permitted to vote required a quorum that was determined by the number of male members in attendance (Friedman 1985: 11–18). Moreover, men typically managed matters of church discipline from its investigative and trial stages to the enforcement of sanctions. Although accusations of engaging in offensive acts were more often brought against male church members than against their female counterparts, allegations directed at men typically revolved around activities viewed as minor infractions such as drinking or dancing. Investigations of female members, though less frequent, generally centered around offenses deemed far more serious—for example, adultery, fornication, abortion. "Women who were accused of sexual offenses were suspended from the church if they were contrite, excluded if they were not, but they were reconciled with the church only after they were punished" (Friedman 1985: 16; see also Juster 1994: chap. 5).

These offenses associated with women's embodiment were viewed with such concern because many Victorians feared that feminine sensuality could ignite men's desire. And clearly, according to many of these evangelicals, church discipline was crucial because of women's natural predilection for defiance and irresponsibility—feminine character traits that often tempted men to sin. After all, were not all women the direct descendants of a primordial wife, Eve, whose lack of self-control and undue influence over her husband ushered sin into the world? This reasoning legitimated a "gendering of sin" (Juster 1994: 148) in evangelical theological discourse at this time: "Every time a sister was excluded for fornication, or lying, or (most damning of all) spreading evil reports about a fellow communicant, the image of woman as seductress (i.e., as Eve) was confirmed in the eyes of the community" (Juster 1994: 170). Defenders of these patriarchal churches and their disciplinary double standards contended that such social control mechanisms actually provided direct benefits to their female membership by protecting unscrupulous women from masculine aggression.

Despite this general shift from egalitarianism to patriarchy, male dominance in nineteenth-century evangelical churches and families sometimes met with dogged resistance. The restriction of voting rights to male congregants generated heated controversy within many Baptists churches of the South. "Baptist supporters of the right of women to vote in the church argued . . . [for] the principle of equality. . . . Furthermore, church suffragists believed that if women were denied the vote they would not be responsible for the purity of the church. The latter argument hit at the crux of female leadership. If women did not participate in the exercise of discipline, how could they constitute a church?" (Friedman 1985: 13).

Although many of these patriarchal churches placed very real constraints on female members, individual women in many instances did not simply acquiesce to the congregational enforcement of these disciplinary double standards. Although the sex-specific enforcement of church discipline did sustain a highly gendered social order in the rural evangelical South, this order was challenged to a significant degree by many of the women who resisted such regulation in word or in deed with "remarkable audacity": "In cases of disorderly conduct some women remained independent of the church while others refused to submit to its discipline. Even those reconciled to the church first had their say and did so in no uncertain terms" (Friedman 1985: 15).

Similar tensions manifested themselves within the households of many nineteenth-century Southern Baptists. Definitions of wifely domesticity inspired by the convergence of evangelicalism and Victorian gender norms were particularly rigorous in the rural South. Because the family had remained a unit of economic production in the rural South for quite some time, the domestic responsibilities of southern evangelical women were defined far more broadly than those to which northern urban women were expected to attend (Friedman 1985: chap. 2). Women's domestic chores in the South were not restricted to the household proper, but also included working in the field, attending to dairy chores, spinning, managing a household industry and selling the goods produced by it, and acting as "deputy husband" when the situation demanded it. Given the lengthy list of daily chores facing them, rural southern wives needed to be more industrious than their husbands (Friedman 1985: 22–23, 128–129). The boundaries demarcating men's domestic responsibilities generally excluded household chores and child care.

This radically unequal and deeply gendered household division of labor among Southern evangelical couples stood in stark contrast to the egalitarian theological principles upon which these marriages were founded. Many of the same evangelical wives who comported themselves to this rigorous version of Victorian domesticity nevertheless embraced an ideal of marital equality. This ideal was sustained, in thought if not in practice, by artifacts of egalitarianism that continued to define evangelical marital unions in Victorian America.

Theoretically, marriage united two individuals who were to perform gender-related roles, but mutual support was to lead to the true spiritual union.

Although the marriage ceremony enjoined obedience on the wife but not on the husband, ministers still stressed mutuality of responsibility. The couple vowed to keep "a high esteem and mutual love for one another; bearing with each other's infirmities and weaknesses . . . to encourage each other . . . to comfort one another . . . in honesty and industry to provide for each other's temporal support; to pray for and encourage one another in the things that pertain to God, and to their immortal souls." (Friedman 1985: 34)

This egalitarian vision of evangelical marriage, which likened the ideal husband-wife relationship to the spiritual union between Christ and his church, often remained just that—a vision and an ideal. Women generally took this spiritual call to marital partnership quite seriously, "but husbands resisted their wives' efforts. The marital union then was a struggle to reconcile these perspectives" (Friedman 1985: 35). Given the exigencies of daily life in the Victorian South, along with the concentration of economic resources and decision-making authority in the hands of the evangelical family's husband, marital struggles were frequently resolved in his favor.

As evidenced by Friedman's intriguing study of southern evangelical wives' diaries and recorded dreams, the contradictions manifested in these women's marriages produced for them a profound sense of cognitive dissonance. Many women were confronted with the dual tasks of counterbalancing such egalitarian ideals with gross practical inequities and reconciling their own personal desires with the pressures and obligations of the religious community in which they lived. Evangelical women adopted various strategies to deal with these cross-pressures, ranging from either outright rejection or acceptance of evangelical ideals to creative negotiation of these contradictions (Friedman 1985: 52, 129).

The cultural accommodation of evangelicalism in the late eighteenth and early nineteenth centuries led to the gradual convergence of evangelical and Victorian gender ideals. In fact, the cultural dominance of Victorian gender norms was accompanied by the rise to prominence of evangelical religion in America: the upstart evangelical sects of the eighteenth century had effectively moved, during the course of the nineteenth century, from the cultural periphery to the religious mainstream. In the wake of these historical shifts, "the androgynous essence of evangelical religion was eroded by repeated encounters with the profane world. . . . No longer positioned outside (and against) the world, the evangelical church was now fully *of* the world" (Juster 1994: 107, 113, emphasis in the original).

The Demise of Victorian Gender Ideals and the Rise of Protestant Fundamentalism, 1875–1930

Victorian conceptualizations of gender began to erode by the close of the nineteenth century (DeBerg 1990: 24–41). Victorian notions of public-sphere masculinity were being progressively undermined by the shift from small-scale cottage industries to a more corporate, bureaucratic form of capitalism. "'Manly' work in one's own shop, office, vehicle, or factory gave way to employment in bureaucratized, sterile corporate offices. . . . When American business became big business, men's ability to play the 'economic warrior' was reduced since many small businesses failed or were bought out and men became mere bureaucratic cogs in large business organizations" (DeBerg 1990: 25), including U.S. Steel, Standard Oil, and American Telephone and Telegraph.

In addition, the patriarchal Victorian family was becoming less and less practical. With the long work hours and commuting times ushered in by this corporate wave of industrialization, husbands and fathers were spending less time in the household. The absentee Victorian father was fast becoming a patriarch in name only. "As male participation in childrearing decreased . . . women had more say in the decisions made about their children than did men. And with the responsibility for the training and guidance of the young came much real and symbolic power" (DeBerg 1990: 35).

The demise of Victorian gender ideals was also fostered by the influx of women into the previously male-dominated public sphere during the late nineteenth century (DeBerg 1990: 25–35). The post-Victorian New Woman, aided by first-wave feminism and women's rights activists, made significant inroads into educational institutions, the paid labor force, and organizations involved in political action. Social activists and new female employees were confronted with the choice of either clinging to outmoded beliefs or revising prevailing definitions of womanhood in light of their public-sphere commitments. Many women chose the latter course of action. "There were simply too many cases, even in respectable middle-class society, in which the highly differentiated gender definitions and roles [of Victorian America] had little congruence with the way people actually lived their lives" (DeBerg 1990: 38).

Consequently, women became less dependent on men, marriage, and motherhood: "Women, especially educated ones with more opportunities to support themselves in the workplace, were no longer bound to stay in marriages and used divorce to escape. The fact that women had more options—divorce and/or self-support—than they had previously meant that they gained a better bargaining position within the marriage relationship. Their stronger position further weakened the supports of male domination and control of family life" (DeBerg 1990: 38).

Evangelical churches felt the reverberations produced by these dramatic social changes (Friedman 1985: chap. 6). Many late-nineteenth- and early-twentieth-century evangelicals who were beholden to the religion's perfectionist roots and reformist impulses championed women's entrance into the public sphere.[3] Prominent women of this era, such as leaders of the Women's Christian Temperance Union (WCTU), drew on the reformist zeal of evangelicalism to argue for women's suffrage, child labor laws, and the formation of a juvenile justice system. In light of these facts, religious historian Nancy Hardesty and others have argued that nineteenth-century perfectionist evangelicalism actually gave rise to early feminist social reform efforts and subverted the Victorian Cult of True Womanhood: "Nineteenth-century American feminism was deeply rooted in evangelical revivalism. . . . The revivalists' emphasis on conversion and commitment gave women and men a mission to save the world which applied not only to souls but also to bodies, minds, social relations, and the body politic. The same strategies used in evangelism—the spreading of the gospel per se—were also used to spread the gospel of reform" (Hardesty 1984: 9–10).

Although such evangelical-inspired social activism could be seen merely as civic housekeeping, this view is less than compelling when weighed against historical evidence. Women's political activism during this time subverted domesticized femininity and challenged narrow definitions of Victorian womanhood. Women gained practical political experience and developed leadership expertise through their affiliations with such organizations as the WCTU. "Through such [social reform] organizations, women across the country, but particularly urban middle-class women, burst into the public sphere with a reforming zeal rooted in evangelical religion and the cult of domesticity. These wives and mothers may not have been employed, but leave the house they did, and men no longer could claim the political world as their own" (DeBerg 1990: 32). Evangelical women's participation in denominational missionary efforts also gained momentum at this time. Methodist churches were among the first to promote women's missionary efforts; their Baptist and Presbyterian counterparts soon followed suit. Alongside the political activism of parachurch groups like the WCTU, denominational missionary outreach fostered evangelical women's participation in public sphere activities.

Nevertheless, it would be erroneous to conclude that evangelical Protestants as a whole championed these social changes. The rise of women's missionary societies produced significant tensions concerning the appropriate role of women in evangelical religious organizations. Baptist women's outstandingly successful fundraising efforts in support of missionary activities, in particular, produced considerable ambivalence among the members of the Baptist Convention. After initially meeting resistance to their missionary activities, Baptist women eventually elicited public praise from the Convention for their efforts. Still, these energetic women had to be careful not to appear to be usurping the authority of the male-dominated missionary boards. In a committee report crafted in 1885, these women "asked [the Convention] that they be allowed to continue working 'in a quiet and unostentatious way' " (Friedman 1985: 116). Consequently, women's entrance into the public sphere produced within evangelicalism a profound cultural paradox. By the end of the nineteenth century, "traditional attitudes concerning women's domestic role existed simultaneously with acceptance of women's religious and social leadership" (Friedman 1985: 127).

These broad historical changes within American society, combined with such contradictory trends within evangelicalism, posed a serious challenge to Victorian beliefs about the dichotomous distribution of masculine and feminine traits among men and women respectively. Moreover, such momentous changes raised questions about the gendered familial and social roles these essentialist conceptualizations supported. Given the vexing questions such shifting historical forces raised about men, women, family life, and even the fate of the nation as a whole, it is not surprising that the growing reaction against Victorian gender and family relations produced a significant degree of ideological ferment within both American society at large and evangelical Protestant churches. DeBerg (1990: 25) concludes that by the turn of the century "women's nature and sphere of activity became the battleground on which men fought for their own identity as men. Could men be true men if women were no longer true women?" It was in response to this social ferment that Protestant fundamentalism was born.

Fundamentalism, so named because of its association with the perceived "fundamentals" of Protestant Christianity, initially coalesced as a reaction against modernism (DeBerg 1990: chap. 6). Whereas modernism stood for the "progress" of human reason and encouraged the application of higher criticism to scriptural study, fundamentalists embraced dispensational premillenialism and defended the inerrancy of the Bible. Premillennialism broke with earlier, more perfectionist versions of evangelical theology (often referred to as postmillennialism) by positing that the establishment of the kingdom of God was not founded upon the moral progress of humanity. Rather, the second coming of Christ was now thought to be preceded by a historical period of rampant immorality, widespread apostasy, and mass infidelity (Hardesty 1984: 158). In light of the demise of Victorian ideals, many religious conservatives were swayed by the pessimism of fundamentalist theology. A radical about-face in the theological stance of Dwight L. Moody (the most prominent evangelical-turned-fundamentalist) reveals the power of the Protestant fundamentalist message for many turn-of-the-century religious conservatives. With the rise of fundamentalism, Moody abandoned his earlier, more optimistic postmillennial evangelical convictions in favor of a more pessimistic premillennialist view (McLoughlin 1968: 24).

Biblical inerrancy—the belief that the Bible is the literal and infallible Word of God—also achieved a privileged status in first-wave fundamentalist Protestantism. Early fundamentalists not only understood the Bible to be historically accurate, but construed scripture as the ultimate source of moral truth for individual believers. First-wave fundamentalists therefore rejected other sources of revelatory inspiration (e.g., speaking in tongues). Instead, they strove for a more codified and stable theological base—the timeless truths of the Bible—in the face of rapid social change. This shift was a strategic move on the part of first-wave fundamentalist leaders—who were, by and large, men. By identifying the Bible as the ultimate standard through which God's will could be deciphered and by portraying their own scriptural readings as the authoritative interpretation of biblical mandates, these leading spokesmen were able to legitimate their pastoral authority in a religion that had initially called into question virtually all forms of social hierarchy.

The sweeping social changes that began to take hold in post-Victorian America provided many first-wave fundamentalists with clear evidence of premillennial moral decay. In the face of these upheavals, many leading fundamentalists argued for the restoration of Victorian notions of assertive masculinity and passive femininity, a patriarchal household structure, and the ideology of separate spheres (Bendroth 1993: chap. 5; DeBerg 1990: chaps. 2 and 3). Moreover, the fundamentalist rehashing of these Victorian gender conceptualizations now infused such pleas with direct appeals to the inerrant truths of the Bible.

Androgyny was criticized by leading first-wave fundamentalists as a violation of God's intent for clarity, harmony, and complementarity in creation. First-wave fundamentalists sought to reassert the importance of essential gender difference by sharply contrasting what they perceived as the masculine predilection for strength and aggression with the more subdued and naturally deferent feminine character. One leading first-wave fundamentalist contended: "In man, the Scriptures emphasize the active virtues. . . . In woman, they emphasize the passive virtues. . . . When this difference is lost and man becomes womanish, or woman becomes mannish, then the proper balance is lost, and harmony gives way to discord" (as quoted in DeBerg 1990: 45).

First-wave fundamentalists also supported a return to the patriarchal family. In contrast to the liberated New Woman of the early twentieth century, evangelical wives were alternately encouraged to emulate the selflessness and long-suffering of Jesus Christ; to reenact the subordination of Eve to Adam (God was thought to have instructed the fallen first wife to submit to her husband's authority); and to mirror the submission of the Church to Christ's leadership—the latter in bold distinction to more egalitarian idealizations of the Christ-Church union that pervaded nineteenth-century evangelicalism. In any case, these apologists for the patriarchal family envisioned a divine hierarchy that featured, in a descending order of authority: God, Christ, man/husband, woman/wife, children.

A woman's natural callings as wife and mother were a favorite topic of many leading fundamentalists during the early twentieth century. Because they viewed the post-Victorian New Woman, rising divorce rates, and women's invasion of the public sphere as signs of the End Times, many early fundamentalists urged women to return to their proper God-ordained role as supportive wife and self-sacrificing mother. Women were encouraged not to dirty themselves by participating in politics, higher education, or economics. They were warned not to jeopardize their family and, indeed, the fate of the nation by abdicating their divinely prescribed domestic role. After all, early fundamentalists strategically contended, the home more than even the church itself was the bastion of true religion and the cornerstone of a strong Christian nation.

In the face of the revolt against marriage waged by the New Woman and first-wave feminists, fundamentalist Protestants sought to reinstate the Victorian Cult of True Womanhood, now buttressed by references to carefully chosen biblical passages. Women's call to motherhood was thereby legitimated not only by appeals to their once-removed civic power ("the hand that rocks the cradle . . .") but by ever more strident religious rhetoric and scriptural appeals. One leading fundamentalist offered the following appraisal: "If there be any difference in degree touching the importance of the spheres assigned the two sexes, surely the palm goes to the woman, since according to God's own decree and word, she is in a position to mold the character and determine the destiny of the race" (as quoted in DeBerg 1990: 46).

Although first-wave fundamentalists remained a dominant force in American Protestantism around the turn of the century, the gender relations advocated by these religious conservatives were not without their own internal contradictions. Early fundamentalists were hardly a monolithic group of like-minded religious conservatives. Given the firm, though by no means identical, convictions of these religious conservatives, historians have called attention to the infighting that often plagued this movement despite its common distaste for modernism (DeBerg 1990: 97). Thus, although many fundamentalists sought to delimit women's influence in their churches (including the right to address assemblies), the move to do so sparked heated debate among religious conservatives (DeBerg 1990: 76–79; Hassey 1986). Some evangelicals expressed deep suspicion about the fundamentalist call for "loyalty to creed" over "loyalty to denomination." Indeed, because many evangelicals placed great importance on denominational membership, "the most caustic Fundamentalists spent more time attacking other southern Evangelicals than anyone else and quickly lost influence in their own denominations" (Flynt 1981: 29). Internal divisions within turn-of-the-century conservative Protestantism were also quite evident in fundamentalist appraisals of the evangelical-inspired Women's Christian Temperance Union (WCTU). Fundamentalists who wished to silence women in church gatherings could hardly support the WCTU, whose female members frequently used the pulpit to articulate their messages (DeBerg 1990: 77).

Practical dilemmas forced many fundamentalist churches to rely heavily on women's labor power and available time. Given the shortage of manpower in many of these congregations, fundamentalist preachers became ever more diligent about infusing their religious rhetoric with themes of virility, militarism, and Christian heroism (DeBerg 1990: 86–97). Forces perceived to be opposed to fundamentalism (e.g., modernism, liberalism, and mainline Christianity) were denigrated as "feminine" or "womanish." In a clear break with their evangelical forebears, fundamentalist preachers "rejected the feminized Jesus of Victorian evangelical piety and identified Jesus with traditional notions of masculinity. . . . Fundamentalist ministers asserted their masculinity by presenting Christianity as a faith for real men and the prime Christian example, Jesus, as a manly man" (DeBerg 1990: 92–93). Military metaphors were in abundant supply among early fundamentalist preachers, as men were called to be "warriors in God's army" and "soldiers of Christ" (DeBerg 1990: 93, 95).

Still, preachers in many of these congregations could not afford to turn their attention from their predominantly female membership. Women's labor was needed for the movement to flourish. As such, women were urged to consider careers of a sort in mission work or Christian education (DeBerg 1990: 80). Ultimately, a Protestant commitment to the priesthood of all believers and the populist impulse of early evangelicalism was overturned in favor of hierarchical distinctions that placed ordained clergy (typically men) over and above church laity (predominantly women). Thus, while these churches depended heavily on women's labor power for their very survival, women were barred from leadership positions in them. One fundamentalist "made the distinction between public preaching, which was 'inimical' to women's sphere, and women's legitimate sphere within the church, which he called 'ministration'" (DeBerg 1990: 81). Women's ministries within many early fundamentalist churches were auxiliaries in the truest sense of the term (DeBerg 1990: 82–83).

Although this religious movement could hardly be construed as a victor in the war against modernism, the unique and lasting imprint of first-wave fundamentalism on evangelical gender and family discourse is unmistakable. Fundamentalists successfully masculinized evangelical religion. The fundamentalist husband—no longer the economic warrior for his family due to the rise of corporate capitalism—could become a soldier of Christ. Furthermore, male fundamentalist clergy codified conservative Protestant theology by raising the Bible as the ultimate standard—an inherently rational, masculine standard—that lent logical clarity to pressing moral, familial, and social issues.

Family Relations in Evangelical and Fundamentalist Protestantism: From Postwar to Present

Rapid changes in twentieth-century American society (especially after World War II) exacerbated rather than allayed the anxiety of leading fundamentalists and many evangelicals. As aptly catalogued by Margaret Lamberts Bendroth (1984, 1993), prominent fundamentalist commentators—from the postwar years to the rise of the New Christian Right in the late 1970s and early 1980s—were alarmed by what they perceived to be the individualism and social disconnection that characterized American society.

Despite the ushering of women back into the domestic sphere soon after World War II, marriage and family life were once again being redefined in ways that made many religious conservatives uneasy (Bendroth 1984: 130–131). As a result of postwar suburbanization, economic expansion, and increasing geographic and social mobility, the individualistic dimensions of family life were quickly obviating the more traditional functions of marriage—long-term relational commitment and societal stability. "Personal fulfillment had replaced social utility as the primary purpose of marriage" (Bendroth 1984: 131).

It was on the heels of these social changes and redefinitions of family life that feminist criticism of women's traditional roles emerged. Feminist critiques drew force from these cultural shifts toward personal fulfillment, called into question the unequal treatment of American women, and gained considerable momentum well into the 1970s. Second-wave feminist manifestos such as Betty Friedan's *The Feminine Mystique* were "in many ways a product of this confusion rather than a simple call for justice. Women's restlessness and discontent mounted as their role in the home appeared to lose much of its moral and social significance" (Bendroth 1984: 131).

Despite the largely negative reaction of fundamentalists to these socio-economic shifts and to the burgeoning women's movement, evangelicals—many of whom had experienced upward social mobility after World War II (Flynt 1981: 26–27)—were decidedly polarized on these issues (Bendroth 1984). Some evangelicals sought to shore up traditional conceptualizations of gender roles in the family and society at large (Bendroth 1984: 131–132). However, given the scope of mid- to late-twentieth-century gender role transformations (most notably, a dramatic increase in women's participation in the labor force), a simple appeal to traditional Victorian gender ideals buttressed by some carefully chosen biblical passages about innate feminine vulnerability, wifely submission, and women's inborn penchant for domesticity would prove inadequate. Therefore, like their fundamentalist kin, many leading conservative Protestants during this time again threw aside the perfectionist trappings of early evangelical religion and began to place greater emphasis on an intractable order-of-creation argument to justify women's circumscribed social roles, church responsibilities, and subordinate position in the family (Bendroth 1984: 131–132). "The order of creation idea," which stressed that Adam's creation preceded that of Eve, "was clearly an intensification of the traditional notion of male and female spheres. Instead of basing women's status in the Fall and the curse of Genesis 3:16, the newer theory rooted female subordination in creation itself. Thus, because they were created after men, women ranked below them in a divinely instituted hierarchy. Further, as a fundamental principle of creation, this order was not affected by the work of Christ" (Bendroth 1984: 132). Proponents of this brand of evangelical theology contended that women's secondary status in the creative order forestalled any arguments that men and women could become equals in this lifetime.

This theological maneuver was directed not only against the ideals of the secular women's movement, but also against a growing coterie of evangelical feminists who had begun to gain a hearing within conservative Protestantism during the early 1970s, and who continue to enjoy considerable popularity today. Evangelical feminism argues for gender equality and a withdrawal of the familial and ecclesiastical restrictions often directed at women in conservative Christian churches (Bendroth 1984, 1993; Fowler

1986; Hardesty 1984: 159–161; Ingersoll 1995; Stacey and Gerard 1990). Contemporary evangelical feminism (or biblical feminism, as it is often called) initially drew force from the women's liberation movement during the early 1970s, when its leading proponents mobilized and issued a formal statement condemning sexism within theologically conservative Protestant denominations. Soon after issuing this declaration, biblical feminists formed the Evangelical Women's Caucus, endorsed the Equal Rights Amendment, and began producing a parallel Christian advice literature. Directed primarily at evangelical women, this critical advice literature included periodicals such as *Daughters of Sarah* and popular polemical treatises such as *All We're Meant to Be* (Scanzoni and Hardesty 1992), the latter of which has won publishers' awards and has been revised and reissued twice since its original printing in 1975.

To nonevangelicals, biblical feminism may seem like a contradiction in terms. To be sure, biblical feminists do not attract as much media and political attention as traditionalist evangelical counterparts such as James Dobson, Tim and Beverly LaHaye, and Jerry Falwell. However, biblical feminism has had a significant impact on contemporary evangelical gender discourse. The Evangelical Women's Caucus, founded in 1973, has spawned a second organization, Christians for Biblical Equality, which is also opposed to much of the traditionalist rhetoric advanced by leading evangelicals. And perhaps most notably, evangelical feminists continue to attract sustained criticism from more traditional-minded religious conservatives. So great is the perceived threat of evangelical feminists that their conservative Protestant critics have recently mobilized to form an explicitly anti-biblical-feminist organization, the Council on Biblical Manhood and Womanhood. After convening a conference of their own and producing a point-by-point denunciation of biblical feminism and egalitarian strands of evangelicalism, this organization has recently published a critical tome of nearly six hundred pages, aptly titled *Recovering Biblical Manhood and Womanhood: A Response to Evangelical Feminism* (Piper and Grudem 1991). Yet this group of neoconservatives has not had the last word. Biblical feminists and egalitarian evangelicals have responded in kind, offering strong criticisms of the materials produced by the Council on Biblical Manhood and Womanhood (e.g., Groothuis 1994; Van Leeuwen 1990). It would be erroneous to conclude that this state of affairs has effectively undermined any further transformation of evangelical spousal role conceptualizations. Evangelical gender and family discourses continue to undergo significant transformation. Biblical feminist criticism of the patriarchal family has successfully problematized notions of husband-headship and wifely submission. A melange of traditional and progressive gender ideals are evidenced within Christian social movements, such as the Promise Keepers (Bartkowski 1999, 2000), and within evangelical Protestantism at large.

Part II
Contemporary Conservative Protestant Gender Discourse
Elite Evangelical Prescriptions for Family Life

Philosophers, theologians, and social scientists often make reference to epistemology (assumptions about how people come to know what they take to be true), ontology (presuppositions regarding the nature of the world and the essence of humanity), and soteriology (assumptions religious believers make about God's requirements for spiritual salvation). Evangelicalism provides distinctive answers to these three pivotal issues.

Scripture, Sin, and Salvation:
The Rules of Evangelical Discourse

Epistemologically, contemporary conservative Protestantism is defined by an unswerving commitment to the inerrancy of the Bible. Not unlike their first-wave fundamentalist forebears, contemporary evangelicals generally agree that the Bible is the word of God and believe that scripture provides reliable instructions concerning an array of personal, spiritual, and social issues. Jerry Falwell (1980: 54) unambiguously defends the merits of biblical inerrancy: "A thorough study of the Bible will show that it is indeed the inerrant Word of the living God. The Bible is absolutely infallible, without error in all matters pertaining to faith and practice." Given this interpretive posture, leading evangelicals admonish conservative Protestants against "reading into" scripture. Such an approach to scriptural study is thought to undermine the text's ability to function independently as the word of God. Indeed, it would seem that virtually all leading evangelicals concur on this epistemological commitment to biblical inerrancy, regardless of their orientation toward other theological and social issues. Prominent evangelical feminists echo the same commitment to biblical inerrancy advanced by more politically conservative evangelicals. Rebecca Merrill Groothuis (1994: xi) claims straightforwardly: "Any argument for any position that is not based on or compatible with scriptural teaching is useless and dangerous. The Bible— not tradition, not modern society—is our only authoritative, inerrant guide" (see also Scanzoni and Hardesty 1992: 5).

Many of these same authors draw links between a general commitment to biblical inerrancy on the one hand and a deep concern for the literal meaning of individual biblical words and phrases on the other. Letha Scanzoni and Nancy Hardesty (1992: 9–10), for example, conclude that "in dealing with a specific [biblical] passage, we must know what it actually says, what the words literally mean. Sometimes, particularly on issues concerning women or prophecy or sexuality or other emotional issues, we let our theology tell us what the words mean rather than let the words tell us what the writer meant!" Again, this preoccupation with the literal meaning of scriptural words and passages is embraced not only by evangelical feminists, but also by conservative Protestant family commentators generally. James Dobson (1991: 226) claims that his understanding of God's plan for families is "not based on guesses and suppositions, of course. It is drawn from the literal interpretation of God's Word [i.e., the Bible]" (see also Falwell 1980: 110). And popular evangelical author Mary Pride (1985: 138) maintains that "every word in the Bible is true," while Fred Littauer (1994: 148) contends that "nothing is in Scripture by chance. Every word, every 'jot and tittle' is by design and is placed, in the original manuscripts, exactly as God intended."

Consistent with this broader commitment to the unimpeachability of the Bible and its component books, these commentators agree that scripture speaks authoritatively to family issues of all sorts. Darien Cooper (1974: 10) recounts how "after an intensive study of the Bible, I saw that God had definite solutions to life's problems. And a detailed outline of how a successful marriage should be maintained." In a similar vein, Dobson (1991: 109, 1975:

69) declares, "Biblical principles offer the most healthy approach to family living," adding that "the prescription for a successful marriage is found in the Bible, where the concept of the family originated. God, who created the entire universe, should be able to tell us how to live together harmoniously" (see also LaHaye 1968: 7, 9). In keeping with this commitment to biblical inerrancy, evangelical feminist Patricia Gundry (1980: 13) tells readers of her advice manuals to check the ideas contained therein (as well as those found in other Christian advice books) against prescriptions provided by the Bible: "You will want to use biblical principles in working out your marriage and deciding what it will be. But be careful in deciding which principles really are biblical. Just because someone who writes a book or has some kind of following or credentials says it is biblical does not guarantee that it is. . . . Read the Bible yourself. . . . Go as God leads you."

Despite this widespread conservative Protestant commitment to biblical inerrancy, closer scrutiny reveals that inerrant scriptural readings that hold sway among contemporary religious conservatives are informed by particular hermeneutic (interpretive) strategies leading evangelicals employ to ascribe meaning to the biblical text (Bartkowski 1996; Boone 1989). Evangelical readings of scripture are largely contingent on two pivotal theological presuppositions within this community—namely, a belief in human sinfulness and a commitment to submit to God's plan for human salvation.

Conservative Protestants' ontological position regarding human sin and depravity evinces an elective affinity with their understanding of the Bible's Book of Genesis. Leading religious conservatives interpret the creation account in the book of Genesis to mean that although human beings (i.e., Adam and Eve) were originally made perfect or in God's image, this primordial husband and wife defied God's instructions and thereby doomed all of humanity to live in a sinful world (e.g., Bilezikian 1985: chaps. 1 and 2; Dobson 1975: 39, 1991: 224–225; Falwell 1980: 53–54; Gabriel 1993: 40–41; Pride 1985: 3). They maintain that because Adam and Eve defied God and committed the original sin, all human beings are infected with a predilection for sinful or selfish behavior.

Stemming from this assumption about the fallen state of human nature, conservative Protestant soteriology is predicated on the notion that the only certain path to spiritual salvation lies in a personal striving to submerge or submit one's self-will to some form of external authority. Yet, despite this general point of theological agreement, there is sharp disagreement among religious conservatives concerning precisely how submission should be defined and how it should be implemented in human relationships. Although some leading evangelicals urge all individual believers to submit directly to the authority of God, Jesus Christ, or the Bible (e.g., Bilezikian 1985; Follis 1981; Gabriel 1993; Fred Littauer 1994; Scanzoni and Hardesty 1992; Van Leeuwen 1990; Wagner 1994), others argue for a hierarchical ordering of human relationships in which believers occupying subordinate roles are enjoined to submit to divinely appointed human authorities (e.g., Christenson 1970; Cooper 1974; Dobson 1975, 1991; Elliot 1976; LaHaye 1977). These assumptions about the inerrancy of the Bible and the depravity of human nature, in addition to theological disputes concerning the Bible's instructions for reconciliation with God, all inform conservative Protestant gender and family discourse.

Three

Discourses of Masculinity, Femininity, and Sexuality

Evangelical Debates over
Gender Difference

In many respects, competing definitions of masculinity, femininity, and sexuality provide the foundation for all other disagreements about gender-related issues among conservative religious elites. What is the "essence"—the defining characteristics, if any—of masculinity and femininity? Are women and men essentially different from one another, or are they largely the same? How is gender related to human sexuality? In the past three decades, these questions have stimulated a rancorous debate among leading evangelicals.

Essentialism Embraced: Elite Evangelical Support for Gender Difference

A large number of best-selling evangelical family commentators argue for an essentialist conceptualization of gender. This essentialist gender ideology posits that masculinity and femininity are naturally distinct from one another.[1] Moreover, according to this essentialist view, all normal men exhibit masculine characteristics while women naturally manifest feminine traits. The dominant evangelical discourse consequently highlights what are perceived to be innate differences between men and women.

Many evangelical authors' understandings of essential masculine-feminine difference begin by placing a premium on physical differences between men and women, focusing largely on men's allegedly greater strength, propensity for physical aggressiveness, and more active orientation toward life's challenges (e.g., Dillow 1986: 119–120; Dobson 1991: 178–182; Falwell 1980: 130–131; Fred Littauer 1994: 57, 66; Smalley 1988a: 14–15, 1988b: 31–32). At the same time, this coterie of advice authors stresses women's distinctive reproductive features and physiological capacities (e.g., breasts, womb, menstruation, childbearing, lactation, menopause) and their ostensible connection to family relations (e.g., Cooper 1974: 65; Dobson 1982: 404–405; Elliot 1976: 61–62; Lewis and Hendricks 1991: 114; Pride 1985: 41–42). According to many of these commentators, then, biological sex and socially enacted gender roles are closely connected.

In speaking of sexual relations between a husband and a wife, it is difficult to imagine that Tim LaHaye is not also contrasting masculinity with femininity. LaHaye (1968: 61) describes the husband as "the instigator" of sex and the wife as "the receiver"; in addition, he graphically contrasts the "titanic explosion" of the male orgasm with that apparently experienced by women—"a warm sense of gratification and satisfaction" (see also LaHaye 1968: 63–65). Using remarkably similar language, Elisabeth Elliot (1976: 59) contends that "the physical structure of the female would tell us that woman was made to receive, to bear, to be acted upon, to complement, to nourish."

Several of these commentators contrast women's need for meaningful sexual intimacy (thought to necessitate hours of precoital romance and emotional tenderness) to men's hypersexuality. Men's desire is portrayed as the product of an indiscriminate and insatiable appetite for sex (e.g., Dillow 1986: 119–120; Getz 1974: 29–30, 1977: 92–94; Fred Littauer 1994: 63, 81; Smalley 1988a: 16–17, 1988b: 154). Again, Tim LaHaye (1968: 63–65) claims that the "sex drive in a man is almost volcanic in its latent ability to erupt at the slightest provocation. . . . Most women do not have the problem of looking at a man and lusting after him. . . . A woman responds to kind words and acts and a tender touch." James Dobson (1975: 116) concurs, arguing that "sex for a man is a more physical thing; sex for a woman is a deeply emotional experience." According to Dobson, prostitution, pornography, and rape have little to do with gender, and may be traced largely (if not wholly) to men's virtually insatiable sexual appetites (Dobson 1975: 115, 1982:

402–403, 1991: 31–32)—i.e., to the "sheer biological power of sexual desire in a male" in contrast to the "feminine inertia" that marks women's sexuality (Dobson 1975: 115, 117; see also Getz 1974: 32). If his female readers haven't already gotten the message about their sexual obligations within the marital relationship, Dobson (1975: 118) warns them explicitly that "abstinence is usually more difficult for men to tolerate" and adds that men who are not treated to frequent sex at home may look outside the marital relationship to have their sexual needs met (Dobson 1975: 130).

Given the biological "fact" of masculine hypersexuality, the disciplining of women's bodies is a prominent feature of essentialist advice manuals written for evangelical wives. Several of these manuals for women provide detailed grooming prescriptions, beauty tips, and body management advice that evangelical women can employ to attract—and perhaps reign in—their husbands' wandering eyes (e.g., Cooper 1974: chap. 11; LaHaye 1976: 60–61). Such manuals also feature explicit advice designed to teach a wife how she can satisfy her husband sexually in order to forestall any thought of extramarital relations on his part (e.g., Cooper 1974: chap. 12; Dillow 1986: chaps. 9 and 10; LaHaye 1976: chap. 13). On this score, some authors recommend feminine restraint combined with a wife's virtually boundless availability to her husband's need for "sexual release." Beverly LaHaye (1976: 130–131), for example, warns women with dynamic, assertive temperaments that they risk "demasculiniz[ing] a man by dominating and leading him in everything—including sex"; LaHaye goes on to argue that such a woman "ignores her husband's ego at her own peril," adding that "the success of her marriage may well depend upon her performance and willingness to let her husband maintain leadership in this [sexually] intimate area of their life." Tracts such as these encourage evangelical women to maintain a close surveillance of their own bodily and sexual practices in order to appease their man's virtually boundless desire.[2]

These authors also contend that men and women are different in a range of psychological and social capacities. Within this discourse, men are viewed as inherently more logical than women (e.g., Dobson 1975: 27; Elliot 1976: 146; Florence Littauer 1994: 9; Fred Littauer 1994: 123; Smalley 1988b: 30–31; Weber 1993: 114). Some authors contrast the masculine predilection for rationality with feminine reliance on emotional sensitivity, intuition, and interpersonal communication (e.g., Cole 1982: 96; Farrar 1990: 174; LaHaye

1968: 65; Florence Littauer 1994: 8–14; Fred Littauer 1994: 57–58; Smalley 1988a: 12–15, 1988b: 12–13). Dobson (1975: 27), for example, argues that such innate gender distinctions are unambiguously reflected in men's sharper mathematical reasoning and women's greater verbal acumen (see also Dobson 1991: 178; Weber 1993: 107). Such cognitive distinctions are thought to undergird the different talents men and women bring to family relationships. The masculine penchant for logic and rationality is thought to be consistent with men's ability to act as visionaries. Men's big-picture thinking is contrasted with feminine sensitivity to nuance and detail. According to best-selling author and Promise Keeper speaker Ed Cole (1982: 147): "Men are headliners, women are fine-print people" (see also Cooper 1974: 66; Dillow 1986: 118; Dobson 1991: 182–183; Elliot 1976: 145–146; Lewis and Hendricks 1991: 56, 126; Weber 1993: 24, 27, 114).

These evangelical advice authors contend that masculinity is driven by instrumental concerns. Viewed as initiators, men are thought to thrive on challenge, competition, instrumental achievement, and accolades (e.g., Dillow 1986: 106; Dobson 1991: 183; Elliot 1976: chap. 13; Fred Littauer 1994: 67; Smalley 1988a: 100, 1988b: 76–77). Crabb (1991: 212), for example, argues that "men are designed to enter their worlds . . . with the confident and unthreatened strength of an advocate." Cole (1982:63) encourages his readers to cultivate the same manly traits exhibited by Jesus Christ: "Jesus was a fearless leader, defeating Satan, casting out demons, commanding nature, rebuking hypocrites. . . . Since to be like Jesus—Christlike—requires a certain ruthlessness, manhood does also."

In contrast, women are portrayed as naturally more expressive, nurturing, relational, and responsive. As responders, women are thought to crave stability and security rather than challenge and are believed to value intimate ties to friends, family, and their surrounding environment rather than instrumental achievement (e.g., Dobson 1991: 32; Elliot 1981: chap. 14; Getz 1974: 205; LaHaye 1977: 179–180; Fred Littauer 1994: 126; Smalley 1988a: 13–15, 1988b: 13, 30–31). Again, Crabb's (1991: 212) definition of essential femininity contrasts markedly with his understanding of deep masculinity: "Women are designed to invite other people into a non-manipulative attachment that encourages the enjoyment of intimate relationship." In this same spirit, Mary Pride (1985: 39) refers to mothers as "natural nurturers" (see also Lewis and Hendricks 1991: 54–55, 88), and Darien Cooper (1974: 46–47,

64–65) exhorts her female readers to accept the protection that all husbands long to provide, in turn supporting their husbands' instrumentalist efforts on behalf of the family with wifely praise, encouragement, and admiration (see also Dillow 1986: chap. 6; Lewis and Hendricks 1991: 120–124).

Essentialism Contested: The Evangelical Discourse of Gender Sameness

Ideological dispute over the essence of gender and sexuality is very much in evidence in the contemporary evangelical family advice genre. Despite the dominance of essentialist rhetoric in conservative Protestant gender discourse, a growing number of evangelical commentators have begun to challenge the prevailing essentialist view. These critical commentators argue that masculinity and femininity are not composed of dichotomous sets of traits that are categorically distributed among men and women. Instead, they emphasize an androgynous overlap between men and women and point to what they perceive to be the largely ungendered distribution of emotional sensitivity, rationality, responsiveness, and assertiveness (e.g., Follis 1981: 108–109; Gabriel 1993: 39; Groothuis 1994: 162; Scanzoni and Hardesty 1992: 167–174). In her best-selling *Woman Be Free!,* Patricia Gundry (1977: 22, 31) maintains that "male and female hold much more in common than they do in difference" and argues that "masculinity and femininity are indefinable qualities." Gilbert Bilezikian claims: "Nowhere does the Scripture command us to develop our sex-role awareness as males or females. It calls us—both men and women—to acquire the mind of Christ and to be transformed in His image. . . . Both men and women are called to develop . . . their basic personhood in cooperation with the Holy Spirit . . . a character that exhibits 'love, joy, peace, patience, kindness, goodness, faithfulness, gentleness, self-control' (Galatians 5:22–23). Biblically, such qualities pertain neither to masculinity nor femininity. . . . Genuine Christian spirituality is located beyond the entrapments of sex roles" (Bilezikian 1985: 208–209).

Consistent with this overriding argument for gender sameness, gender distinctions are thought to result from pernicious forms of gender socialization, self-serving male domination in a fallen world, and outmoded stereotypical thinking (e.g., Gabriel 1993: 63; Siddons 1980: 43–45; Wagner 1994: 44). Therefore, psychological tests commonly employed to prove gender differences are dismissed by these authors as artifacts of a male-dominated culture. Scanzoni and Hardesty (1992: 11) assert: "Having projected dualism and dichotomy onto the human race, men have then woven it into culture" (see also Van Leeuwen 1990: 54–60, 83–88). Such debates about the empirical bases of gender difference are, of course, remarkably similar to academic and popular disputes on the subject.

Consequently, these evangelical advocates of gender sameness offer a general indictment of the oppressive gender stereotypes that operate within society at large, and are especially critical of the invidious notions of gender difference so often promulgated by leading evangelical Christians (see for example Bilezikian 1985: 295; Gabriel 1993: 45; Gundry 1977: 25). Ginger Gabriel maintains: "In some 'Christian' literature the 'feeling' characteristics are referred to as 'feminine' and women are urged to be more emotional. The 'thinking' characteristics are considered to be 'masculine.' Men are told to be more cerebral. The reality is that these characteristics are spread across the genders. . . . God created man and woman to reflect his own image. God intended both men and women to be both thinking and feeling. A whole person is in touch with both sides" (Gabriel 1993: 45).

In stark contrast to the dominant evangelical notions of gender difference described above, Gabriel (1993: 46) reminds her female readership: "God created you to be both initiating and nurturing" (see also Gundry 1980: 170). Consequently, biblical feminists' prescriptions for initiation are often directed at wives and are cast in very broad terms. Several encourage wives to act on their "true [sexual] feelings and desires" rather than striking a more "stereotypical pose" where "the husband is a Macho Man and the wife is a Fascinating Female" (Gundry 1980: 158, and see 158–159; Scanzoni and Hardesty 1992: 167–174). Gundry concludes her discussion of this subject by comparing the traditional evangelical perspective with what she believes is a more enlightened view of Christian sexuality: "Rather than focusing on supposed differences between the sexes and what this means sexually, the equal couple is free to focus on each other. They want mutuality in their sexual experiences, not conformity. . . . Consideration for the other can replace wondering how you are as a sex partner. . . . The sharing nature of a marriage based on mutual submission brings a consideration and comfortableness to sex that can make it what you want it to be at any given time—fun, physical desire, or a way to express intimacy" (1980: 158–159).

While some of these biblical feminist authors recognize the subordinate status of their ideas within male-dominated evangelical churches, many of them remain optimistic about the prospects for debunking notions of gender difference. Bilezikian (1985: 210) charges: "As members of the [evangelical Christian] community where 'there is neither male nor female for you are all one in Christ Jesus,' we should strive to exhibit to the world our 'sameness' in Christ." In the final analysis, then, these authors not only argue that gender equality is a worthy goal for which to strive as a society, but add that evangelical Christians should play a leading role its pursuit.

Post-Feminist Reconfigurations:
Radical versus Moderate Essentialism

Recent years have witnessed two decidedly different reactions among evangelical essentialists to the rise of gender-sameness rhetoric. Several leading evangelical commentators argue for what might most appropriately be termed *radical essentialism*. These commentators view gender differences as fixed. A series of best-selling family advice manuals authored by James Dobson frequently return to this claim that gender differences are largely immutable (see also Elliot 1976, 1981). Dobson begins by arguing that male inexpressiveness is neither simply a product of socialization nor a mutable quality that wives should expect husbands to overcome after years of marriage: "Many men—not just those who were taught to be inexpressive—find it difficult to match the emotions of their wives. They *cannot* be what their women want them to be. . . . He has seriously attempted to rearrange his basic nature on five or six occasions, but to no avail. A leopard can't change his spots, and an unromantic, uncommunicative man simply cannot become a sensitive talker. The marital impasse is set in concrete" (Dobson 1991: 132, emphasis in original).

Dobson underscores this point about immutable gender difference repeatedly in his manuals, surmising at one point that "nothing can be done to change the assignment of sex made by God at the instant of conception. That determination is carried in each cell, and it will read 'male' or 'female' from the earliest moment of life to the point of death" (1991: 179). Therefore, Dobson concludes by warning his vast readership that attempts to overcome such inborn differences are doomed to failure: "in fact, the sexes differ so markedly in ways that are not subject to change—anatomy and physiology—that it is a serious mistake to ignore [these differences] or try to make them disappear" (Dobson 1975: 131. See also 1975: 62–63, 114, 120; 1991: 178).

Given their uncompromising commitment to gender difference, many radical essentialists are overtly critical of individuals whose behavior they believe has departed from God's design for men and women. Feminists, gays, lesbians, socialists, humanists, the media and entertainment industries, and even sociologists, as well as any other individuals perceived to challenge God's design for radical gender difference, are open to criticism from many of these authors. Given their antipathy toward social engineering, several of these male authors are especially critical of men they think have capitulated to feminism by bargaining away their God-given predilections for rationality, strength, and dogged perseverance in exchange for more sensitive (i.e., feminized) varieties of manhood. Chuck Swindoll (1991: 26–27) reviles the contemporary "spineless wimps who've never disentangled themselves from mama's apron strings" and waxes nostalgic for the days "when men were men . . . [and] you could tell by looking." Female authors in this genre refashion antifeminist sentiment for their women readers (e.g., Elliot 1991; Pride 1985: 6–13,154–160). The rise of feminism is seen as delegitimizing the life choices of women who are committed to traditional family roles (e.g., Elliot 1976: 27, 93, 1991; Pride 1985: 157, 160). Consequently, several of these authors tell their female readership that women's true liberation is found in opposition to feminism.

In contrast to radical evangelical essentialists, other conservative Protestant commentators committed to gender difference seem more willing to entertain the mutability of masculine-feminine distinctiveness. These commentators, who construe male-female difference as predispositional rather than immutable, can be best described as *moderate essentialists* (Florence Littauer 1994; Fred Littauer 1994; Smalley 1988a, 1988b; see Bartkowski 1997). Moderate essentialists are committed to the view that gender differences are important and God-ordained (see, e.g., Florence Littauer 1994: 10; Fred Littauer 1994: 57, 66) but are quick to add that such differences are not cast in stone (Fred Littauer 1994: chap. 6; Smalley 1988a: chap. 4, 1988b: chaps. 4–10). Gary Smalley, the most prominent of these commentators, offers an extensive illustration for his readership. Smalley begins by likening women to "the butterfly," which "is sensitive even to the slightest breeze . . . notices the beauty of even the tiniest flowers," and is fragile: "If a tiny pebble were taped to its wing, the butterfly would be severely injured and eventually die." Smalley then proceeds to liken men to the buffalo, which is "rough and calloused. It's . . . not even affected by a thirty-mile-an-hour wind. . . . Tape a pebble to the buffalo's back and he probably won't even feel it" (1988b: 29–30). Smalley goes on to contend that the "buffalo's toughness is a tremendous asset. His strength, when harnessed, can pull a plow." Yet, despite the grain of "truth" Smalley believes his readers will find in this female-butterfly, male-buffalo analogy, he argues that such seemingly "fundamental" male-female differences are indeed mutable: "The analogy ends in that the buffalo can never take on any of the butterfly's sensitivities, and the butterfly will never benefit from the buffalo's strength. Such is not the case with your marriage. Your husband can learn how to be gentle, sensitive, and romantic, but he probably won't learn by himself; that's why I've written this book . . . to show how you can help him. You must realize that your husband doesn't understand how much his cutting words or indifferent attitudes actually affect your feelings. He can learn, but you'll need to help him" (Smalley 1988b: 30). Thus, Smalley argues that while husbands are naturally inclined toward callousness and indifference, they can indeed cultivate several desirable traits—e.g., sensitivity and compassion—that seem to come so naturally to women.

Moderate essentialists also directly encourage their male readership to cultivate such characteristics in their men's manuals. Authors such as Smalley (1988a), Fred Littauer (1994), and Gary Oliver (1993) offer themselves as prime examples of husbands who, after years of emotional detachment and obliviousness, were able to cultivate a "new-found sensitivity" (Smalley 1988a: 58–59, 97–99; see also Fred Littauer 1994: 51–52, 64–65). Underlying the moderate essentialist commitment to mutable gender difference and sensitized manhood is an imperative to engage in selective gender blending. In fact, rather than decrying the devaluation of masculinity, moderate essentialists celebrate what they perceive to be the virtues of femininity—sensitivity, compassion, and understanding.

Littauer therefore urges men to resist cultural pressure to engage in hyper-rational, emotionally insensitive displays of masculinity. Instead, he encourages his male readership to emulate what he perceives to be the paragon of sensitized manhood, Jesus Christ. Littauer (1994: 61) argues:

"Jesus, the strongest, most courageous man who ever lived, was not ashamed to show emotion. He was the 'man of sorrows' (Isaiah 53:3). He 'wept' (John 11:35)."

Perhaps aware of the resistance such observations might meet among evangelical husbands in the face of contrarian advice provided by James Dobson, Elisabeth Elliot, and radical essentialists, moderate essentialist authors proceed to catalog what they believe to be the devastating consequences of husbands' insensitivity in the home: a demonstration of his selfishness and unreliability at the expense of other family members, increasing emotional distance between husband and wife, and the impairment of his children's development (e.g., Fred Littauer 1994: 24, 65, 104–105; Smalley 1988a: 17–18).

The Bible and the Essence of Gender

Interestingly, conservative Protestant essentialists and evangelical purveyors of gender sameness each look to the Bible to lend support to their particular conceptualizations of femininity, masculinity, and sexuality. Yet the Bible does not contain one coherent message concerning these issues.

Scriptural Rationales for Gender Difference

Despite internecine disagreements regarding the relative mutability of gender traits, evangelical essentialists are generally united in the view that the Bible provides divine confirmation of masculine-feminine difference. First, many of these commentators read the creation story recounted at the end of Genesis 1 and continuing through Genesis 2 as proof that God intentionally created men and women to be different from one another (e.g., Crabb 1991: 140–141; LaHaye 1968: 62; Lewis and Hendricks 1991: 26–27; Fred Littauer 1994: 57–58, 92; Smalley 1988a: 13). Dobson offers the following interpretation of what these authors construe as a key passage in Genesis 1: "The Bible says emphatically, 'Male *and* female created he them' (Genesis 1:27, King James Version, emphasis added [by Dobson]). Not one sex, but *two*" (Dobson 1991: 179, emphasis in original).

In addition, essentialist authors interpret Genesis 2 to mean that men and women were not only created to be different from each other, but were designed by God to complement one another. These authors interpret Genesis 2:18 ("The Lord God said: 'It is not good for the man to be alone. I will make a helper suitable for him'") as evidence of divinely ordained gender complementarity (see, e.g., Dobson 1975: 185; Fred Littauer 1994: 57; Pride 1985: 41; Smalley 1988a: 14, 1988b: 13; Weber 1993: 108). And they reason that gender difference and complementarity have been transmitted to the sons of Adam (i.e., all men) and the daughters of Eve (i.e., all women), because 1 Corinthians 11:9 explains that God "created woman for man" (Elliot 1976: 107, 114; Getz 1977: 13, 103, 134; Lewis and Hendricks 1991: 101; Weber 1993: 108. See also Cole 1982: 130; LaHaye 1968: 7).

Thus, the assertiveness and perseverance believed to be characteristic of Adam's masculinity is thought to be found in all men. Larry Crabb argues: "Ever since Adam first had to work up a sweat to make the ground yield more food than weeds, men have wondered if they have what it takes to get the job done. The question mark is inherited, passed on from father to son through an arrogant nature that is determined to find adequate resources within oneself" (1991: 206). Crabb also points out that 1 Kings 2:2 reads, "Be strong and show yourself as a man" (1991: 148).

This understanding of bound-and-determined masculinity stands in stark contrast to the scriptural legitimations essentialist authors use to depict essential femininity. Several of these authors contend that 1 Peter 3–4 aptly portrays the traits endemic to essential femininity—a gentle nature and a subdued manner (see also 1 Timothy 2:11): "[Wives,] your beauty should not come from outward adornment, such as braided hair and the wearing of gold jewelry and fine clothes. Instead, it should be that of your inner self, the unfading beauty of a gentle and quiet spirit, which is of great worth in God's sight" (see, e.g., Cooper 1974: 41; Crabb 1991: 193, 205; Dillow 1986: 145; Elliot 1991: 398; Getz 1974: 136, 1977: 16, 133–140; Smalley 1988b: 67). Elliot concludes from this scriptural verse that "the essence of femininity" is characterized by "self-abandonment," "humble obedience," "surrender," and "the willingness to be only a vessel, hidden, unknown. . . . Femininity *receives*" (1991: 398, emphasis in original). Similarly, Getz interprets this passage to mean that "'quietness' is related to [a woman's] very God-created nature and, in turn, appeals to the God-created nature in man" (1977: 136).

How are women to avoid violating God's intent for feminine meekness? Some of these commentators highlight several other biblical verses that might serve as an additional incentive for women who experience difficulty in conforming to this ideal, including: "Better to live on a corner of the roof than to share a house with a quarrelsome wife. Better to live in a desert than with a quarrelsome and ill-tempered wife. . . . A quarrelsome wife is like a constant dripping on a rainy day"—Proverbs 21:19 and 27:15 (see Crabb 1991: 204–205; Dobson 1991: 132); "An excellent wife is the crown of her husband, But she who shames him is as rottenness in his bones"—Proverbs 12:4 (Lewis and Hendricks 1991: 122; see also Cooper 1974: 47); "For a man . . . is the image and glory of God, but the woman is the glory of the man" (Cooper 1974: 39); and "Let a woman learn in quietness and entire submissiveness"—1 Timothy 2:11 (Cooper 1974: 41). In a similar fashion, many essentialist authors believe that the biblical characterization of wives as "weaker vessels" (1 Peter 3:7) provides scriptural evidence of the more delicate nature of women (Cooper 1974: 70; Falwell 1980: 131; LaHaye 1977: 167; Lewis and Hendricks 1991: 82; Smalley 1988b: 76–77. See also Pride 1985: 187; Weber 1993: 121–122). Smalley asserts to his female readership: "The Greek word for weaker means more 'sensitive' or more 'fragile' (1 Peter 3:7; Romans 14:1). Since women tend to be more aware of relationships and the nurturing aspects of life, it is reasonable to assume that your husband is not as aware as you are that something is missing between the two of you" (1988b: 76).

Finally, some commentators—particularly radical essentialists—argue that scriptural allusions to God and Jesus as male and to the Christian church as female reveal that God Himself recognizes the validity of gender distinctions not just among individual human beings but for the structuring of society and the ordering of the world. Several essentialist authors argue that God is in fact male and should be understood as and addressed as "Father" (Dillow 1986: 52; Elliot 1981: 61; Getz 1974: 162; LaHaye 1977: 127; Pride 1985: 37; Weber 1993: 133, 143, 151. See also Cooper 1974: 26). Drawing connections between the male God imagery in the Bible and the manly predilection for "big-picture" thinking, Stu Weber (1993: 133) describes God in unabashedly masculine terms as "the ultimate King and Pro-visionary."

Scriptural Rationales for Gender Sameness

Evangelical proponents of gender sameness reject the foregoing scriptural interpretations in favor of those that support their androgynous conceptualizations of gender. These critical commentators begin by interpreting several biblical passages as indicators of gender equality. They read the account of human origins in the Book of Genesis to mean that both men and women were originally created in the image of God (e.g., Bilezikian 1985: 211; Gundry 1977: 19; Scanzoni and Hardesty 1992: 21–22). Genesis 1:26 figures prominently in this interpretation: "Then God said, 'Let us make man [i.e., human beings] in our image, in our likeness, and let them rule over the fish of the sea and the birds of the air, over the livestock, over all the earth, and over all the creatures that move along the ground.' " Many gender-sameness authors place an interpretive emphasis on chapter 1 of the Genesis creation story, which describes human origins in generic and ungendered terms (see, e.g., Gundry 1980: 82; Siddons 1980: 43–44; Van Leeuwen 1990: 38–40). This interpretive strategy enables them to relativize or deemphasize its chapter 2 counterpart, in which the creation of Adam is depicted as having preceded that of Eve. Scanzoni and Hardesty conclude that scripture reaffirms "not [men's and women's] distinctives but our similarities" (1992: 106). Similarly, Gilbert Bilezikian argues that "both man and woman were uniquely made of the same human substance" (1985: 26, 31). In addition, these commentators are fond of citing a verse from Paul's New Testament letter to the Galatians (3:28), which states that "in Christ Jesus . . . there is neither Jew nor Greek, slave nor free, male nor female, for you are all one in Christ" (Gundry 1977: 24–25; Scanzoni and Hardesty 1992: 315–316).

Gender-sameness authors place great emphasis on scriptural passages about apparently strong, capable, and vibrant female personages (e.g., the stories of Deborah the Judge and Prophet, Sarah the wife of Abraham, and the sexually uninhibited wife of Solomon, as well as of the unflagging commitment of Jesus' female disciples such as Mary Magdalene). Such accounts, according to these authors, call into question prevailing evangelical constructions of feminized weakness, gentleness, and sexual passivity (see, e.g., Bilezikian 1985: 69–71, 199; Follis 1981: chap. 9; Gundry 1977: 90–104, 1980: 45–46, 129–130; Scanzoni and Hardesty 1992: 79–91, 170–172; Siddons 1980: 44).

Related to this broader commitment to the androgynous character of gender, biblical references commonly thought to support essentialism (i.e., women as "weaker vessels" or naturally more "quiet and gentle" spirits) are radically reinterpreted by these dissident commentators. Scanzoni and Hardesty (1992: 109) argue that women are hardly the "weaker" sex when one accounts for cultural expectations about masculinity and defines strength more broadly—for example, women's greater stamina and longer life span (see also Bilezikian 1985: 192; Siddons 1980: 75). They proceed to endorse the commentary of biblical interpreters who have argued "that 'weaker' as used [in 1 Peter 3:7] does not mean physical or mental deficiency but refers to one who is socially and politically without honor. Thus the admonition to honor the woman, because society did not" (Scanzoni and Hardesty 1992: 109). According to this reading, then, women's apparent "weakness" is traced to patriarchal oppression (Bilezikian 1985: 301).

As for women's allegedly essential "gentle and quiet spirit," Gundry offers the following rejoinder to the interpretations provided by evangelical purveyors of gender difference: "The provincial [early Christian] woman who wanted to impress [her peers] would tend to copy the Roman women. But Peter warned against this. Women were told to clothe themselves instead with a gentle and quiet spirit. Rather than attributes of universal femininity as sometimes claimed, these are the fruits of the Spirit which all Christians are to exhibit (Galatians 5:22, 23). Those women were to put off ostentation and let God's Spirit clothe them with qualities which would attract their husbands to Christ" (Gundry 1977: 82; see also Bilezikian 1985: 208–209).

In contrast to the prevailing masculinization of God (as Father) and the corresponding allusions to Jesus Christ's manliness, many gendersameness authors highlight what they perceive to be scriptural evidence for the largely androgynous character of God. These authors contend that God is both initiating and nurturing, and that God's androgynous character is clearly articulated by the use of both masculine and feminine divine imagery in the Bible (e.g., Follis 1981: chap. 10; Gabriel 1993: 38–40; Groothuis 1994: 126; Mollenkott 1983). Based on her reading of the Bible, Gabriel (1993: 39) concludes: "God is neither male nor female. God is both." On the heels of such scriptural interpretations, Scanzoni and Hardesty (1992: 130) contend that "Jesus Christ is our example, our paradigm. We are not told in Scripture to seek what it means to be a 'man' or a 'woman' in our society, but what it means to be Christ-like. We are called to mature personhood in Christ's image (Ephesians 4:13)." Other dissident advice authors agree, with some using scriptural references to argue that Jesus can justifiably be called a feminist (e.g., Siddons 1980: 56). To underscore such arguments, these authors contend that Jesus himself subverted essentialist conceptualizations of masculinity and femininity that prevailed in biblical times. They interpret his displays of gentleness with men, women, and children alike, as well as his frequent public displays of emotion, as a refusal to capitulate to the restrictive masculine mold of his day (Bilezikian 1985: 118; Scanzoni and Hardesty 1992: 129; Siddons 1980: 49–57).

Finally, whereas essentialist commentators believe that the marital unity described in the Bible necessitates gender difference and complementarity, dissident evangelical advice authors argue that scriptural imperatives for marital oneness and unity rest instead on androgynous notions of gender and shared interests between marriage partners (Bilezikian 1985: 33–35; Gundry 1980: 33; Wagner 1994: 70–71; Scanzoni and Hardesty 1992: 26, 28–29, 137–138, chap. 8; Siddons 1980: 50). Glenn Wagner contends: "Meeting the mutual and realistic expectations we have for marriage is part of the 'oneness' that defines a biblical union (Genesis 2:24, Matthew 19:5, Corinthians 6:16–17, Ephesians 5:31)" (1994: 14). Similarly, Bilezikian (1985: 35) explains his interpretation of Genesis 2:24, which depicts a husband and wife as "one flesh": "The concepts of reciprocal dependency and mutuality in equality are intrinsic to the doctrine of oneness. . . . [B]ecause husband and wife are mutually dependent in a relationship of equality, they 'become one flesh' and their bond is characterized by permanency."

Four

Wifely Submission or Mutual Submission?

Evangelical Discourses of Family Power

Gender debates within conservative Protestantism are not confined to disputes about the essence of gender. They also include competing prescriptions regarding the exercise of family power. When choices arise concerning the family's welfare, how should such decisions be made? What practical strategies should spouses employ to resolve marital disagreements? On what grounds can the exercise of authority within the home be legitimated?

Patriarchy Extolled: The Dominant Discourse of Husband-Headship and Wifely Submission

A large number of popular conservative Protestant gender and family commentators advocate a patriarchal family structure (e.g., Cooper 1974: 43; Dillow 1986: 122–145; Dobson 1991: 92–94; Farrar 1990: 157–183; Getz 1977: 124–129; Pride 1985: 196–203; Weber 1993: 83–98). In practical terms, these authors argue that husbands—not wives—are ultimately responsible for making decisions that affect the welfare of the family and its members. James Dobson states flatly: "The primary responsibility for the provision of authority in the home has been assigned to men. It will not be popular to

54

restate the age-old Biblical concept that God holds *men* accountable for leadership in their families. . . . God apparently expects a *man* to be the ultimate decision-maker in his family" (Dobson 1991: 92–93, emphasis in original; see also Cole 1982: 70–71; Farrar 1990: 179–180 for similar statements).

To be sure, none of these authors discourage husbands from seeking the input of their wives prior to making decisions, and many commentators even inject egalitarian rhetoric—for example, equal in value, different in function—into their prescriptions for patriarchal spousal relations (see Cooper 1974: 62, 65; Getz 1977: 129–131; LaHaye 1976: 72; Pride 1985: xiii). Dobson, for example, does not altogether rule out discussion, compromise, and negotiation as a means of familial decision making (e.g., Dobson 1975: 93–94; see also Crabb 1991: 173–174; Getz 1974: 162–164, 1977: 120–123). To the contrary, he cautions husbands to avoid exercising a "nineteenth century authoritarianism" in which patriarchs could recklessly disregard the wishes of other family members (Dobson 1982: 409; see also Crabb 1991: 197; Dobson 1982: 411, 1991: 97, 184).

Yet, despite such strong warnings against dictatorial domestic leadership, many of these commentators seem to agree that husbands are not obligated to solicit (much less heed) wifely advice or admonitions. Ultimately, these authors contend, God holds husbands accountable for exercising familial leadership that is in keeping with biblical principles. Therefore, even as Dobson (1975: 69–70, 1991: 130) maintains that men are to exercise familial authority in a benevolent and selfless fashion, he concludes: "for those who accept God's design for the family, it is clear that husbands bear the *initial* responsibility for correcting . . . [domestic] problem[s]. This obligation is implicit in the role of leadership assigned to males" (Dobson 1975: 70, emphasis in original; see also Dobson 1982: 409–410).

Evangelical wives, on the other hand, are often construed as "executive vice presidents" in the family (e.g., Cooper 1974: 65–66; Dillow 1986: 122–145; see also LaHaye 1976: 71). Many of these authors liken the family to other social institutions—e.g., corporate, military, or government organizations—that operate according to the principles of hierarchy and submission to duly appointed authorities (Cooper 1974: 61, 85; Pride 1985: 198–199; see also Farrar 1990: 179–180). As executive vice presidents in the family, wives are told that they are far from powerless. They are instructed to offer input as requested or deemed necessary with regard to family decision making (e.g., Cooper 1974: 67; Dillow 1986: 128). At the same time, however, evangelical wives are enjoined to submit themselves to and obediently implement their husbands' ultimate "presidential" decisions, even if those choices are in direct contradiction to their own "vice-presidential" wishes (Cooper 1974: 68–88; Dillow 1986: 128; LaHaye 1968: 109–110; LaHaye 1976: 78): "the president's success depends on the vice president's help in carrying out the policies. When new decisions have to be made, the president may consult the vice president for advice, but he assumes responsibility for the final decision. Once a policy is decided, they work together as a team to carry it out. . . . In this relationship, they share a oneness, good communication, emotional peace, and security, provided the vice president is not struggling to gain control of the organization!" (Cooper 1974: 66). Given their crucial role in administering their husbands' directives pertaining to family life, wives are strongly discouraged from manifesting a grudging obedience to their husbands in cases where spouses do not share similar views (Cooper 1974: 90–91; Dillow 1986: 126–128, 139). But how are wives to avoid harboring such resentment?

Alongside such reminders about the importance of their distinctive familial responsibilities, evangelical wives are encouraged to cherish their diminished decision-making power in the family. Darien Cooper's best-selling *You Can Be the Wife of a Happy Husband* (1974: 61–99), which boasts thirty-three printings and more than 700,000 copies in print, treats this issue at length. First, Cooper contends that familial leadership is accompanied by a burdensome responsibility for making the correct decision. Thus, she maintains that in wifely submission lie the true seeds for women's liberation: "Let go! Relax. You can enjoy the freedom of knowing that, along with the right to make the final decisions, your husband carries the responsibility for the consequences of his decisions" (Cooper 1974: 78; see also Dillow 1986: 139–140; Elliot 1976: 65–67; LaHaye 1976: 71).

Second, Cooper argues that a spirit of submission will ultimately yield personal satisfaction for wives. Stories abound in wives' advice manuals of women whose submission to their husbands' leadership, in the final analysis, brought their wishes to fruition (putatively, via the handiwork of God). Cooper herself provides four such examples illustrating the practical benefits of wifely submission, including one story recounting how a wife's submission led to the conversion of her non-Christian husband despite his initial displeasure with his mate's churchgoing habits (Cooper 1974: 78–79, 86–89; see also Dillow 1986: 140–142; LaHaye 1976: 79–80). Pointing to these and other practical merits of wifely submission, Cooper urges wives: "Resist temptations to interfere with his leadership because you feel his decisions or actions are too forceful, harsh, or wrong. Don't argue your point or try to manipulate him. Respond to his leadership in a relaxed manner, and you will find that your husband usually wants to please you" (1974: 78).

Finally, women are told that husbands who seem reluctant to lead their families will be encouraged to do so by their wives' submissive posture (Dillow 1986: 125, 140–142; LaHaye 1976: 73–74, 141–142): "You will encourage your husband to take the lead by being a good follower and telling him how much you enjoy his taking charge. As you display trust in his ability, he will be more eager to continue as head of the house. Interestingly, as you follow, your husband will lead; but if you become aggressive, he may regress. You nag, and he will rebel. If you desire to please him, he will want to please you" (Cooper 1974: 79).

Patriarchy Contested: The Oppositional Discourse of Mutual Submission

In stark contrast to the prevailing evangelical notion of wifely submission, a burgeoning group of dissident commentators argues for mutual submission in the home (e.g., Gabriel 1993: chap. 11; Gundry 1980: 22–26; Fred Littauer 1994: 150–152; Smalley 1988b: 156; Van Leeuwen 1990: chap. 12). In general, proponents of this oppositional perspective maintain that both partners—not just the wife—have a mutual obligation to submit themselves directly to God, thereby disavowing their individual interests for the collective good of the marital relationship (Bilezikian 1985: 162–171; Follis 1981: 94–95; Fred Littauer 1994: 145–146; Groothuis 1994: 163–165; Scanzoni and Hardesty 1992: 151–152; Wagner 1994: 38). This perspective, which seems to have originated with evangelical feminists, has now become common currency among equality-minded religious conservatives and moderate essentialists. Evangelical feminist Rebecca Merrill Groothuis outlines the meaning and perceived merits of mutual submission: "Rather than eliminating submission altogether, biblical feminism calls for more submission. . . . Unlike the established power of hierarchy or the grab-for-power of anarchy, mutual submission sets aside the power struggle and yields to the rule of love. . . . No marriage fails for lack of authority and control; rather, marriages fail for lack of mutual love and submission. . . . Would not two-way submission then be twice as good" as one-way wifely submission (Groothuis 1994: 164–165)?

In place of patriarchal leadership, these oppositional voices outline several different strategies for familial decision making: (1) In-depth discussion and compromise, including the input of both spouses or all family members who will be affected by the decision (Gundry 1980: 136, 139; Fred Littauer 1994: 155–156, 163; Scanzoni and Hardesty 1992: 160; Smalley 1988a: 135–139, 1988b: 164–165, 1994). (2) A general agreement not to take action on a particular decision until both spouses or all involved parties are of similar mind (Gundry 1980: 139–140; Florence Littauer 1994: 124; Fred Littauer 1994: 166–167; Scanzoni and Hardesty 1992: 160; Smalley 1988a: 129–131, 1988b: 165). (3) Deference to the spouse who exhibits the most competence in that area or who has the most at stake in the decision (Follis 1981: 92–93; Gundry 1980: 139–140, 144; Fred Littauer 1994: 155; Scanzoni and Hardesty 1992: 160–161). (4) An alternation of duty periods in which one spouse serves as the decision maker for a given time, then the other serves a similar duty period (Scanzoni and Hardesty 1992: 160). (5) The use of quid pro quo, a this-for-that trade of favors exchanged by spouses facing minor disagreements (Gundry 1980: 145).

These commentators extol what they perceive to be the practical benefits of mutual submission and joint decision making: learning to respect each partner's personal interests and boundaries; averting abusive patriarchal oppression; fostering marital intimacy and sexual responsiveness for both spouses; modeling appropriate conflict-resolution tactics for children; and relieving husbands of the burden of sole responsibility associated with patriarchal decision making (e.g., Groothuis 1994: 164–165; Gundry 1980: 151–163; Fred Littauer 1994: 156; Scanzoni and Hardesty 1992: 160–174; Smalley 1988a: 133–134, 1988b: 165). Ginger Gabriel, best-selling author of the revised and expanded *Being a Woman of God* (more than 250,000 copies in print), supports this perspective via a critical counterexample: "Many a woman has memorized the submission Scriptures, gone to women's study groups on submission, gone forward in church to recommit her life to submitting to the role of wife, only to blow up hours later at an insensitive husband. . . . The solution is not to try to show more respect to your husband.

The solution is to experience God's healing" (Gabriel 1993: 104, emphasis in original).

Servant-Leadership and the Reappropriation of Mutual Submission Rhetoric: Neopatriarchal Discourse and Biblical Feminist Rejoinders

Given the rise of egalitarian evangelicals' pleas for mutual submission within the home and broader cultural shifts toward gender equality, definitions of patriarchal headship offered by traditionalist voices within conservative Protestantism have changed significantly over the past three decades. In fact, recent years have witnessed the rise of new-guard evangelical purveyors of domestic patriarchy. New-guard advocates of patriarchy have sought to incorporate feminist critiques of male domination into their vision of marital relations while still envisioning the husband as the family's leader (e.g., Crabb 1991; Lewis and Hendricks 1991; Piper and Grudem 1991). Evangelical advocates of this neopatriarchal ideology employ two key rhetorical strategies to advance their cause.

First, rather than defining headship solely as male domestic decision-making authority, new-guard proponents of the patriarchal family commonly speak of male family leadership as a husband's responsibility to take the lead in serving the needs of family members. In an attempt to clarify their complicated definition of male family leadership, many of these authors (including several leading Promise Keepers) have appropriated a neologism—servant-leadership—from popular organizational consultant Robert Greenleaf (e.g., Crabb 1991: 191; Lewis and Hendricks 1991: 67–78; Piper and Grudem 1991: 63; Weber 1993: 97. On Greenleaf's original conceptualization, see Fraker and Spears 1996; Frick and Spears 1996). Although critics catalog servant-leadership as an oxymoron, several of these authors take great pains to draw distinctions between Christ-like servant-leadership on the one hand and autocratic, dictatorial, and potentially abusive forms of male family headship on the other (e.g., Crabb 1991: 48–59, 197–202; Lewis and Hendricks 1991: 67–78; Piper and Grudem 1991: 61–65). So, despite their defense of male family leadership, many of these authors decry unilateral decision making on the part of husbands and express great anxiety over the abuse of women in the home (see Crabb 1991: 108–110, 152, 197; Lewis and Hendricks 1991: 75–77; Piper and Grudem 1991: 62).

Robert Lewis—who has written most extensively on this topic of servant-leadership in evangelical homes—contrasts servant-leaders with lording leaders. His conciliatory orientation toward critics of male family leadership is noteworthy:

> In a biblical marriage, the husband's role revolves around "leadership." Now if you hold to a more egalitarian position, you may react and cry "foul"! You may jump to the conclusion that I'm just a chauvinist advocating the oppression of women through a hierarchical model of male dominance. Nothing could be further from the truth. . . . Wives, are you afraid that if your husband is the "leader," he'll dominate you? . . . Too many homes, including Christian ones, have degenerated into this style of leadership. Women have suffered untold hurt and humiliation as a result. But that kind of leadership totally contradicts biblical teaching. . . . The kind of leadership Jesus defines for His followers has to do with: *Responsibility,* not privilege. *Service,* not being served. *Support,* not superiority. (Lewis and Hendricks 1991: 51–52, emphasis in original)

According to several of these authors (see Lewis and Hendricks 1991: 75–78), husbands are instructed to lead not by retaining rights to a final say in decision making but by initiating discussions on matters of common concern to family members (after all, according to these authors, men are "initiators"); by planning for the family's future with their wives and jointly mapping out the trajectory of their marriages (especially since many of these authors argue that men are gifted with "big-picture thinking"); and by initiating valuable family traditions (again, manly leadership is seen as consonant with masculine initiation).

A second rhetorical strategy employed by these new-guard advocates of domestic patriarchy involves a recasting of submission rhetoric. Several new-guard proponents of the patriarchal family rhetorically meld prescriptions for wifely submission with references to mutual submission in their advice manuals (see Crabb 1991: 173; Dillow 1986: 127–128; Farrar 1990: 162, 180–182; Piper and Grudem 1991: 62–63; Weber 1993: 86). Farrar's *Point Man* (1990) provides several illustrations of his distinctive conceptualization of mutual submission. For example, this manual contains a chapter titled "Husband and Wife Teamwork in the Marriage Cockpit" that melds mutual submission rhetoric with a vision of the "marriage cockpit" predicated on relations of hierarchy and differential authority—the husband acts as the superordinate pilot while the wife occupies a subordinate copilot position.

Anticipating that this melding of authority-minded allusions (pilot versus copilot) and equality-minded rhetoric (mutual submission, teamwork) will cause confusion, Farrar attempts to clarify this issue for his male readership, quite tellingly, via a football metaphor. Farrar argues that although a quarterback and wide receiver share the "same objective" and must operate as an "effective unit" to achieve success, the quarterback "has the final say because he's the quarterback" (1990: 164). According to Farrar's logic, the quarterback's position as play caller on the football field demands the exercise of authority that, while receptive to feedback from his subordinate teammates, must prevail in the face of disagreements or indecision. This attempt to naturalize hierarchy as an essential feature of all social relationships via sports metaphors (quarterback-husband, receiver-wife) is strikingly similar to the political or military metaphors used by old-guard evangelical defenders of the patriarchal family; however, the quarterback–wide receiver metaphor is arguably less dictatorial-sounding than political or military illustrations, as teammates should ideally be more disposed toward negotiation than are inherently unequal political officeholders or military personnel.

Like other authors in this emergent genre, Farrar seeks to redefine mutual submission within the context of a husband-headship family model:

> Let me be clear. Mutual submission does not mean that the husband and wife take turns being the head of the home. That is the man's permanent assignment. It does mean that the husband demonstrates and models the concept of submission in his own life when the situation calls for such a response. Mutual submission is just another way of describing servant-leadership for the husband and loving submission for the wife. *It is at the core of both biblical headship and biblical submission.* (Farrar 1990: 181, emphasis in original)

In this way, then, new-guard proponents of the patriarchal family embrace the general idea of mutual submission even while they redefine the phrase to be consistent with their specific dictates for male family leadership.

Several recently published biblical feminist manuals offer rebuttals of new-guard patriarchal rhetoric that casts the husband as the family's servant-leader (e.g., Groothuis 1994: 27–28; see also Van Leeuwen 1990: 244). In

assessing the increasing prominence of this term among leading evangelicals, Groothuis contends:

> Traditionalists maintain . . . [that] the husband's authoritative headship is
> deemed essential for the biblical integrity of the family. . . . The husband's
> "servant-leadership" is said always to work for the wife's benefit. . . . But
> as long as the definition of woman's difference entails the need for her to
> come under the protective guidance of a man and to gear her entire life
> around helping that man as he leads her, the implication of her inferiority
> and inequality will be very real indeed. (1994: 26–27)

Consequently, evangelical feminists conclude that Christian readers of
neopatriarchal family advice manuals should not be swayed by the recent
attempts of leading religious conservatives who inject egalitarian rhetoric
into their ideologies of male dominance.

Wifely Submission, Mutual Submission, and Debates over Gender Difference

One important source of dispute between evangelical defenders of
the patriarchal household and conservative Protestant critics of male family
leadership concerns competing assumptions about the essence of gender—
i.e., the extent to which masculinity and femininity are envisioned as radically
distinctive or largely homologous. In general, evangelical proponents of a
patriarchal family structure view masculinity and femininity as radically different from one another and argue that distinctively masculine traits—including logic, strength, assertiveness, and instrumentalism—uniquely qualify
men for familial leadership and for the burden of responsibility that accom-
panies this superordinate position (e.g., Cooper 1974: 50, 66–67; Dobson
1982: 401, 1991: 93–94; Elliot 1976: 58–60, 64). Among those who promulgate
these radical essentialist rationales, Elisabeth Elliot (1976: 178) maintains
that a husband's "virile drive for domination [is] God-given and necessary in
fulfilling his particular masculine responsibility to rule," while Dobson (1991:
94) argues: "Boys and girls typically look to their fathers, whose size and
power and deeper voices bespeak leadership."

At the same time, these authors maintain that women's psychological
responsiveness, desire for relational stability, and innate vulnerability pre-
dispose them to submit willingly to their husband's household leadership

(e.g., Christenson 1970: 33; Cooper 1974: 66–67, 74–75; Dobson 1991: 184; Elliot 1976: 58–62). Tim LaHaye, cofounder of the Moral Majority, asserts that a "man is the key to a happy family life because a woman by nature is a responding creature. . . . That is one of the secondary meanings of the word *submission* in the Bible. God would not have commanded a woman to submit unless he had instilled in her a psychic mechanism which would find it comfortable to do so" (LaHaye 1977: 178, emphasis in original).

In contrast, many egalitarians and evangelical feminists use gender-sameness arguments to justify egalitarian decision-making authority in the home (e.g., Gabriel 1993: 45–47; Groothuis 1994: 126, 162; Gundry 1977: 22–25; Scanzoni and Hardesty 1992: 125–126). Ginger Gabriel, a critic of the "male-thinking" and "female-feeling" ideals that pervade evangelical gender discourse, explicitly encourages her female readership not to yield to the authority of their husbands: "God created you to be both initiating and nurturing" (1993: 46). Patricia Gundry adds: "Only weak men demand weak women" (1977: 111; see also Gundry 1980: 130–131). In this way, many advocates of mutual submission contend that husbands and wives alike possess the requisite capacities for exercising family leadership.

Interestingly, not all advocates of mutual submission envision the relationship between gender and household authority in this fashion. Rather than arguing that male-female differences are inconsequential, moderate essentialists believe that leadership in the home requires a thoroughgoing commitment to teamwork precisely because patriarchal authority is impaired by an array of uniquely masculine biases. Specifically, these commentators argue that men's inherent lack of sensitivity, compassion, and intuition, combined with the apparent abundance of these qualities in women, necessitates joint decision making among couples (see esp. Fred Littauer 1994: 155–156; Smalley 1988a: chaps. 7 and 9). Fred Littauer (1994: 155) remarks: "God . . . gave [our wives] understanding and perception that we husbands often don't have. They can see things we don't see. Therefore they need to be a part of the decision-making process about everything that affects the family." To convey this point more readily, these authors frequently cite incidents in which a wife's insight and intuition about a problem actually spared—or would have spared, had she been consulted—families from the dire consequences of a hasty, uninformed husband's unilateral decision (e.g., Florence Littauer 1994: 8–9; Fred Littauer 1994: 162–163; Smalley 1988a: 107–109,

132–133). Consequently, moderate essentialist Florence Littauer urges her female readership not to subordinate their feminine intuition to their husbands' penchant for logical argumentation: "God gave us women intuition. Let's not throw away the gift" (1994: 10). Therefore, although these evangelical critics of patriarchy disagree about the nature of masculinity and femininity, they concur that husbands and wives should share decision-making responsibilities.

Family Power and the Bible

Alongside scriptural disputes about the nature of gender difference are divergent evangelical understandings of the Bible's references to the exercise of rightful authority within the home. Key portions of the Bible seem to command the wife's submission to her husband, while other passages appear to support mutual submission and shared marital authority by husbands and wives.

Patriarchal Interpretations of the Bible

Evangelical commentators who embrace a patriarchal family structure construe several key biblical passages as advocating male headship and wifely submission in the home. Most popular among these are verses 22 through 24 from chapter 5 of the Bible's book of Ephesians (Cooper 1974: 16–17, 77, 84–85; Dobson 1975: 69, 1982: 409, 1991: 128; LaHaye 1968: 106–107; Pride 1985: 197): "Wives, submit to your husbands as to the Lord. For the husband is the head of the wife as Christ is the head of the Church, his body, of which he is the Savior. Now as the church submits to Christ, so also wives should submit to their husbands in everything." Focusing on the first of these passages (i.e., Ephesians 5:22), many patriarchal commentators frequently remind wives that submission to their husbands serves as an indicator of their commitment to Jesus Christ, for whom their husbands are serving as a divinely appointed proxy (e.g., Elliot 1976: 140–141; LaHaye 1976: 72–73): "It should be comforting to know that God will, literally, show you His will for your life through your husband. . . . You are rebellious to Christ's leadership to the same degree that you rebel against your husband's leadership" (Cooper 1974: 75–76).

These commentators also interpret several other biblical passages as divine commands for patriarchal household authority—for example, Colossians 3:18; 1 Peter 3:1–6; 1 Timothy 3:4–5; Titus 2:3–5 (Cooper 1974: 18, 56–57, 81, 85, 90; Dobson 1982: 409–410, 1991: 92; LaHaye 1968: 106–107; Pride 1985: xi, 196–197, 203), as well as 1 Corinthians 11:3: "Now I want you to realize that the head of every man is Christ, and the head of the woman is man, and the head of Christ is God" (e.g., Cooper 1974: 20–21, 62; Pride 1985: 197). These authors contend that the divine hierarchy of God-Christ-Church mirrors the divinely ordained familial hierarchy of husband-wife-child. According to these writers, this passage is clear in its implications for family life: the husband is biblically commanded to exercise headship over his wife and children (e.g., Cooper 1974: 62–65; Weber 1993: 86–87).

In addition to these New Testament passages, many of these specialists maintain that the Old Testament's Genesis 2 account of human origins and the Genesis 3 depiction of the entrance of sin into the world underscore both the primacy of patriarchal authority and the pitfalls of feminine leadership in the home. These commentators interpret the Genesis 2 order-of-creation narrative in which the creation of Adam predates that of Eve as a divine endorsement of patriarchal authority among this primordial couple (Cooper 1974: 17; Elliot 1976: 134, 145ff). Pointing to this account of human origins, these commentators stress that Eve was not only created after Adam, but from his body (namely, his rib), to relieve Adam of the sense of incompleteness that plagued him. Elliot (1976: 67, 145–146) and others therefore conclude that God created women (the daughters of Eve) "from and for" men (the sons of Adam). In practical terms, these authors construe the order of creation as unambiguous evidence that wives are to serve as "helpmeets" to husbands, who in turn are to exercise authority over wives (e.g., Dobson 1991: 129; Weber 1993: 89–90).

Many of these patriarchal commentators interpret the Genesis 3 account of humankind's "fall" from grace as a confirmation of the pitfalls of feminine leadership in marriage (e.g., Christenson 1970: 39; Cooper 1974: 21; Elliot 1976: 24–25; Pride 1985: 3). According to these commentators, sin entered the world because Adam's divinely ordained position of authority was usurped by his wife Eve, who had decided on her own accord to eat the forbidden fruit from the Tree of Knowledge of Good and Evil. Some of these commentators also indict Eve for using her feminine wiles to undermine further her husband's authority. By enticing Adam with the forbidden fruit she had initially eaten, Eve convinced her husband to follow her into original sin (see Cooper 1974: 21; Farrar 1990: 167): "It was, in fact, the woman, Eve, who saw the opportunity to be something other than she was meant to be—the Serpent convinced her that she could easily be 'like God'—and she took the initiative. We have no way of knowing whether a consultation with her husband might first have led to an entirely different conclusion" (Elliot 1976: 24–25).

Based on this interpretation of Genesis 3, these family commentators place great emphasis on what they perceive to be the gender-specific indictment God meted out to Eve for inviting sin into the world: "your desire will be for your husband and he will rule over you" (Genesis 3:16; see also 1 Timothy 2:13). These authors understand this passage to mean that God's punishment of Eve included the reinforcement of patriarchal authority in marital relations. They conclude that if Eve was at all uncertain about her subordinate place in the created order, God further clarified his marital chain of command after Eve led the first couple into original sin.

Egalitarian Interpretations of the Bible

In stark contrast to the biblical interpretations that hold sway among conservative Protestant defenders of domestic patriarchy, egalitarian commentators highlight key scriptural passages to support their commitment to mutual submission. Most notably, they emphasize that the series of biblical passages often used to legitimate wifely submission (Ephesians 5:22–24) are preceded (and, in their view, superseded) by a verse—Ephesians 5:21—that commands mutual submission: "Honor Christ by submitting to each other" (see Bilezikian 1985: 162–164; Gabriel 1993: 102; Fred Littauer 1994: 150; Mason 1985: 153; Scanzoni and Hardesty 1992: 148ff; Wagner 1994: 73). Similarly, these commentators interpret 1 Peter 3:7 as evidence of divine support for mutual submission. Not unlike Ephesians 5, 1 Peter 3 allows for divergent interpretive emphases that yield contradictory scriptural readings. Although some of the opening verses from 1 Peter 3 are interpreted (and strongly emphasized) by advocates of patriarchy as directives for wifely submission, 1 Peter 3:7 somewhat ironically describes husbands and wives as "joint heirs" or "fellow heirs" of God's grace. It is to this latter passage (verse 7) that defenders of mutual submission give interpretive primacy (Gundry 1977: 83; Fred Littauer 1994: 147; Smalley 1988a: 41; Scanzoni and Hardesty 1992: 140–143; Wagner 1994: 105). In addition to these passages, other verses such as Romans 12:10 ("Be devoted to one another in brotherly love") and Romans 15:7 ("Accept one another just as Christ also accepted us to the glory of God") are cited by some of these authors as evidence of God's imperative for marital equality (see Fred Littauer 1994: 56, 125, 147; Smalley 1988a: 139, 1988b: 91).

Given such views, many egalitarian authors directly challenge the veracity of biblical interpretations that conclude that husband-headship and wifely submission are a divine imperative for the family. Some of these dissident authors construe headship—translated from the Greek word *kephale*—as a literal reference to the chronological order of creation. They consequently argue that the literal meaning of the term *kephale* is not "authority," but rather "origin" or "source" (e.g., Bilezikian 1985: 241–243; Gundry 1977: 71, 1980: 116; Scanzoni and Hardesty 1992: 150; Siddons 1980: 62–63; see Ingersoll 1995). Therefore, 1 Corinthians 11:3—in which the (allegedly Pauline) author writes, "Now I want you to realize that the head of every man is Christ, and the head of the woman is man, and the head of Christ is God"— is interpreted as a chronological description of creation rather than a timeless prescription for hierarchical spousal relations. These authors contend further that the equation of the creation order with patriarchal authority is inconsistent with other seemingly egalitarian biblical passages, such as 1 Corinthians 11:11–12: "In the Lord, however, woman is not independent of man, nor is man independent of woman. For as woman came from man, so also man is born of woman" (see Fred Littauer 1994: 147; Groothuis 1994: 67–68; Gundry 1980: 107; Scanzoni and Hardesty 1992: 30, 316).

Many of these critics of the patriarchal family contend that if the Pauline word *kephale* is translated literally to mean "head," it must refer to an actual head on a human body (Bilezikian 1985: 247–249; Gundry 1977: 64; Littauer 1994: 153–154; Scanzoni and Hardesty 1992: 33–37). These equality-minded commentators are quick to point out that body parts operate interdependently, and they are prone to stress other Pauline scriptural references—1 Corinthians 12:14–25, Colossians 2:19—that indicate that the head is not to be privileged over other body parts such as hands, feet, ears, or eyes (Bilezikian 1985: 248; Fred Littauer 1994: 146, 153–154; Scanzoni and Hardesty 1992: 35). Evangelical feminists (Follis 1981: 97–103; Gundry 1977: 77, 89–104; Scanzoni and Hardesty 1992: chap. 5) buttress their criticism of husband-headship by pointing to women in the Bible who exercised authority and leadership in the family (e.g., Sarah, the spouse of Abraham) and who were leaders in the early church (Phoebe, a deaconess and minister) and in society at large (e.g., Deborah, a prophet and judge, as well as Queen Esther).

Consequently, these equality-minded commentators contend that portrayals of women (i.e., daughters of Eve) as more prone to sin and therefore in need of male authority do not hold up under scriptural scrutiny. They claim that because Adam and Eve both partook of the forbidden fruit in Genesis 3, they shared joint responsibility for humankind's original sin (e.g., Bilezikian 1985: 39–50; Gabriel 1993: 95, 104; Gundry 1977: 20–21; Scanzoni and Hardesty 1992: 37–44; Van Leeuwen 1990: 42–48), a view some commentators support by reference to Romans 3:23: "All have sinned and fall short of the glory of God" (Scanzoni and Hardesty 1992: 9). Patriarchal interpretations of the Bible that place culpability on Eve for humanity's fall from grace are characterized as being distorted by the importation of cultural biases into scriptural study (Bilezikian 1985: 49–50, 263–264; Groothuis 1994: 67–68, 111; Gundry 1977: 20–21; Scanzoni and Hardesty 1992: 33, 134–135). Indeed, some of these authors seem more willing to indict Adam's behavior in this incident, for he alone is said to have received an admonition directly from God not to eat the forbidden fruit (Bilezikian 1985: 39–50). Even more importantly, according to these authors, Eve was tempted by Satan disguised as a serpent—an adversary superior in cunning to any human being—whereas Adam was gullible enough to eat the forbidden fruit without question simply upon the suggestion of Eve, who was his equal (Bilezikian 1985: 48–50; see also Scanzoni and Hardesty 1992: 45).

Finally, several of these equality-minded commentators maintain that what is frequently interpreted as God's normative statement that Adam would "rule over" Eve after their collective fall was not a prescriptive endorsement of a patriarchal family structure. Rather, they interpret this verse as a predictive lamentation offered by an omniscient God who foresaw the hardship patriarchal oppression would cause for women in a male-dominated family and a sinful world (Bilezikian 1985: 54–56; Gabriel 1993: 95, 109; Gundry 1977: 61; Scanzoni and Hardesty 1992: 1–2, 43–44; Siddons 1980: 43; Van Leeuwen 1990: 44–45). Scanzoni and Hardesty explain: "Perhaps the most famous of God's pronouncements to women is . . . [that from Genesis] 3:16: 'He shall rule over you.' A better translation is found in The Jerusalem Bible: 'He will lord it over you' " (1992: 43).

Five

Separate Spheres or Domestic Task Sharing?

Evangelical Debates over Financial Provision, Housework, and Child Care

A final component of contemporary evangelical gender debates centers on divergent elite prescriptions pertaining to household responsibilities. These debates hinge on three key issues: financial provision, housework, and child care.

The Evangelical Discourse of Separate Spheres

Dominant evangelical gender ideals are characterized by a strong commitment to fixed and dichotomous spousal roles. Many of the most popular evangelical advice authors equate masculinity with public-sphere pursuits (most notably, economic provision) and link femininity with private-sphere involvement (i.e., housework and child care). These authors typically argue that the same masculine assertiveness that uniquely equips husbands for household leadership provides men with the requisite capacities for economic competition and financial provision for their families (see Christenson 1970: 127–128; Cooper 1974: 80; Dillow 1986: 119–121; Dobson 1991: 25–26; LaHaye 1977: 26; Lewis and Hendricks 1991: 87; Swindoll 1991: 47; Weber 1993: 92). James Dobson argues:

Suddenly, we see the beauty of the divine plan. When a man falls in love with a woman, dedicating himself to care for her and protect her and support her, he suddenly becomes the mainstay of the social order. Instead of using his energies to pursue his own lusts and desires, he sweats to build a home and save for the future and seek the best job available. His selfish impulses are inhibited. His sexual passions are channeled. He discovers a sense of pride—yes, masculine pride—because he is needed by his wife and children. Everyone benefits from the relationship. (1991: 32)

Given men's achievement-minded orientation toward life, these authors contend that a husband's attachment to other family members is channeled through his economic provision for the household (Cooper 1974: 72; Elliot 1976: 114; LaHaye 1977: 23, 176; Weber 1993: 92). Likewise, women's innate sensitivity, relationality, and submissive orientation are thought to equip wives for domestic responsibilities that include selflessly meeting the needs of her husband and children (e.g., Crabb 1991: 158; Dillow 1986: chap. 6; Swindoll 1991: 47–49; Weber 1993: 104). Beverly LaHaye (1976: 88) queries her female readership: "God created women to be helpers, and where better could we begin than right in our own home?" Similarly, Dobson (1975: chap. 1) describes a mother as the family's "domestic engineer," while Mary Pride (1985: 20) compares the values of true "wifeliness" (i.e., "long-term *commitment* and daily *self-sacrifice*" for her family) with the lamentable " 'me'-marriage [that] reflects the feminist value of self-fulfillment" (emphasis in original). Linda Dillow (1986: 134–135) instructs her female readers to prioritize their life commitments in light of their own self-denial: God first, followed by (in descending order of importance) the wife's husband, children, home, the wife herself, and finally her own personal commitments outside the home.

Yet again, several of these authors refer to what they perceive as clear-cut biological differences between the sexes to justify such divergent gender roles in the family.[1] Men's physical capacity for hard work is contrasted with women's maternal instinct (e.g., Dobson 1975: 131; LaHaye 1976: 97; LaHaye 1968: 34, 1977: 24, 28, 169), and such divergent capabilities are seen to justify gendered household responsibilities (Lewis and Hendricks 1991: 114). Stu Weber asks his male readership:

What do you see, after all, when you look at the vehicle of a man's physical body? What was it made for? Check it out. In contrast, what does a woman's body tell you that a woman was made for? Every twenty-eight days or so her body tells her she was made for giving life and its sustenance. Her breasts remind her that she was made for giving life and nurturing life. What does a man's body tell you? Not a thing! Why? Because the purpose for a man is out on the horizon. A man was made to be a provisionary, a wagon scout, out there in front, looking ahead. The purpose isn't inside. . . . We must find that purpose outside of ourselves. (1993: 212)

Competing Reactions to Dual-Earner Families among Separate Spheres Advocates

The rise of dual-earner families in recent decades has caused some degree of ideological dissent among evangelical proponents of separate spheres. One faction of these authors is opposed to dual-earner familial arrangements with very few exceptions (e.g., Christenson 1970: 127–129; Dobson 1982: 349–358; Elliot 1976: 53; Lewis and Hendricks 1991: 191–195; Pride 1985: part 4). Tim LaHaye puts the matter bluntly in *How to Be Happy Though Married* (more than 800,000 copies in print): "The most important [danger of dual-earner arrangements] is that if the wife works and keeps her money separate from her husband's, it breeds a feeling of independence and self-sufficiency which God did not intend a married woman to have. . . . I am convinced that one of the reasons young married couples divorce so readily today is because the wife is not economically dependent upon her husband" (1968: 29; see also, e.g., Cooper 1974: 74–75; Dobson 1991: chap. 15; Elliot 1976: 113).

Some evangelical advice authors offer wives and mothers currently in the labor force practical tips, informational resources, and personal vignettes that might serve as an additional incentive for quitting their paid jobs so that these women can dedicate themselves fully to serving their families and especially their children (see Burkett 1995; Cooper 1974: 155–156; Pride 1985: 211–214; Lewis and Hendricks 1991: 200–202). One recent tome on this subject, more than three hundred pages long, is targeted explicitly at evangelical wives and mothers. Aptly titled *Women Leaving the Workplace: How to Make the Transition from Work to Home,* this particular advice manual surveys evidence concerning the allegedly negative impact of women's growing labor-force participation on the family. Among such negative repercussions are the hidden financial costs purportedly incurred by wives who have abandoned their domestic roles (e.g., expenses associated with securing out-of-home child care, eating out, hiring domestic help). Even more significant, from this viewpoint, are the costs of mothers' employment that are incurred by children. Larry Burkett, the author of this manual, laments: "too often these blessings [i.e., children] are ignored because of the focus on the pressures of everyday life. To provide the material things they think their kids 'need,' all too often parents overwork themselves, which results in emotional neglect of the very ones they are trying to provide for. But those [children] who spend any portion of their young lives in day care appreciate how valuable a mom is. Only a mother can love like a mother" (Burkett 1995: 239).

The solution to these problems, from Burkett's vantage point, is not found in a more equalized division of labor among dual-earner couples; rather, Burkett urges women to return to the domestic realm and implement the various money-saving strategies provided throughout his book—tightly budgeting money and time; practicing bartering in lieu of paying cash; establishing a home business if needed; and thrifty gift-giving, among other suggestions. To make his case, Burkett marshals images that underscore the importance of a protected childhood, replete with spiritual motifs:

> It's a tough world for kids, and it's going to get a lot tougher. They will need all the support they can get to avoid the pitfalls Satan has skillfully laid for them. . . . I understand the negatives of some stay-at-home moms, and the positives of a second income, but weighed in the balance I believe the scale tips decidedly toward full-time moms. . . . Positive self-worth and godly character are very important to your children. Maybe they will get this outside the home, but are you willing to take the chance? Your children only have one childhood and you only get one chance. (Burkett 1995: 246–247)

Another faction of pro–separate spheres evangelical authors is more willing to deem wives' and mothers' labor-force participation legitimate provided that employed women do not allow their work commitments to compromise their family obligations (Linamen and Holland 1993: chaps. 8 and 12; see also Dillow 1986: 81–82; Getz 1977: chaps. 11 and 12). Reacting with some ambivalence to the massive influx of women into the labor force in recent decades, many of these authors wish to make sure that evangelical families—and particularly conservative Protestant wives—do not fall prey to the apparent financial and relational costs of relying on two incomes rather than just that provided by the husband.

Such misgivings about women's labor-force participation strongly impact these authors' conceptualizations of the household division of labor in dual-career families, as evidenced most clearly in a recently published manual—*Working Wives, Workable Lives,* written by Karen Linamen and Linda Holland. This manual, as its title implies, is targeted specifically at employed evangelical wives. Although employed wives are encouraged to institute family task sharing, to purchase convenience foods, and to cultivate lowered expectations of domestic tidiness (Linamen and Holland 1993: 34–35, 43–44, 90), the authors seem guided by the underlying assumption that the domestic sphere is in fact the wife's realm. Consequently, career-minded women are admonished to attend diligently to their meal preparation responsibilities: "Serving junk food to your family isn't mentioned in the 'Thou Shalt Nots' of the Ten Commandments. Nor will it land you time in jail. But if the most balanced meal your kids eat in an entire week is PopTarts and milk, then you probably deserve whatever guilt you're feeling [about being a working mother]. . . . If you want to live to see grandkids (and have your kids healthy enough to bear some), take action now" (1993: 113–115). Echoing this theme, best-selling author Linda Dillow (1986: 81) tells her employed female readers that they need to be "even more organized than the full-time homemaker—make dinners on the weekends, get up early to get everything in order, and so on" (see also Lewis and Hendricks 1991: 200).

Gendered Prescriptions for Housework and Parenting

Following closely from this broader commitment to distinctive spousal roles, evangelical commentators who embrace a separate spheres ideology typically support a gendered division of household labor. As part of their primary providership responsibilities, husbands are generally charged with implementing the family's budget, paying bills, and overseeing financial records (Cooper 1974: 53, 75; Dillow 1986: 90, 141; Dobson 1975: 68–69, 1991: 140–141; LaHaye 1968: 27–28; Lewis and Hendricks 1991: 77, 87; Swindoll 1991: 32). Other masculinized tasks identified in such manuals include outdoor chores and minor household repairs (Cole 1982: 149; Cooper 1974:

33, 39, 70; Dillow 1986: 91–92; Dobson 1975: 62, 1991: 140–141; Elliot 1976: 91; Weber 1993: 42).

By contrast, evangelical wives are charged with the vast majority of domestic responsibilities. A wife's household tasks are often spelled out in painstakingly explicit detail by these authors (e.g., Dillow 1986: 70–77; Getz 1977: 49, 109). Wives are portrayed as exercising primary responsibility for the following household tasks: shopping for basic household necessities; laundry; food preparation and cleaning up after meals; and indoor cleaning and housekeeping (e.g., Cooper 1974: 52, 134–137; Dillow 1986: 21–23; Dobson 1975: 166, 1991: 132; Elliot 1976: 111; Getz 1977: 49, 109; LaHaye 1976: 78, 89; Pride 1985: 148–149). Several of these authors define a wife's housekeeping responsibilities very broadly. For example, wives are not simply deemed responsible for general household cleaning but are also encouraged to tidy up—without "nagging"—messes left behind by husbands who may have an aversion to cleaning (e.g., Elliot 1976: 84; LaHaye 1976: 62–64, 88–91).

These authors typically view task sharing as a temporary and voluntary act of compassion on the part of husbands. When asked by one of his readers, "How do you feel about a man doing his share of the housework and helping with the meals at home?" James Dobson replies forthrightly: "My opinion on that subject is not likely to win me great numbers of friends among the women of the world, but I dislike seeing a man work all day at his job and then be *obligated* to confront his wife's responsibility when he comes home" (1975: 166, emphasis in original). Dobson is disheartened by full-time homemakers "who have browbeaten their puppy-dog husbands into cooking and washing dishes every night of the year." While he concedes that "there are times when a loving husband will choose to bail out his overworked wife," he is quick to add: "Personally, I balk when I think that my wife is demanding that I go beyond the call of duty; I like to help her on a *voluntary* basis, and often do so" (1975: 166, emphasis in original). Echoing this theme, Elisabeth Elliot (1976: 131) is highly critical of spouses who would attempt to divide household chores equally between them, stating outright: "Marriage is not a fifty-fifty proposition." She contends that the "picayune scorekeeping" needed to insure task equality guarantees little more than a "business partnership" of a marriage.

Alongside such recommendations for the dichotomous allocation of domestic chores, several of these authors claim or imply that mothers should attend to the lion's share of childcare responsibilities (see Cooper 1974: 50–53; Dillow 1986: 66–70; Dobson 1982: 349–358; Getz 1977: chap. 8; LaHaye 1976: 96–108; Lewis and Hendricks 1991: 102–104, 185–190; Pride 1985: 35–82). Women are thought to be characteristically equipped for this task, not only biologically but psychologically. Robert Lewis marvels at his wife's ability to juggle her domestic chores and myriad parental responsibilities: "I'm amazed at how [my wife] Sherard can keep track of what's going on all over the house. She'll be in the kitchen baking, focused on a certain recipe, and yet is somehow still able to carry on a conversation with our four-year-old. Meanwhile, she's in touch with what's going on in the next room with our nine-year-old *and* with our teenage daughter upstairs. Don't ask me how she does it! A man's brain simply does not have that kind of power. . . . For a focused male brain, four kids talking at the same time is torture! But not for Sherard. Somehow she can serve a meal *and* carry on a four-way—no— a five-way conversation at the same time. Incredible!" (Lewis and Hendricks 1991: 109, emphasis in original).

Many of these authors are alarmed that such an esteemed view of motherhood no longer holds sway in many American homes and has even eroded within some evangelical households. Mary Pride (1985: 39) prompts maternalistic feelings among her female readers whose babies count on their compassionate moms to make their child's "yucchy little bottom all clean and sweet," and to wipe the youngster's "gooey face, innocently awash in carrot and rice cereal." Pride queries: "Doesn't it make you feel special that God has entrusted you to nurture and protect this tiny morsel of helpless humanity?"

James Dobson, who comments at length about parental responsibilities within his best-selling *What Wives Wish Their Husbands Knew about Women* (nearly two million copies sold), laments that "many American women have apparently decided that raising children is an enormous interference and sacrifice" (Dobson 1975: 170; see also Getz 1977: 75). He then proceeds to link rapid increases in child abuse, child neglect, and even the murder of children by their own parents to what he perceives as American parents'—and especially mothers'—growing desire to put their own career pursuits ahead of their children's needs. Dobson (1975: 160–164) is expressly critical of employed mothers of preschool children; he argues forcefully against the use of daycare and even implies that children who lack sufficient parental contact as youngsters are considerably more at risk of becoming convicted felons in adulthood. Lee Harvey Oswald and Charles Manson are the two most notorious examples he mentions (see also Pride 1985: 116–120, 128). Dobson dismisses arguments about how a mother's "quality time" with her children should be her primary concern: "Who says that a working mother's evening time with her children is necessarily of greater quality than it would have been if she remained at home all day? Her fatigue would make the opposite more likely.... Let's give our babies both quality *and* quantity" (Dobson 1975: 164, emphasis in original). Not surprisingly, the following admonition occupies a prominent place on the "list of practices for mothers to avoid" reproduced in Dobson's manual: "Don't take a full-time job or otherwise make yourself largely unavailable to the child during [the infant/toddler] period of his life" (1975: 170).

This vision of the mother as primary parent does not exclude the father from childcare activities altogether. To the contrary, authors of these manuals regularly enjoin fathers not to become so over-involved in their careers that they neglect the needs of their families and, especially, their children (e.g., Cole 1982: 137–143; Dobson 1982: 411–412; LaHaye 1977: 184–185; Lewis and Hendricks 1991: 88; Weber 1993: 144–145). Paternal involvement is deemed crucial by many of these authors precisely because of the special "masculine" personality characteristics (e.g., decisive leadership) fathers alone are expected to bring to the process of child development. Therefore, these commentators typically argue that both husband's and wife's respective family roles must be modeled in a gender-specific fashion to maturing sons and daughters (e.g., Cooper 1974: 40; Dobson 1982: 415; Elliot 1976: 133; Getz 1977: 86; LaHaye 1968: 81–82; Lewis and Hendricks 1991: 88, 207; Weber 1993: 163–168). Dobson (1975: 159) remarks that "both the masculine and feminine personalities are needed in modeling of roles for children," while Robert Lewis argues that "as parents, we should instill in our young sons this vision of providing financial security for a wife. It should be their goal in life to bring in enough income so that their future wives are not forced to work" (Lewis and Hendricks 1991: 88). Farrar's *Point Man* (1990) contains several lengthy chapters on the importance of gendered parenting strategies (see also Weber 1993). One chapter, titled "How to Raise Masculine Sons and Feminine Daughters," is designed to give fathers the tools they need "to point their children to an accurate, God-given, sexual identity"

(Farrar 1990: 201, and see chap. 2; Weber 1993: chap. 11). Farrar asserts: "A child with a clear sexual identity and a liberal amount of self-confidence will not be afraid or anxious of assuming the role of husband or wife when the proper time comes. Such children will know who they are and what they are to do in establishing a home" (1990: 220–221).

The Evangelical Discourse of Domestic Task Sharing

In contrast to the foregoing authors' defense of separate spheres for husbands and wives, biblical feminists and a growing coterie of egalitarian evangelicals advocate fluid spousal roles, domestic task sharing, and coparenting. Indictments of dual-career families are conspicuously absent from these manuals, and many of these authors even offer stinging criticism of traditionalist evangelical commentators who promote a separate spheres ideology (see Bilezikian 1985: 271–272; Follis 1981: 88–90; Groothuis 1994: 11, 126, 163–164; Florence Littauer 1994: 47–48; Van Leeuwen 1990: 231–234). Scanzoni and Hardesty (1992: 167) contrast the prevailing evangelical perspective on spousal roles with their own more egalitarian views: "The couple who wants an equal-partnership marriage must . . . strive to avoid falling into the stifling trap of gender-role stereotyping, which stresses differences and separate spheres, driving men and women apart rather than drawing them together. Christian marriage should be the kind of relationship that encourages both spouses to grow in Christ to exhibit the fruit of the Spirit (Galatians 5:22–26)." Indeed, freedom and flexibility are the principles that guide many of these authors' critiques of prevailing evangelical advice concerning family roles and responsibilities (e.g., Gundry 1980: 159–160; Siddons 1980: 75–76; Van Leeuwen 1990: 179–185).

Several of these authors highlight what they perceive to be the potential pitfalls of a coercive wifely domesticity (e.g., financial dependence, psychological depression), and in many cases encourage their female readership to pursue suprafamilial commitments (including labor force participation) if desired (Follis 1981: 46–47; Gabriel 1993: 126–127; Groothuis 1994: 169; Gundry 1980: 132, 170; Scanzoni and Hardesty 1992: chaps. 8 and 13; Van Leeuwen 1990: 182–185, 207). These commentators provide many illustrations of family life featuring women who are actively engaged in work outside the home and greatly satisfied with such pursuits (Follis 1981: 93; Gabriel 1993: 7, 38, 118; Scanzoni and Hardesty 1992: 291–293; Smalley 1988a: 76–77;

Van Leeuwen 1990: 142–143; Wagner 1994: 67, 74, 97). Rather than simply counseling men to avoid overcommitments to their occupational pursuits (a perspective that implicitly equates a husband's role with breadwinning), several of these authors admonish both spouses to avoid careerism (see Scanzoni and Hardesty 1992: 164; Wagner 1994: 35; Van Leeuwen 1990: 207–208).

In addition, these commentators encourage their male readership to provide moral and practical support for their wives' suprafamilial ambitions (Scanzoni and Hardesty 1992: 301–302; Smalley 1988a: 33, 77, 123–125; Wagner 1994: 69–70; see also Gundry 1980: 159–160). In his chapter-long treatment of spousal abuse, Fred Littauer provides his male readership with a survey designed to gauge their "potential for aggression" (correlated with affirmative answers to the questions posed). Among these questions, Littauer inquires of husbands: "Do you insist that your wife stay home and not work or have her own income, even when she wants to?" (Littauer 1994: 133; see also Smalley 1988a: 76–77).

Both evangelical feminists (Bilezikian 1985: 35; Follis 1981: 46, 93; Gundry 1980: 170; Scanzoni and Hardesty 1992: 158–159; Siddons 1980: 76–75) and moderate essentialists (Fred Littauer 1994: 133, 64; Smalley 1988a: 76–77) justify such recommendations, in part, by appealing to values such as equity, autonomy, and personal fulfillment. Yet, unlike biblical feminists who eschew masculinized definitions of protection and providership (see, e.g., Follis 1981: 45–46; Scanzoni and Hardesty 1992: 161), moderate essentialists redefine prevailing conceptualizations of male protection and provision broadly enough to encompass an imperative for husbands to be understanding and supportive of their wives' educational and professional aspirations (e.g., Fred Littauer 1994: 6–7, 64; Smalley 1988a: 76–77, 123–125).

Dissident Injunctions for Shared Housework and Coparenting

Consistent with this broader commitment to fluid and overlapping spousal roles, readers of these manuals are encouraged to share household tasks equally and to engage in coparenting. These same readers are given a long list of practical benefits ostensibly associated with such domestic arrangements: the emotional fulfillment emanating from the couple's display of mutual commitment to the marriage through task sharing and coparenting; the option of spending more time together working jointly on projects or engaging in shared leisure activities; the sense of relief enjoyed by husbands and fathers who might feel unduly burdened by being cast as the family's sole provider; and the opportunity to model gender-role flexibility for children (e.g., Fred Littauer 1994: 64; Groothuis 1994: 11, 165–166; Gundry 1980: 132, 151–155, 178–180; Scanzoni and Hardesty 1992: 162; Smalley 1988a: 121–122; Van Leeuwen 1990: 125–163; Wagner 1994: 67–68, 77).

Yet, in light of dominant evangelical support for highly dichotomized spousal roles and husband-providership, several of these commentators seem acutely aware that their advocacy of task sharing and coparenting may encounter resistance among their male readership (e.g., Scanzoni and Hardesty 1992: 161–162, 300; Wagner 1994: 68; see also Van Leeuwen 1990: 145–147, 162). Popular author, Promise Keeper speaker, and president of Today's Family Gary Smalley cautions his male readers: "Do not expect a band to play whenever you help with the housecleaning" (1988a: 33). In a similar vein, Promise Keeper Glenn Wagner (1994: 68) seems to assume that his male readership may not know how to implement his recommendations for domestic task sharing on their own initiative: "Ever try telling your wife, 'Give me a list of things you want done this weekend, and I'll see that they're accomplished?' After you help her regain consciousness and composure, you can follow through on your shocking intentions." Despite the somewhat humorous tone of such passages, these commentators are quite serious about urging husbands to be attentive to an array of domestic chores, including shopping for various household items, doing the laundry, cooking meals, and cleaning the home (e.g., Bilezikian 1985: 117; Fred Littauer 1994: 64; Scanzoni and Hardesty 1992: 162, 164, 300; Smalley 1988a: 33, 34).

These commentators are particularly critical of husbands in dual-earner marriages who expect their wives to come home to a second shift of domestic chores or solo parenting after a full day at work (e.g., Scanzoni and Hardesty 1992: 362–363; Smalley 1988a: 117–118). Thus, in contrast to purveyors of dichotomized spousal roles (whose solution to working wives' second shift is for these women to leave the work force or simply become more organized household managers), many dissident commentators argue that this problem should be resolved via dramatic increases in husbands' domestic labor and childcare contributions. One manual written specifically for dual-earner evangelical couples takes to task husbands who may be neglectful of their "cohomekeeper" role: "When you are a truly liberated man, you will see beyond the stereotypes. You will not only accept your wife as a coprovider, but you will be secure enough in your manhood to wash a dish or change a diaper" (Balswick and Balswick 1995: 102).

Even as husbands are enjoined to make greater contributions to the family's domestic labor requirements, wives are encouraged to throw off the shackles of economic incompetence by becoming more actively involved in the family's financial affairs (e.g., Florence Littauer 1994: chap. 5; Gundry 1980: 170; Wagner 1994: 36). These authors encourage the sharing of financial information among spouses and are strongly critical of husbands who would attempt to withhold such information from their wives (Florence Littauer 1994: 61–62; Fred Littauer 1994: 38, 164, 167–168; Siddons 1980: 27). In contrast to the stereotype of feminine financial incompetence, Florence Littauer (1994: 43) contends: "We are each born with certain talents. The question is not whether a male or female is best at certain tasks, but which personality can do the job best. Not all men have a feel for finances and not all women have a fear of figures" (see also Siddons 1980: 76).

If any women in her female readership remain unconvinced about the importance of these issues, Littauer alerts them to the inherent dangers of fiscal passivity. She provides for her readers a series of vignettes about women who submissively entrusted their husbands with the family finances, only to find themselves in near economic ruin from their husbands' financial mismanagement (Florence Littauer 1994: 48–55). Consequently, in cases in which the husband acts as the family's financier, Littauer warns wives (1) to become aware of their legal obligations as specified by the laws of the state in which they live—she reviews some of the basic differences in various states' financial codes (1994: 56–58); (2) to read widely on the subject of family finances and fiscal investments—she provides a recommended reading list of financial self-help books (1994: 59, 205); (3) to insist that their husbands make available to them all financial records and documents—she provides a predesigned checklist of important financial papers (1994: 62–65); and (4) to budget and monitor expenses as a couple—she provides a complete expense ledger (1994: 57). Several of these authors therefore contend that godly husbands will readily share with their wives this important information (Florence Littauer 1994: 61–62; Fred Littauer 1994: 38, 164, 167–168), while only abusive husbands bent on control will hold fast to the reins of financial decision making (Wagner 1994: 36).

As was the case with financial provision, there is a significant degree of diversity in these commentators' justifications for task sharing and coparenting. Biblical feminists and other equality-minded evangelicals defend task sharing and coparenting as more equitable and as a means of liberation from restrictive gender stereotypes (e.g., Follis 1981: 88; Gundry 1980: 138–139; Scanzoni and Hardesty 1992: 161–165; Siddons 1980: 76). Scanzoni and Hardesty, who treat this issue in great detail, argue: "New ways of family living can emerge in equal-partner marriages. New approaches to the most menial household tasks may come about, with everyone pitching in to help as much as possible. . . . The older dependency image can be cast off, as wives pursue new ways of aiding their families—without fears of 'losing femininity' or 'damaging husbands' egos'" (1992: 163–164).

Moderate essentialists approach this issue from a somewhat different angle. Although they clearly agree that principles of fairness and equity necessitate joint responsibility for domestic chores, they also legitimate a husband's contribution to the domestic workload with injunctions for men to protect their more fragile wives from overwork (Fred Littauer 1994: 64; Smalley 1988a: 118–119, 124). Gary Smalley contends that "many men . . . maintain the inward conviction that women should remain in the kitchen cooking or cleaning while they play golf, hunt, or watch the game on TV. . . . Think of your wife's special limitations before expecting her to take on *added* responsibilities. Such forethought will avoid extra strain on your relationship and protect your wife's mental, spiritual, emotional, and physical life" (Smalley 1988a: 121, emphasis in original).

Smalley also reminds his male readers to take up the reigns of parental responsibility as one means of protecting their wives from the rigors of child-rearing (e.g., Smalley 1988a: 101, 122, 124). In his popular manual written for husbands, Smalley confesses his failure to exercise leadership in this area of family life: "During our early years of marriage, when my children would cry during the night, I automatically expected my wife to get up and take care of them. And she did. Never did I feel compelled to get up and take care of the kids. Be tender and alert to her physical needs. Be the leader in taking whatever steps are needed to insure that your wife gets the rest she needs" (Smalley 1988a: 122). In the event that evangelical fathers are not swayed by the rhetoric found in his best-selling men's manual, Smalley provides strategies Christian mothers might use to solicit their husbands' domestic participation: "You must paint a picture of yourself for your husband's benefit. Let it portray your physical limitations and your unique needs. . . . Explain how many times a day you change your son's diapers, chase the children out of the street, and pick up after them. Help him picture the fatigue and pressure you face, knowing you'll never catch up with housework. Open his eyes to the boredom you feel as you fold and refold, straighten and re-straighten, tie and retie" (Smalley 1988b: 135). Smalley reassures his female readership that the resulting guilt felt by uninvolved husbands may in fact convert such otherwise distant fathers into committed coparents.

Competing Scriptural Interpretations for the Allocation of Domestic Labor

Rival coteries of elite evangelicals marshal an array of scriptural passages to justify their injunctions for dichotomized or, alternatively, shared domestic task allocation.

Separate Spheres and the Bible

Evangelical purveyors of separate spheres draw on several carefully selected scriptural references to support their vision of dichotomized household roles and responsibilities. First, these commentators point to a series of verses in the book of Genesis that seem to support masculine breadwinning and feminine domesticity. According to these commentators, Adam served as the provider and leader of the primordial family while Eve acted as his helper—that is, an assistant under his charge (see Cooper 1974: 20; Elliot 1976: 113–114; LaHaye 1977: 23; Lewis and Hendricks 1991: 99–102; Pride 1985: 196; Weber 1993: 47, 92). These authors reason that Adam's position of providership is the rightful inheritance of all men who come after him. They stress that this masculinized role in the family was reinforced by God's punishment of Adam following the primordial couple's original sin: "To Adam [God] said . . . 'Cursed is the ground because of you; through painful toil you will eat of it all the days of you life. . . . By the sweat of your brow you will eat your food'" (Genesis 3:17–19). Tim LaHaye reminds husbands of their providership responsibilities by citing 1 Timothy 5:8, which reads, "But if any provide not for his own, and specially for those of his own house, he hath denied the faith, and is worse than an infidel" (1977: 185; see also Cooper 1974: 71). These same commentators argue that the repercussions of Eve's sinful act (Genesis 3:16, 20) hinged on her domestic concerns and maternal responsibilities—subjection to her husband, pain during childbirth. Formerly named "Woman," this primordial mother was thereafter called "Eve"—the latter interpreted to mean "mother of all living" (Crabb 1991: 157; Christenson 1970: 39–40; Cooper 1974: 71; LaHaye 1977: 23, 185; Weber 1993: 112).

Second, separate spheres authors interpret several Pauline references in the Bible's New Testament as a divine imperative for domesticized femininity (e.g., Cooper 1974: 18; Crabb 1991: 158; Getz 1977: 105–107; Lewis and Hendricks 1991: 99–104; Pride 1985: 136–138). Most notable among these is Titus 2:3–5, which reads: "Likewise, teach the older women to be reverent in the way they live. . . . Then they can train the younger women to love their husbands and children, to be self-controlled and pure, to be busy at home, to be kind, and to be subject to their husbands, so that no one will malign the word of God." According to many of these same evangelical authors, 1 Timothy 5:14 reiterates this message, as it instructs young widows "to marry, to have children, to manage their homes and to give the enemy no opportunity to slander." And finally, 1 Timothy 2:15 states that "woman will be kept safe through childbirth, if they continue in faith and holiness with propriety"—which Getz (1977: 80) interprets to mean that a married woman's "most significant fulfillment will come by being a good wife and mother," and which Mary Pride (1985: 41) understands as God's articulation of the principle that "childbearing is a wife's basic role." Perhaps sensing her readers' suspicion of such bold proclamations in late twentieth-century America, Pride seeks to allay any such concerns: "We don't have to be timid in approaching this passage. Childbearing *is* woman's 'peculiar function.' . . . Having babies and raising them is our role" (1985: 42, emphasis in original).

So that there may be no doubt about the specific responsibilities evangelical wives are to undertake while being busy at home, separate spheres authors encourage their female readership to emulate the Ideal Wife described in chapter 31 of the Book of Proverbs (Dillow 1986; Pride 1985: 147–152; see also Cooper 1974: 58–59; Dobson 1991: 129; LaHaye 1976: 88; Lewis and Hendricks 1991: 202–203). This dedicated and selfless woman is said to have awakened early in the morning and retired late in the evening in order to meet her various and sundry domestic obligations, including shopping ("She is like the merchant ships bringing food from afar"—verse 14); cooking ("She gets up while it is still dark, she provides food for her family"—verse 15); and sewing ("In her hands she holds the distaff and grasps the spindle with her fingers. . . . She makes coverings for her bed"— verses 19, 22). In their view, the Ideal Wife depicted in the Bible was the paragon of homemaking and motherhood: "She watches over the affairs of her household and does not eat the bread of idleness. Her children arise and call her blessed, her husband also, and he praises her: 'Many women do noble things, but you surpass them all'" (verses 27–29).

Scriptural Arguments for Domestic Task Sharing

Evangelical advocates of fluid spousal roles, domestic task sharing, and coparenting offer competing theological rationales to legitimate their distinctive conceptualization of familial responsibilities. According to these authors, the Bible provides no explicit instructions for husbands to adopt a breadwinning role or for wives to focus on domestic pursuits (Bilezikian 1985: 24; Follis 1981: 88; Scanzoni and Hardesty 1992: 130, 161–162). Moreover, these commentators radically reinterpret the biblical passages commonly cited to support a separate spheres ideology.

Several of these equality-minded authors begin by pointing out that the initial role of Eve in the Book of Genesis consisted of exercising joint dominion over Creation with her husband Adam (Bilezikian 1985: 25–26, 41; Gabriel 1993: 41; Gundry 1977: 23, 61; Siddons 1980: 43, 63; Van Leeuwen 1990: 41–42, 171–172). They add that Adam's oppressive role restrictions for Eve emanated from his fallen, sinful pursuit of self-interest (e.g., Bilezikian 1985: 50–58; Gabriel 1993: 95; Gundry 1977: 24; Siddons 1980: 43, 85; Van Leeuwen 1990: 44–45). Part of the fall, from this viewpoint, was Adam's (not God's) attempt to reduce Eve and all women from full personhood to their reproductive capabilities: "Adam tries [to rule over Eve after the Fall]. Whereas in Genesis 2:23 Eve was called 'Woman,' in [Genesis] 3:20 she is reduced to 'mother of all living.' Her function and sphere have been cut in half" (Scanzoni and Hardesty 1992: 44; see also Van Leeuwen 1990: 172–173).

In addition, equality-minded commentators contend that New Testament passages such as Titus 2:5 and 1 Timothy 5:14 are context-specific injunctions that instruct first-century Christian wives to be "busy at home." Focusing on the last phrase in each of these biblical verses, this group of commentators reminds evangelical spouses that Paul offered such instructions to first-century Christian women only "so that no one will malign the word of God" and so early Christians would not "give the enemy [i.e., the political opposition of their day] opportunity for slander" (e.g., Bilezikian 1985: 289; Gundry 1980: 124–127).

To lend legitimacy to such controversial biblical interpretations, these authors contend that role flexibility, task sharing, and coparenting are in fact supported by a careful reading of the Bible. Many of these commentators argue that the Bible's injunction that husbands exhibit a Christ-like and sacrificial love for their wives (Ephesians 5:25–30) demands no less than role flexibility, an equalized division of household tasks, and shared parental responsibilities (see Follis 1981: 89; Siddons 1980: 75–76; Smalley 1988a: 35, 119; Wagner 1994: 67–68): "Husbands, love your wives, just as Christ loved the church and gave himself up for her. . . . Husbands are to love their wives as their own bodies. He who loves his wife loves himself. After all, no ever hated his own body, but feeds and cares for it, just as Christ does the Church—for we are members of his body."

Scanzoni and Hardesty are highly suspicious of chivalrous definitions of selflessness that equate Christ-like sacrificial giving with the husband protecting his wife even unto death. They contend that it is "easier for men" to imagine being martyred for their family "than being asked to share household tasks . . . since the former situation isn't likely to arise very often!" (Scanzoni and Hardesty 1992: 152). They counter: "If Jesus could pick up a towel and wash the disciples' feet, why can't a Christian husband in imitation of Christ's love pick up a towel and wash the dishes? Or cook a meal as the risen Savior did on the Galilean beach? Wives can learn to handle money matters wisely as did the woman in Proverbs 31" (Scanzoni and Hardesty 1992: 164). To underscore this point, many of these authors also highlight the New Testament account (Luke 10:38–42) of Jesus rebuking Martha for her preoccupation with domestic tasks. Jesus' reprimand followed Martha's criticism of her sister Mary, who had set aside her domestic responsibilities to listen to Jesus' teachings (Bilezikian 1985: 95; Follis 1981: 116–117; Gundry 1977: 20, 1980: 46; Scanzoni and Hardesty 1992: 75–76; Siddons 1980: 53). Scanzoni and Hardesty conclude that Jesus "did not shoo Mary back into the kitchen but reprimanded Martha for getting too involved in it" (1992: 129).

In a similar vein, many of these authors offer their distinctive understanding of the Ideal Wife described in Proverbs 31. They suggest that while she is said to have attended to select domestic chores, she was also a shrewd businesswoman whose income was valued by her family: "She considers a field and buys it; out of her earnings she plants a vineyard. She sets about her work vigorously; her arms are strong for her tasks. She sees that her trading is profitable, and her lamp does not go out at night. . . . She makes linen garments and sells them, and supplies the merchants with sashes"—verses 16–18, 24 (Bilezikian 1985: 68–78, 193–206; Follis 1981: 89; Gabriel 1993: 41, 44; Gundry 1977: 103, 1980: 54; Florence Littauer 1994: 116; Scanzoni and Hardesty 1992: 82–91).

Part III

Tandem Gender Negotiation among Evangelical Spouses

How do the discursive prescriptions promulgated within these popular advice manuals inform family ministry within evangelical congregations and gender relations among conservative Protestant husbands and wives? What impact do recent changes in elite evangelical family discourse exert on the social experiences of conservative Protestant couples? To address these questions, I turn now to a case study of family ministry and spousal relations at the Parkview Evangelical Free Church, a conservative Protestant congregation located in a large metropolitan area of Texas. The case study approach to social research aims to provide "an in-depth multi-faceted investigation, using qualitative research methods, of a single social phenomenon. The study is conducted in great detail and . . . relies on the use of several data sources" (Orum, Feagin, and Sjoberg 1991: 2). Because I seek to examine how cultural and organizational resources inform local gender negotiations among conservative religious couples, I have chosen to complement my analysis of popular evangelical family manuals with a case study of family ministry and spousal relations at Parkview. This case study draws primarily on participant-observation and in-depth interview data, supplemented by select primary survey data collected from interviewed couples. My goal in the remaining chapters of this study is to situate the patterns and particularities of my subjects' couple relationships within the broader context of Parkview's family ministry program and the ideological rifts that currently characterize elite evangelical gender discourse. I seek to highlight the points of conformity, contradiction, and struggle manifested in their experiences.

As its name indicates, the Parkview Evangelical Free Church is a member of a parent denomination, the Evangelical Free Church of America (EFCA). Many members of the local congregation simply refer to the church as "E-Free" or "EV-Free." The name Evangelical Free is noteworthy, because this denomination is bound together by a commitment to select *evangelical* principles (e.g., biblical inerrancy, the historicity and divinity of Jesus Christ) beyond which member congregations are *free* to explore and apply their Christian faith commitments as they see fit (see Hanson 1990). There is a productive tension at Parkview between a strong commitment to specific evangelical convictions (most notably, biblical teaching) and an enduring respect for diversity in applying those convictions. These countervailing tendencies make this congregation an intriguing case study in the organizational and subjective negotiation of gender. Given its commitment to such a select number of doctrinal principles, churches within the denomination describe themselves as inclusive rather than exclusive.

Several pastors and many members of Parkview call attention to the Evangelical Free label in a very positive way. They argue that, not unlike many nondenominational Bible churches that compete for adherents in the local religious marketplace, this congregation is in large part locally governed and controlled. Article 10 in the EFCA Statement of Faith says as much (Hanson 1990). As one pastor explained at a class for new and prospective church members: "Our church, like those of the New Testament, is evangelical in doctrine and orientation, and free in its structure and church government." Yet, at the same time, this congregation's affiliation with the Evangelical Free Church of America provides its local membership with valuable organizational ties to other churches across the United States and to missionary efforts throughout the world. Thus, despite the overwhelmingly white membership of this church, Parkview is somewhat cosmopolitan in character. Parkview engages in extensive outreach to various disadvantaged populations within its home city and also helps to sponsor myriad overseas missionary efforts (e.g., Central America, Eastern Europe). Thus, to the extent that the term "evangelical" literally means "evangelizing nonbelievers" by exposing non-Christians to the Gospel, this church is located squarely within the evangelical Protestant tradition.

Parkview is also representative of evangelical Protestantism in its strong commitment to an inerrantist reading of the Bible. This theological commitment to biblical inerrancy is evident in much of my observational data and is particularly apparent in the church's doctrinal creed. The first and most important doctrinal statement in this church, as well as in its parent denomination, reflects this high view of scripture: "We believe the Scriptures, both Old and New Testaments, to be the inspired (2 Tim. 3:16; 2 Pet. 1:20–21) Word of God (1 Cor. 2:13; John 6:63; John 17:8), without error in the original writings, the complete revelation of His will for the salvation of men (Matt. 11:27, 16:27; Gal. 1:11, 15–16), and the Divine and final authority for all Christian faith and life (Matt. 5:17–20; John 10:34–35)." The importance of the Bible in this church is further emphasized by one of this organization's mottos: "Where Stands it written?" This question implies that the legitimacy of ideas and practices should be evaluated in light of the Bible's teachings. In the words of one influential member, this motto encourages individuals to "distinguish 'the Word of God' from 'the opinions of man.'" Moreover, the first of five purpose statements suggests that the church members are to "exalt God through Bible-centered worship both privately and publicly."

Weekly services, Sunday school classes, and prayers contain frequent references to the authoritativeness of the Bible as "God's Word" or, simply, "the Word." One Sunday school class teacher made this point by way of counterexample. He expressed his deep disenchantment with some contemporary Christians who "have a loose interpretation of Scripture." This teacher referred to such individuals as " 'cafeteria Christians,' because they take a little of this, a little of that, and throw away the rest. They want to do things man's way." He continued by voicing his displeasure with a new "politically correct" version of the Bible that had just been released. This version of scripture was distinguished by its use of ungendered terminology: "Did you know that there is a new Bible out recently which has done away with gender terms? It's a P.C. version of the Bible. I don't buy this. My understanding of Scripture is that the Bible doesn't change from the first century on. God is not female. This is one of those very subtle ways that Satan gets to us. The Bible is no longer the Holy Bible for the publishers of this new Bible. It, unfortunately, has become man's Bible."

In a more positive fashion, the head pastor of this congregation took pains to explain to me that the very location of the pulpit in this church—tellingly placed front and center—symbolizes this congregation's commitment to the centrality of the Bible in its worship services. These same inerrantist convictions were evident in my in-depth interviews with pastors and members. Among the members I interviewed, a quite common response to the question "Why do you attend Parkview E-Free?" was because of the biblical teaching that occurs there—particularly from the pulpit, but also during Sunday school classes. Moreover, when asked to identify those beliefs that are most important to them as Christians, many of my respondents reflected on their conviction that the Bible is in fact God's Word. Virtually all of those spouses interviewed made some mention of the sinful or fallen nature of humanity; argued that Christ personally saved them from their sin; and claimed that the most reliable information for living a godly life and avoiding sin can be found in following God's and/or Christ's teaching as articulated in the Bible.[1]

Some of my respondents who had prior familiarity with non-evangelical churches, or who had converted from mainline Protestant denominations, even remarked on their frustration with non-evangelical religious leaders whose sermons consisted of little more than "personal anecdotes" or "stories." When asked what first attracted him to Parkview, one respondent stated tartly that the pastorship there "taught out of the Bible. . . . It's not some liberal, wishy-washy, Protestant mainline church." A prominent woman and active teacher in the church made much the same point. Her husband was raised Methodist but is now evangelical; she was raised in a strict Southern Baptist household. On one occasion, she explained to attendees at her women's Bible study: "My husband's religious instruction as a child was less biblical than mine." Since she was raised as a strict Baptist, she sometimes chided him about the social-club type of atmosphere commonly thought to pervade mainline churches: "He attended what I refer to as 'social services' on Sunday," she told us, drawing laughter from all in attendance.

Parkview provides clearly defined Christian values in a very relativistic world. Words like "relativism" and "postmodern culture" are epithets church members use to criticize mainstream American values. The hunger for clear, unambiguous religious values that pervades this congregation is particularly salient among new college students attending the church, themselves a fast-growing group within this church's burgeoning membership. In one pastor's estimation, these young evangelicals are among the most conservative factions within the church. The pastor explains that some of these young adults were raised by parents who came of age in the 1960s and 1970s, "where they had very little boundary. And now these kids grew up without boundaries, and they're going, 'Man, I want to feel secure and safe. Tell me that there is a final word about something.' "

At the same time, Parkview pastors and congregants concede that the Bible was never meant to be used as a history book or a medical manual. At Parkview, the Bible is believed to be without error concerning the issues to which it speaks—marriage, family relations, and spiritual welfare. Many congregants state that they embrace *the fundamentals* of the Christian faith as articulated by conservative theologians earlier in this century while rejecting the fundamentalist label in favor of the term evangelical. Fundamentalists, from this vantage point, espouse simplistic and inaccurate interpretations of scripture. As it was explained to me by one pastor at the church, fundamentalists reject and insulate themselves from secular culture, whereas evangelicals seek to engage and transform the secular realm.

Even as this church neatly fits the typical evangelical profile through its support of missionary activity and its commitment to biblical inerrancy, it is atypical in other noteworthy ways. Perhaps most notably, this congregation is composed of a predominantly middle-class and upper-middle-class membership. Although evangelicals as a group tend to be less educated than their non-evangelical counterparts, the professional class leaders and members of this church are quite well educated. Couples on the lower end of the income continuum were often in the midst of pursuing an advanced educational degree of some sort that ultimately would help them transition into a professional career. The impact of this congregation's family ministry programs on married couples' gender negotiations is the subject of the next three chapters in this study.

Six

Vive la Difference?

Gender Difference in Family
Ministry and Domestic Life

Evangelical discourse concerning the essence of masculinity, femininity, and sexuality is fragmented. Evangelical advocates of gender essentialism argue that masculinity and femininity—and, by extension, men and women—are inherently different. Using biological and scriptural justifications for their views, these authors claim that men are naturally assertive, inherently logical, and motivated largely by instrumental concerns. Many of these same family advice authors contend that women are delicate responders who are innately more nurturing than men. However, the dominance enjoyed by this elite discourse of gender difference within contemporary evangelicalism is eroding. A growing number of leading conservative Protestant authors—biblical feminists and others—have directly challenged these essentialist notions by arguing that men and women are not fundamentally different from one another. A new breed of moderate essentialist advice authors encourages spouses to complement their gender-specific predilections with desirable cross-gender traits. Where do the leaders and members of the Parkview Evangelical Free Church stand with respect to these competing discourses? How do these divergent discourses impact the local negotiation of gender among the church's family ministers and spouses?

Reformulating Gender Difference: Pastoral Teaching on the Essence of Gender and Sexuality at Parkview

Consistent with the dominant evangelical discourse of gender essentialism, many of the pastors and teachers at Parkview believe that men and women are fundamentally different not only in the obvious physical ways but in several other respects as well. However, gender difference rhetoric at the church is much more nuanced and qualified than is the boldly essentialist language found in many popular evangelical family advice manuals.

Microwave Men and Crockpot Women: Gender Difference and Sexual Desire

A commitment to categorical gender difference figured quite prominently in one Sunday school discussion for engaged and newly married couples led by a young family minister at the church, Pastor Bill. The topic for the day is sex within the marital relationship, and the scripture guiding our discussion consists of the Song of Solomon, the most eroticized book in the Bible. The Song of Solomon, we are told during this Bible study, "provides principles for intimate relationships" and consists of a man (Solomon, referred to in the Bible as "Lover") and a woman (his fiancée, described as "Beloved") expressing their erotic feelings for one another.

Pastor Bill begins our discussion by asking the couples in the class: "Scripturally, is the male or the female supposed to be the relational aggressor? Who says that the male should be the aggressor?" Ten hands shoot up. "Female?" No hands are raised. "And who thinks the Bible doesn't say?" Three hands are raised. Notably, Bill himself does not suggest which of these possible responses is correct. He simply directs us to open our Bibles to the first chapter in the Song of Solomon. Apparently, the Bible itself will provide the answer to this question for us. During the next hour, various members of the class read a chapter at a time from the Song of Solomon, interspersed with commentary by the young minister deciphering for us the most salient biblical messages regarding the sexual component of marriage. In the end, Bill leans toward a scriptural interpretation that characterizes the man, not the woman, as the divinely ordained initiator within the marital relationship. Early in the discussion, our young pastor urges the husbands in this class to emulate Solomon in eliciting sexual response from their wives. "Men," he inquires, "do your brides have a Song-of-Solomon passion for you?" What, precisely, is a "Song-of-Solomon passion?" During the Bible study, we linger over several verses that portray Solomon in highly sexualized terms (a "stag"), compared with passive and delicate imagery used to describe his Beloved ("cooing . . . doves"). The pastor takes this opportunity to underscore the profound sexual differences between men and women: "How is Solomon described here? He is a stag. He is pumped and coming! How is the woman described? She is likened to a dove and is hiding in the rocks. She is precious and vulnerable." Based on this exegesis, Pastor Bill concludes that the Bible confirms the depth of men's and women's sexual differences. Opting for a more contemporary sexual metaphor, he explains: "At the risk of sounding crass, men are microwaves and women are crockpots. It takes just seven seconds for men to become aroused. But for a woman, foreplay begins when you wake up in the morning. It takes all day long for a woman."

Our consideration of men's and women's sexual differences, however, is not the final word for that day's discussion. Indeed, this astute pastor seems to recognize the potential problem with such static depictions of radical male-female sexual difference in a way that many leading evangelical essentialists do not: If men and women are worlds apart regarding both the quantity and quality of sexual desire they experience, how can any marital relationship provide couples with mutual satisfaction? Would not such great disparities in sexual appetite produce an enormous degree of marital conflict and effectively undermine the couple's commitment to one another?

Seemingly aware of the problem inherent in radical notions of gender difference, this family minister ends our discussion by strategically amending his microwave versus crockpot metaphor for masculine-feminine sexual difference. Rather than leave us with that image, he concludes by advancing a moderate essentialist plea for men's cultivation of desirable feminine sexual traits and for women's cultivation of benevolent masculine sexual characteristics. Pastor Bill explains: "Research indicates that many young married women—especially Christian women—have trouble consummating marriage and enjoying sex because all of their lives they are told that sex is bad and that they should avoid it. This view that sex is bad is not biblical. [Sex] is good, within the context of marriage. God is honored by our sexual relationships. Isn't it great that our God understands us enough to be honored by something so wonderful? . . . Women, sex is a beautiful thing. You should anticipate it and you should enjoy it. Sexual desire is not evil."

Turning his attention toward the men in the group, the minister now enjoins them to become more sensitive to the emotional needs of their wives: "Men, affirm your wives. If your wife is sexually dormant, you're not doing your job. If your sex life is bad, you are probably not affirming your wife throughout the day. . . . Men, sex does not begin when you take your clothes off." Effective family ministry, in this church at least, entails crafting a portrayal of gender differences that includes complementarity and compromise.

Escaping the Specter of Sexism:
Mixed Metaphors and Gender Contradictions

Bill is not the only pastor at Parkview who embraces notions of gender difference. The senior minister at the church, Pastor Al, does so as well. During my interview with him, Pastor Al uses the word "initiation" to describe the husband's natural predilection in a marriage. Interestingly, such words do not lead Parkview pastors to champion the virtues of Victorian masculinity. Rather, they aim to emphasize that real masculinity entails actively demonstrating sensitivity to the needs of others, particularly family members.

In fact, for Pastor Al, the male penchant for initiation means that husbands should take more—not less—responsibility for the welfare of the marital relationship: "As a pastor, I would put the largest responsibility [for the well-being of the marriage] on the man. When I am in counseling [with couples], I really want to know how he loves his wife. Because typically," Al pauses, searching for the right words. "I want to be careful about this, but in my counseling I notice that women typically are not the initiators. I mean, they respond more. As they're loved, it's easier for them to love. And, as they're cared for, it's easier for them to feel a sense of security. As there is provision made, the women feel like they are safe. And so when I am in counseling, I really try to get to the heart of the man, to understand how he is treating his wife. And [I] find, most of the time, that the greater problem has been in his inability to be sensitive to her needs, causing her years of bitterness and insecurity. So by the time that they come and talk to me, she has no respect for this guy." Al continues by adding an important caveat: "I am not trying to be stereotypical, and I know I probably am in saying this—when I talk about initiators and responders in this way. Now, there are people in our society, women who take more initiative; there are men who are kind of the followers. But I really think God wants the men to be the spiritual leaders in their families. Obviously, [God wants] both of them to love the Lord immensely. But men need to take the initiative."

As my conversation with Pastor Al continues, he notes that despite God's desire for husbands to take the initiative within a marriage, they typically do not do so where the spiritual welfare of the family is concerned. Why is it that husbands, whom "God wants . . . to be the spiritual leaders," relinquish this role so readily in their homes? Pastor Al explains that "perhaps fifty years ago men thought [religion] was more feminine. It was weak to be a submissive man to God. I think our fathers grew up with wars, and they went through the Depression, and they were self-made. And the church was a help to women and to kids." Al, however, is heartened by what he views as "a real change" in the last two decades: "Men [today] are seeing that the greatest power is found in constraint. It's found in control—[like] when you have a thoroughbred horse, and he's got all this power. It's constrained power that's most efficient. [Men now understand] that there's nothing wrong with being God's servant. [They are] understanding that Christianity perhaps was feminized for a while, and now it's come back to men. Men are able to accept it because it's been defeminized."

Al celebrates the fact that evangelicalism has recently broken away from its feminized counterpart—charismatic Christianity—and returned to its Reformationist roots, thereby enlisting the allegiance of men. "It's real interesting. . . . Even during the Reformation period, the hymns were more masculine. They were strong. 'God of Our Fathers,' and 'A Mighty Fortress,' and all of that. [But] when Christianity entered America through the charismatic movement and all, even the music became feminized. It became more feeling-oriented, less objective, less didactic. In the terms we typically use 'feminine' [and] 'masculine,' it just became feely-mealy, fuzzy. Guys hated it for awhile. Now even that's changed. There is a resurgence in the liturgy. . . . People are returning back to more historical roots in faith. I think that's why the traditional worship here works well in our congregation. Because it is strong, didactic teaching."

Al concludes that this development has coincided with another encouraging evangelical trend, namely "guys . . . getting together. And this is almost going to sound like a contradiction, but as guys have accepted that Christianity is for them too, that it's as much a masculine faith as a feminine faith, they're almost showing a feminine side now. They're willing to be vulnerable now that they realize that they can be. . . . So, as guys reach out to guys, there has been a real change in the number of men. Promise Keepers, as you know, have really helped get guys back on track. . . . The vulnerability. I would also say that most of the guys still have trouble doing it with women. They can do it with each other. But they are getting better at it."

Interestingly, Al's definition of masculine initiation is structured around a gendered metaphor that is broad enough to encompass not only masculine attributes (the power of a thoroughbred horse) but their feminine counterparts (emotional openness and vulnerability). Within the framework of this metaphor, feminine attributes act positively to constrain masculine power and—to extend the thoroughbred imagery—tame the horse. And despite his overall belief in gender difference, Al is careful to qualify his overarching commitment to masculine-feminine difference with ideological caveats—i.e., frequent acknowledgment of exceptions to the generalized rule of gender difference. Al takes care to acknowledge, for example, that not all men are initiators nor are all women responders.

Al's facile engagement of gender issues emanates from several sources. Through his extensive involvement with a citywide men's ministry and with many local Promise Keepers, Al has confronted directly the pernicious impact of traditional masculinity on men, women, and families. These topics are quite frequently the point of departure at the well-attended men's Bible studies Al leads in a nearby church. Week after week, two hundred men from diverse ethnic and socioeconomic backgrounds sacrifice their lunch hour, crowd into the basement of a local church, and listen with rapt attention as Pastor Al challenges each of them to become godly men. During these Bible studies, this articulate pastor delineates the ways in which misguided cultural standards of manhood encourage men to objectify women sexually, to hide their emotions, to be competitive to a fault, and to be so terribly negligent of wives, friends, and coworkers. In contrast to these cultural expectations, Pastor Al challenges these men—many of them Promise Keepers and several of them from Parkview—to treat women with respect and dignity at all times, to express their emotions freely, to live more humbly, and to become more aware of the impact of their actions on family members, friends, and colleagues. I often left these gatherings wondering whether I had just attended a Bible study for evangelical men or an all-male gender-consciousness–raising group engaged in a critical analysis of contemporary masculinity.

The many nuances in Al's understanding of gender also stem from the fact that many of the men and women who attend Parkview (including Al's own wife) simply do not fit the sharply dichotomous profiles of initiating masculinity and responsive femininity articulated by leading evangelical proponents of gender difference. Pastor Al himself acknowledged that the men he counsels often have abdicated their role as initiator within the home. Pastor Al's fluid definition of masculinity—comprising both power and vulnerability—is designed to ameliorate this perceived malady.

Quite strikingly, these ambiguous metaphors and gender caveats are cast about with such regularity in a church where women are not allowed, by virtue of their sex, to serve as pastors or elders. Early on in my fieldwork, I began to wonder if these qualified defenses of gender difference were merely a cover for this organization's seemingly sexist practice of not allowing women to hold the pastorship or an elder's position. Yet when asked about the rationale behind the all-male pastorship and Elder's Board, Pastor Al argues that a distinctly masculine ability to interpret the Bible properly or to teach theology has nothing to do with these practices. Al states outright that this congregation's reservation of the pastorship for men "is not a matter of ability, because everybody would recognize, and I know, that there are women that are as gifted as any male teacher. It's not that." Rather, the Bible and scriptural conceptualizations of "spiritual authority" are the central points upon which this question hinges. Al remarks: "The issue really does come back to how you answer the question of spiritual authority. If you see the teaching of the Word [i.e., the Bible], and in particular the teaching of the Word on Sunday from the pulpit, as an exercise of spiritual authority and then you go to the [biblical] text and say, 'She is not supposed to do that,' then you come to the conclusion that she cannot be a pastor. Because of the spiritual authority issue. Now if you separate [teaching from spiritual authority] like [some evangelicals do], then potentially you could have a female pastor."

Despite the fact that this church bars women from exercising formal pastoral power, there are several women who seem, for all practical purposes, to act as surrogate pastors in their ministries to Parkview's female membership. This surrogate pastoral power is bounded by its informality and restrictiveness inasmuch as it entails women teaching female congregants instead of mixed groups. Nevertheless, these women's ministry efforts are greatly appreciated by leaders and members of the church alike. And, as evidenced by women like Angela Butler, the church makes a special effort to encourage such ministry by and for women.

"A Balloon with Slow Leaks": Redefining the Male Ego at a Women's Bible Study

As a male ethnographer in a church where gender is highly salient, my access to female-only Bible studies taught by prominent women in the congregation was limited. Because of my respect for the women-only groups in the church and my fear of alienating spouses by seeming pushy, I was generally reluctant to solicit invitations to women's gatherings. One prominent female teacher of a women's Bible study course, however, did consent to my sitting in on part of her course on Christian womanhood. Angela Butler, the course's teacher, was most gracious to let me sit in, given that the flyer announcing the course to church members read in bold letters, "FOR WOMEN ONLY." As I quickly discovered, Angela had a disarming demeanor that I felt sure was an asset to her women's ministry. When I called Angela, I first asked if I could purchase from her a copy of the text on which her course is based. She agreed without hesitation. Then I asked her if I could attend the class, adding quickly that I would not wish to do so if she or any of the women in attendance might harbor reservations about my presence there. She responded: "Well, it's a nine-week course. I don't imagine you'd want to attend all nine classes?" When I assured her that I was up to the task, she paused momentarily and spoke frankly: "Well, John, I've taught this class for many years. And, for many of the women, this is a ladies' night out. It is a time for the women to fellowship with one another. You could, however, attend tonight's introductory class, which is an overview of the book and the whole class itself." When she confirmed that my attendance would not be an imposition, I readily accepted her offer.

Our evening at Angela's home begins as expected, with "fellowshipping"—informal conversations among the women and introductions of them and me. After twenty minutes, we proceed to the living room. Uncertain about where to sit and wanting to be as unobtrusive as possible, I hesitate to be the first to take a chair. Noticing my hesitancy, Angela directs me: "John, why don't you take the Daddy's chair, up front here next to me?" Blushing at being singled out, I seat myself in the large, maroon, and remarkably comfortable "Daddy's chair."

Angela begins her class by referring to Proverbs 3:1–6 and explaining: "Proverbs is God's love letter to us. Many of the verses in Proverbs refer to a 'son.' I will often change those references to read 'daughter,' because I think it is important that God's message be personalized for us. Of course, I will not change references to God. He is still our Father. Let's open with a word of prayer." Angela proceeds to pray. Her prayer includes an offering of thanks to the husbands who remain at home babysitting this evening so that the women present can attend the class. After discussing the perennially debated merits of various types of Bibles—the New International Version versus the New American Standard Bible versus New Peterson's Bible versus the Bible of Twenty-Six Translations—and formally introducing ourselves to the group, Angela initiates our discussion.

"You are already familiar with one of the themes of this class—the four A's," she says, calling our attention to the mobile we all saw hanging in the kitchen earlier. On the mobile hung a large letter "A" supporting three smaller "A's" underneath it. "These four 'A's' tell us how to act toward our husbands. The big 'A' stands for attitude and it's the most important. I like to say that our attitude is like a hat we put on in the morning. Of course, in Philippians 2:5, the Bible tells us that our attitude should be like that of Christ."

Angela then proceeds to describe the meaning of the smaller "A's" that hung below the overarching "attitude 'A' ": "The first of the three smaller 'A's' is acceptance, which I define as unconditional love. It is discussed in Romans 15:7, and tells us to accept each other as Christ accepts us." She continues: "The next 'A' is for admiration, as described in 1 Thessalonians 5:11." This passage, I discover later, reads: "Therefore encourage one another and build each other up."

At this point, Angela pauses to consider the importance of wifely admiration in marriage. Her commentary clearly invokes the discourse of gender difference, but at the same time provides an interesting contrast to the model of masculine initiation that is so often emphasized by leading essentialist evangelical authors. Using my presence within this women's group to underscore her point, Angela explains: "Now, John here and all other men have very delicate egos. Wives, you must constantly seek ways to build your husbands up. The male ego is like a balloon with slow leaks, or like a bucket with holes in it. If wives don't build up their husbands, then their husbands' egos get soft and men become susceptible to the cute little girl next door or to the lady at work. When I talk on the phone with my mother-in-law, I win points with her and with my husband—who will be on another extension—by building him up to her. I'm able to brag on my husband to his mother, and just as he puffs up with pride about his accomplishments, Mom is very pleased to hear that her son is doing so well."

Angela's description of the leaky-balloon male ego is a most inventive trope when compared with evangelical understandings of gender difference. The content of Angela's gender difference rhetoric diverges notably from dominant evangelical conceptualizations of initiating masculinity and responsive femininity. Angela is able to recast gender difference by depicting the male ego as delicate and "soft"—words that many leading evangelical essentialists often use to characterize femininity and women's bodies. For Angela, masculine initiation in the home would seem possible only to the extent that a wife is able to reinflate her husband's leaky ego. From this vantage point, wives are powerful indeed.

At the same time, Angela's image of the delicate male ego can be seen as sustaining a very traditional, highly constraining form of gender difference for women. The husband's leaky ego would seem to leave his wife shouldering the lion's share of responsibility for the welfare of the marital relationship. It is in this spirit that Angela admonishes wives not to "talk down" their husbands in public: "There is nothing more humiliating for a man than to be talked down in public. Remember, one way to get lots of points with your husband and his family is to brag on him." Similarly, the wives in attendance are told by Angela to avoid explicitly directing their husbands in private settings; rather, given the apparent fragility of the male ego, wives should approach their husbands in a more strategic fashion. Using as a reference John Gray's phenomenally popular book about men's and women's divergent styles of interaction, Angela explains: "Don't criticize your husband. Instead, say 'Harry, I have a problem, and I need your help.' Have any of you ever read the book, *Men Are from Mars, Women Are from Venus?* It says that men are natural problem solvers. So remember that when talking with your husband." Finally, in stating that a wife can be held responsible for her husband's extramarital affair, Angela's rhetoric sustains a sexual and emotional asymmetry between spouses that generally favors men. Husbands "become susceptible to the cute little girl next door or to the lady at work" when wives don't fulfill their proper role of building up and bragging on the manliness of their mates. Angela's gendered metaphor of the leaky male ego therefore invokes the logic of essential difference while recasting the wife as the proactive initiator in a godly marriage.

Dancing with Difference: Masculinity, Femininity, and Identity among Parkview Spouses

Given these nuances in Parkview's family ministry efforts, how do the husbands and wives at this church engage evangelical arguments about the essence of masculinity and femininity? Corroborating Pastor Al's experiences in conducting couples counseling, several Parkview husbands reported struggling with practicing initiation in the home. Some of the men with whom I spoke did not have masculine initiation modeled for them in their families of origin, suggesting implicitly that initiators are socialized into this role. Others currently find themselves in unanticipated life circumstances within their families. Employment difficulties and unforeseen career challenges of various sorts—e.g., an inability to find financially rewarding employment, the exigencies associated with launching a personal business—leave several husbands hard pressed to define masculine initiation as raw public-sphere competitiveness or unbridled instrumentalism.

Clearly, however, such nonconformity to masculine standards of initiation was not the case for most of the men that I interviewed. Taking their remarks at face value, the preponderance of husbands interviewed understand themselves in terms that are highly congruent with masculine initiation. This commitment to gender difference is evidenced in the following statement from a thirty-seven-year-old husband, Ray. As a proud new father of his recently adopted son, Ray finds issues of gender difference highly salient. It is perhaps the adoption of his son that prompts Ray to enlist a psychological, rather than a purely biological, defense of essentialism. Ray contends: "I just think that there is a difference between men and women in terms of the way that they are able to respond to a child. And in the way they think. So they complement each other very well, I think. I think that God created that [complementarity] so the child that is being raised would have the benefit of both."

In response to his remarks, I inquire: "What do you see as the most important male-female differences?"

Ray rejoins, "I think it has to do with the way of thinking. Like, for instance, men—we are doers. We want to *do this,* and we want to *do that.* We want to get things done. We're very project-oriented. Females, in my opinion, are more relationship-type oriented. They want to foster that relationship. [Women have] compassion—more than men have, in my opinion. So, that's the way they complement each other. And we complement each other I think."

In many respects, it is not surprising that the preponderance of the men with whom I spoke portray themselves as proactive initiators. Both within evangelical circles and throughout many sectors of contemporary American culture, the qualities associated with initiation—assertiveness, courage, fortitude—are highly valued. But it is important to note that despite the high value they place upon initiation, these same men are typically quite careful to point out that gender differences—men's "doer" orientation versus women's penchant for "compassion"—need not be rank-ordered. Among these men, such divergent gender orientations are portrayed simply as complementary, not linked in a hierarchical relationship of superiority and inferiority.

This belief that gender differences need not entail the superiority of one set of gender traits over its counterpart is likely a response to feminism and a strategic reaction to increasingly prominent discourses of androgyny within American society at large. An effort to equalize in value masculine initiation and feminine compassion is one way of sustaining a defensible commitment to gender difference in the face of recent critiques against sexism and male chauvinism advanced by proponents of gender sameness. Moreover, qualifiers about gender differences suggest that feminist critiques of sexist dichotomies have effectively challenged the veracity of unqualified generalizations about gender among many Parkview husbands. Concerning his wife's and his own gendered contributions to their son's psychological development, Ray himself concluded our discussion with the caveat that he is *not* saying that a father's and mother's respective contributions to their children's personality development are "mutually exclusive."

What, then, of the women at Parkview? How do the wives I observed and interviewed negotiate the conflicting discourses of gender evidenced within contemporary evangelicalism? As might be expected, Parkview women struggle with issues of gender difference—though these subjective struggles and women's attempts to resolve them take various forms. Many of the women at Parkview find the emulation of ideal evangelical femininity— responsiveness, nurturance—incongruent with their personality traits and their own life experiences. This incongruence is even true for Pastor Al's wife, Jacquie. Whereas she formerly embraced the tenets of evangelical feminism, Jacquie has in recent years become a firm believer in gender difference: "There is something in women that's nurturing; that kind of wants to make a nest, so to speak. These are cliches, but it's really true. . . . It's the beauty of the way men and women are created differently . . . by God."

Despite her rhetorical defense of gender difference, however, Jacquie acknowledges forthrightly that she deviates from a stereotypical feminine norm in many significant ways: "I am definitely more masculine," she says, laughing aloud. "I only know one other person like me and she's my closest friend. I really am . . . kind of different." Referring to her husband, Parkview's pastor, she says emphatically, "I don't need a lot of emotional support from Al. I don't have to talk a whole lot. I can go for days. It doesn't bother me to keep it to myself. It doesn't bother me to be alone. I really am kind of different from most women."

I ask Jacquie, "So, how does that fit with God's plan, if you will, for women and this kind of definition?"

Invoking the strength of the ultimate man in Christian theology, Jacquie asserts: "I see myself as an educator. I say, 'Hey, come on. You don't have to be an emotional basket case.' I say, 'Be strong like Christ.' . . . I can encourage women to be strong with the strength of Christ."

Other Parkview women wrestled with their strong temperaments via a combination of scriptural study, consultation with trusted family members, and theological tropes that redefine God as the author of both family order and gender diversity. At a couples' Bible study, Ellen describes her personal struggle to comport her personality to idealized notions of Christian femininity. "You know, there is that biblical passage that says a woman should have a quiet and gentle spirit. Well, I am neither quiet nor gentle. And I used to really worry about that, thinking 'Why am I so unlike the ideal woman who is described in Scripture?' But then I spoke to my husband about it, and he said: 'That just isn't you.' And you know what? I agree with him. God gave me a personality, and I should not worry that it is different than the quiet and gentle spirit described in the Bible."

Although Jacquie's strength and Ellen's personality deviate from the prevailing norm of responsive femininity, they do not perceive themselves as uncaring or insensitive to those around them nor do they view themselves as unfeminine. But neither are they merely feminine. They, and other Parkview women, appropriate—quite selectively—messages from evangelical discourses of gender difference and sameness and, while holding to essentialism, they dance artfully with the notion of gender difference.

Religious Conviction, Gender, and Embodiment: Of Haircuts and Childbirth

Several Parkview wives' struggles with gender difference center on their bodily practices and experiences of embodiment as women. Jacquie, Pastor Al's wife, recounts how she unilaterally decided to have her long, flowing, mid-back-length hair cut to a one-inch-length "buzz" style haircut—much to her family's shock and dismay. The "haircut experience"—that is, her family's negative response to her unilateral choice—has convinced Jacquie that even the most seemingly mundane and private decisions must take into consideration the feelings of others. The fact that Jacquie's new buzz-cut appearance left her almost unrecognizable to her aghast family members upon their return home has, she says, taught her not to be so impulsive and selfish concerning her appearance and her life.

The intersection of gender, embodiment, and family life was particularly pronounced among Parkview women who had recently given birth or were charged with the full-time care of young infants. In many instances, the heterogeneous life experiences of such well-educated, professional-class women now struggling with the challenges of motherhood produce rich and complex understandings of gender, self, and body. Anne Carson, a thirty-five-year-old mother of two—one of whom is a weeks-old newborn—evinces a striking degree of ambivalence about questions of gender difference and sameness. When first asked about family responsibilities, Anne speaks from her experiences—and, it would seem, women's universal experience—of new motherhood to invoke images of gender difference: "I think that [men and women] are specifically equipped [for different family roles]. Physically, [women's] bodies are made to carry babies in a physical way. So it's kind of natural that we continue that process. Mentally, we're more emotional in general. Expressing more emotions and feeling a wider variety [of emotions] or many at a time. But then we have monthly periods where we go nuts, so we're kind of prepared for that."

Anne then moves on to discuss how women's biological capacity for childbearing informs their temperament and orientation toward the world: "Women tend to look at things differently. More from an emotional perspective than a black-and-white, one-thing-at-a-time perspective. Physically we're equipped for that. Like I say, we carry babies. But also our bodies are softer. And babies like to be against softer bodies. Our voices are lower. Babies like to hear," Anne pauses, then continues. "You know, if you just look at babies, they want to hear a softer voice rather than a gruff voice. I wouldn't say that that's our nature, and if you go against it, then you're going against God. I wouldn't say that. I don't think that's what the Bible teaches. But we have kind of a pre—" Anne hesitates. "Not predestined. Is that the word? But, it's sort of laid our for us. That's more of the natural route to take."

Like popular evangelical purveyors of essentialism, this new mother invokes graphic bodily images to argue that gender differences are divinely ordained. Anne asserts: "I used to believe that a woman can do anything a man can do except pee while standing up. And that if she tried real hard, she could probably do that too. However, [now] I think that if a woman does urinate while standing up, she is going against her nature. She's going to get messy. Her socks will be yellow and it will be a mess. So if she goes with her nature, which is to sit down, which is humbling, things will feel better for her."

Yet, as our conversation moves to explore other facets of Anne's identity—her most formative experiences as a young girl, a mature woman, a trained nurse, and a career-minded MBA—Anne distances herself from the dominant evangelical discourse of gender difference in favor of sameness arguments: "I was never what I would say was a feminist by any means. Because I didn't understand what that really meant. But I felt that women and men were equal. And if she really wanted to do something. I guess I look at it as more of an academic point. Because I remember people saying to me that girls don't do as well in math. Well, I did great in math. I was crappy in

English. So I didn't believe that. Or well, [I heard that] girls can't do as many swings on the monkey bars. Well, I put shorts on under my dress and I could do as many swings as them. So I had some limitations. It was because I wore the dress that I couldn't do as well as the boy."

To underscore men's and women's essential equality, Anne recounts a memorable tale from her youth: "I just never in my mind felt that I was inferior to any male, even as a child. My first day at a new school in the fourth grade, the girls were playing a version of handball. A school version, where you hit the ball against this backboard. The boys were on the other side. The girls' ball went over to the boys' side. And instead of being a nice little boy and handing me the ball back as I went to go get it, he socked it across the yard. It really made me mad. I had never hit anybody in my life, but I beat the crap out of that little boy [laughs]. Age nine and my first day at a new school. And it turned out that he was the bully of the school. Had I known that, I would have thought twice. And I thought, 'I just beat the bully up at this school.' I had great respect from that day on. I never had a problem at that school."

On the heels of Anne's shift to childhood vignettes in favor of gender sameness, I inquire about her present convictions: "So do you still believe that academically and athletically that women are as capable as or are equal to men?" Anne replies, "Yes," and continues by critically evaluating the rhetoric of gender difference in light of her medical training: "And for a long time I struggled with that, because I kept hearing as a new Christian that 'women ought to submit, women ought to submit.' And I thought, 'That just doesn't make sense. Why did He [God] give us a brain then?' [A woman's brain] works the same way. I have studied my anatomy. It works the same way as the man's, physiologically speaking. It needs blood, it needs oxygen, nutrients. OK, yeah, we're not as big-boned. We can't run a marathon as fast. OK, so our nature is a little bit different physically. But we live longer in general. And we carry babies, which is a very strong stress on the body. I mean, every system is affected. Every system is affected." Anne concludes: "And so, in general, I think we may not be strong physically to run a marathon, but we're strong physically to give birth. Mentally, I would say that I see no difference. I really cannot say that a woman is dumber than a man in general. She may not be as educated. But if you took a boy and a girl and they were in the same household environment, and all other things being equal, they would be the same."

Like many Parkview women, Anne artfully rejects the either/or conceptualization of gender implicit in evangelical debates about the nature of masculinity and femininity. Instead, Anne's personal experiences as a wife and mother, combined with her academic and professional training, enable her to traverse the boundaries that demarcate the competing discourses of gender difference and gender sameness. Nowhere is the richness of Anne's gender identity more apparent than in her nuanced understandings of pregnancy, childbirth, and women's bodies. As a mother of a weeks-old newborn, Anne characterizes pregnancy and childbirth as forms of embodiment that are highly salient to her at this moment in her life. And yet, as a registered nurse, Anne is also a technical expert on a range of bodily processes—from pregnancy to neurophysiology, from childbirth to brain chemistry.

Anne's diverse life experiences enable her to draw on a vast repository of cultural resources to make sense of pregnancy, childbirth, and the female body. On the one hand, Anne-the-evangelical-mother links childbearing quite directly with women's predisposition to be more nurturing than men. Anne's commitment to essential difference draws additional force from her gendered references to premenstrual syndrome and the inherent softness of women's bodies. On the other hand, Anne-the-registered-nurse equates childbirth with physical strength, a trait often (mis)understood as a distinctly masculine attribute. This line of thinking invokes images of women's birthing fortitude, and draws force from Anne's childhood scuffle—in which she manhandled the school bully for stealing her girlfriends' ball. Anne's multifaceted narratives of embodiment function here as social texts that are jointly authored through a complex collaboration between Anne's corporeality, her multiple identities as mother and nurse, and the competing discourses (traditional-evangelical, medical-scientific) she can enlist to make sense of such bodily experiences. Because the authorship of these texts is collaborative and dynamic, Anne and Parkview women like her are able to write competing story lines into their narratives of embodiment and identity.

Seven

Negotiating Patriarchy

*Submission, Subversion, and
Family Power*

The dominant discourse of family power among conservative religious luminaries turns on conceptualizations of husband-headship and wifely submission. According to most proponents of this hierarchical family model, husbands have been appointed by God to be the ultimate decision makers within the home, and wives are instructed to submit to the domestic authority of their husbands. More recent variations on this discursive theme construe the husband as the family's servant-leader and express criticism of autocratic decision making on the part of husbands. By contrast, the oppositional discourse of household authority within evangelical circles is predicated on the notion of mutual submission. Most proponents of this model argue that the husband and the wife should exercise joint and equal authority within the home. These commentators implore their readers to implement consensus-building or negotiation-based strategies for conflict resolution. Given the hotly contested nature of this issue among leading evangelicals, what do ministers and members at Parkview believe about submission within the home? And how, if at all, is the practical exercise of authority within these couples' homes impacted by the various discourses of family power promulgated by elite evangelicals?

Pastoral Perspectives on Spousal Authority: Submission in Parkview's Family Ministry Program

At first glance, the issue of submission seems to be a point of disagreement among the Parkview pastors I interviewed. Some family ministers invoke the dominant evangelical discourse of wifely submission to describe their views on family decision making, while others cite the oppositional evangelical discourse of mutual submission. The artful ways in which these pastors invoke such competing discourses is the key to effective family ministry at Parkview.

Pastoral Support for Wifely Submission

For one of the associate pastors at Parkview, Pastor Steven, the biblical word "submission" clearly refers to scriptural verses directed at the wife—not the husband—in a marital relationship. When I ask him how he understands the biblical word "submission," he says tersely that it means "wives, be subject to your husbands." After a lengthy pause, he continues: "Maybe it would be helpful if I also said what I don't think it is. I don't think it is cowering in the corner in fear and submission. And I don't think it's mental suicide."

"Mental suicide being?" I inquire.

He quickly responds: "Being you no longer have any say in this matter, [as in] 'Everything I say goes, no matter what, no questions asked. You do things as I say them or else you're out of here.' I think submission in a large way is essentially submission to the realization in Scripture." Steven pauses momentarily. "Well, one, it is submission to the husband in the marriage. But [it is] submission also to the fact that in Scripture God has placed men . . . in a role of leadership within the marriage. So it is submission to a person. But it's also submission to, as far as we can tell, the plan and how God has designed it for the family throughout Scripture—that the male should be the head of the household [and occupy] the leadership role. But that doesn't necessarily imply, at least it doesn't in my opinion, that the woman is brain-dead and can no longer make decisions, or [that she cannot] help make decisions, or [that she] should not be consulted in making decisions."

"So, in a positive sense, what does it imply or entail?" I ask.

"I think from the woman's perspective, it is a submission to the leadership of the husband, not to the will of the husband," Steven concludes. "It's submission to the leader based on a track record of trust that the leader has proven in the past."

The foregoing exchange demonstrates Pastor Steven's unambiguous belief that submission pertains to the wife's role within the marriage. At no point during this exchange does he use the phrase "mutual submission" to describe his views about authority within the home. Yet, despite his advocacy of wifely submission, Steven's definition of this controversial term is more qualified than that presented by many leading evangelicals who extol the benefits of wifely submission. Steven expends more effort delineating what submission is not than describing what it is. And while Steven indicates that the husband's leadership is divinely ordained, he concludes that a husband's right to leadership must in some sense be earned ("based on a track record of trust . . . proven in the past"). A wife should submit not to her husband's will (caprice, selfish wishes) but to his responsible, tested leadership.

By his own account and that of his wife, Jenna, Steven has earned the right to exercise leadership within the context of their marriage. Steven suggests that submission is really not all that difficult for Jenna because he tries to lead responsibly: "Jenna knows that I would never ask her to do something that would harm her. . . . The leader, myself in this case, I'm not going to ask Jenna to do something that is not good for her or is going to harm her. [My family leadership] does not give me carte blanche to tell her to do anything I want her to do and [it does not mean that] then she's got obey me because she's a woman and I'm a man. That's ridiculous."

Pastoral Support for Mutual Submission

Not all the pastors at Parkview share this interpretation of submission. Pastor Bill, the teacher of the Sunday school class on marital sexuality discussed in chapter 6, is a strong advocate of mutual submission within the home. Bill had in fact delivered a Sunday evening sermon on mutual submission not long before my interview with him.

When I ask him during our interview about a Christian husband's family roles and responsibilities, he shoots back without hesitation: "Submission." Referring to his wife, Linda, he continues: "When I say submission, [I mean] denying myself to meet the needs of other people. Putting Linda before me. I think that is the ultimate thing."

"And in what ways does that manifest itself in your relationship?"

"Just doing things to serve her. Doing things to affirm her. Doing things to build her up in her relationship with Christ. It can be anything from rubbing her back at the end of the day to taking out the trash to," Bill hesitates for a moment. "There's just a million ways. Submission is just putting her desires and her needs above my desires and my needs. I am not very good at it. But it's important and I am trying to work on it."

"So, whose duty is it to submit?"

"It's a mutual deal. She submits to me. I submit to her. We cosubmit in everything. I guess if there was an ultimate decision where we completely didn't agree, we probably would still work to get to an understanding. But then I guess as the spiritual leader, I would take that responsibility. Although really we do pretty well in that. I don't think that I have ever made a decision where I've said, 'We're going to do this,' and she has had to say, 'I really disagree, but I'll submit.' So we can usually work things out and understand one another well enough where either I'll say, 'I understand what you're saying. We'll do that,' or she'll say, 'I understand what you're saying. We'll do that.' "

Interestingly, Pastor Bill imparts vestiges of patriarchal rhetoric into his egalitarian defense of mutual submission. Although he and his wife "cosubmit in everything" and despite the fact that he would not deign to make a unilateral decision about their marital relationship, he still understands himself to be the leader of his family. Nevertheless, his definition of leadership would probably not attract much criticism from even the most avid evangelical feminist purveyors of mutual submission. When asked to define spiritual leadership, Bill explains, "Spiritual leadership, as I see it, is more of a nurturing relationship than it is authoritative. I would never say in the same sentence [to my wife] the two phrases, 'Linda' and 'submit.' I really could not imagine [saying that] unless I was completely joking, and telling her to go fix me a chicken pot pie or something," he says, laughing loudly. "I just would not do that, because that is not showing her Christ's love. And so when I say spiritual leadership, realize that biblical leadership is servanthood. It is Christ, who was the leader, washing the feet of the disciples. And the Christian church is probably not aware of that as much as they need to be. That my being a spiritual leader means I am responsible to serve."

Pastor Al's views also seem highly congruent with the discourse of mutual submission. He begins one of our discussions on this issue by highlighting what some persons—particularly non-evangelicals like myself—might understand as contradictory passages in the Bible. For Al, however, such scriptural verses make perfect sense: "In a couple places, [the Bible] asks the wife to be submissive to her husband. But then at the end of a section that talks about slaves and masters, and husbands and wives, and children and parents, it says 'submit one to another.' So for me, submission isn't two people on two different levels. I believe in mutual submission. And that means that I give up my rights [and] she gives up her rights [for us] to try to live together in peace."

Turning to his own marital relationship, Al explains that he can't ever recall having to make a unilateral decision without his wife, Jacquie, and adds, "if I did, I'd probably regret it. I mean, we work on it until we understand. Until I understand where she's coming from [and] she understands where I'm coming from. And so we really operate as a partnership. I'm not one that would teach guys lording it over their wives in any kind of way. That's not right. That's not biblical. However you understand submission, that's not right. That's not what it's talking about."

Given our joint awareness of the heated evangelical debates over wifely submission versus mutual submission, how would he counsel other evangelical men such as those at Parkview who take the position that a wife is obligated to submit to her husband? Counterposing leadership with lordship, he provides a scriptural explanation for mutual submission that I have never before run across in the myriad advice manuals I have read on the subject: "If you've gotten to the place where you have to pull rank from the Bible, your marriage is in trouble. I mean, that's a problem. If I have to say here at this church, 'John, you're going to do this because I am the pastor. And I am telling you what to do,' I've lost it. I am not a leader anymore. That's a problem. I would never say that. If I ever said that to anybody, I'd know it was time for me to leave. The point is that I think the issue of submission has more to do with leadership than it does with lordship." Al continues: "Jesus says, 'Come to me all ye who labor and are heavy laden and I'll give you rest.' Then he goes on to say, 'Take my yoke upon you and learn from me.' That's what it means. A yoke is where two people get together and they carry the load together. A yoke of oxen. And that's the point."

Pastor Al continues in this vein, now creatively combining an appeal to pragmatism with his scriptural imagery in order to engage authority-minded husbands: "I would help a guy [to understand]. I would say: 'Look, you're try-ing to control your wife, man. I mean, that's not biblical. Back off the control. Do you understand what you're saying to her? She's not listening to you. If you're trying to control her, obviously she's not respecting you. And there's no way that she'd ever come close to your view of submission.' So, that's the kind of thing that I would do. Help him understand that they're not listening. They're not loving their wives as Christ loved the church. And particularly if they're pulling rank through that command, that's a problem."

Yet again, I hear the word "leader" folded into a defense of mutual sub-mission. I query: "It seems like you're saying—and I just want to paraphrase to be sure that I am understanding correctly—that it's not the wife's duty to submit. It's an issue of mutual submission. But the man is the leader in the marriage?"

"Yes, right," he responds.

"So," I then ask, "how would mutual submission square with a husband's leadership in the marriage?"

He replies: "I would say that if I am a good leader as a man—and I should be the leader, I should take initiative—that my wife will feel so nurtured and so loved that it just makes sense for her to follow my leadership."

"In terms of making decisions or . . . ?" I hesitate, struggling for the appro-priate words. "I am trying to grab something practical with leadership."

Al counters with just such an example: "It might be that I say, 'Honey, I think we need a new car.' If I have been communicating correctly, she is going to say, 'I agree. I have known that all along.' So I can hardly think of anything, if my relationship is the way God wants it to be, where I am going to be pulling rank. I don't ever do that."

I remain somewhat confused about how male family leadership can coex-ist with mutual submission, and how mutual submission can then be squared with the husband taking initiative. I beg Al's indulgence and press forward: "So, I realize that this is really pushing the envelope. But just again, [I am] trying to pin down the leadership issue. If leadership isn't making decisions, like having the authority to make decisions, how would you define leadership then? And maybe you've already done that and I've just missed it."

"Well," he replies, "I believe in a model called servant-leadership. My desire as a pastor is to make everybody else successful. And so if I apply that at home, my job is to make my wife successful and my children successful. And the way I do that is by giving myself away. I don't do it perfectly, but that's the way I do it. Jesus said, 'Greater love hath no man than he lay down his life for his friends.' Now I am not that extreme. I am not that good at loving. But if I am helping them to be who God wants them to be, then." Al pauses momentarily, then continues: "I have never had any trouble with people following me, because I build consensus. And I build it at home. I love my kids to think it's their idea almost. It's hard to explain. I haven't analyzed it really." Al concludes, "I think the bottom line [is that] if it came down to a head-knocking, we-both-think-we're-right in my home, we would probably not decide."

"Unless there was consensus, you're saying?" I ask, just to be certain we understand one another.

"Yes," he replies. "Hopefully we're both spirit-filled, submissive to God, and one of us would budge one way or the other."

Submission and Family Ministry at a Women's Bible Study

The embattled state of the submission question within contemporary evangelicalism is also evidenced in Angela's treatment of this issue in her women's Bible study course. As it turns out, authority in the home is represented on Angela's kitchen mobile containing four small "A's" hanging beneath a large "A" that symbolizes "attitude." During the overview of her women's Bible study course, Angela explains: "The final 'A' on the mobile stands for authority. This, of course, refers to submission. First Peter 3:1 tells us to submit to one another out of reverence to Christ. I like to think of submission as 'yielding,' or 'letting someone go ahead of you.' " Taking a confessional tone, Angela concedes: "This has been rather difficult at times for my husband, Andrew, and me. We are both first-born, opinionated, and strong-willed. When spouses are this way, it can make marriage difficult and can breed disrespect. And, sure enough, earlier in our relationship, I did not respect Andrew. He would suggest something and I would think, 'That's a stupid idea,' or 'What do I need with a husband?' And, the world today teaches the exact opposite of biblical submission. This Conference on Women that recently took place in China is a perfect example. This conference will make the world's women miserable. Submission is the oil in the lock and the grease in the gears of your marriage."

Is Angela promoting an ideology wifely submission or mutual submission in the context of her women's ministry? At this point in the group's discussion, it is most difficult to tell. On the one hand, she refers to a biblical passage which she says "tells us to submit to one another"; she proceeds to admit that submission has been difficult for both her husband, Andrew, and herself—implying that submission is incumbent upon both of them. Moreover, she refers to submission in euphemistic and apparently ungendered terms as "yielding" and "letting someone go ahead of you." Yet, on the other hand, Angela uses vignettes from her marriage that can be read to support wifely submission. The submissive wife should not be so critical of her husband. And, although she does not elaborate on this point, she is overtly critical of the 1995 Conference on Women, apparently for the feminist overtones that emerged from it.

In many respects, Angela's ambiguous stance on this issue mirrors the discursive contradictions in evangelical conceptualizations of household authority. An increasing number of evangelical advocates of a patriarchal family have appropriated the phrase "mutual submission" into their advice manuals even as they preserve the husband's authority within the home. This trope of melding the egalitarian terminology with recommendations for a patriarchal family structure is even found in the women's advice manual that serves as the guide for Angela's nine-week class.

Yet, as the discussion moves forward during the evening, Angela's perspective on this issue seems to shift somewhat toward the wifely submission pole of this discursive continuum. Perhaps because she is speaking to an all-women's group rather than a mixed-gender gathering, or perhaps because she really is—in the final analysis—an advocate of wifely submission, she calls our attention to several biblical passages explicitly directing wives to submit to their husbands (e.g., Colossians 3:18–19; Titus 2:3–5). This topic will be the focus of two separate sections of the Bible study, she tells us during her course overview. Nevertheless, it is Angela's own personal struggle with submission to her husband Andrew, as well as her thirteen years of ministering to evangelical women, that have convinced her that many wives wrestle with issues of submission and control in the context of marriage. How does she explain the apparent difficulty wives experience in submitting to the authority of their husbands? After all, isn't wifely submission part of God's plan for married couples? Shouldn't submission therefore come easily for wives?

In addressing this apparent contradiction, Angela appeals to notions of gender difference and complementarity. However, her assessment of this connection between submission and essential masculine-feminine difference diverges markedly from the elite evangelical commentators who argue that God instilled in women a naturally submissive spirit (see esp. LaHaye 1977: 178). Angela explains to us: "Now, women want to be in control. That's our nature. It is also the position we are often put in, when Dad is away from home working or traveling. Women's controlling nature has been a problem since biblical times. Women naturally have a difficult time being submissive and respectful." Angela underscores this point by suggesting some reading material for women who wish to gain more insight into this matter. Consequently, just as Angela contends that men are born with "leaky balloon" egos, she argues that women are born not naturally submissive but rather craving control. Submission, according to Angela, is the corrective for this control-craving, strong-minded feminine orientation she finds manifested in herself and so many other women she has met over the past thirteen years.

Tinkering with Patriarchy: Gender, Power, and the Prospect for Structural Change at Parkview

Rhetorical contradictions within Parkview's family ministry program aside, it is noteworthy that this church does not permit women to serve as pastors; does not allow women to sit on the Elders Board; and, by default rather than by formal rule, does not have any women teaching Sunday school classes—unless they happen to do so as assistants to their husbands. While this organizational hierarchy is considerably less negotiable than the gender rhetoric at Parkview, some of the young adult unmarried women in the church recently began to inquire why women are not allowed to teach Sunday school classes at the church. When confronted with this inquiry, Pastor Al explained to them that there is no written rule at the church that bars women from teaching Sunday school classes; rather, the all-male teaching system at Parkview simply evolved over time because male teachers have always been plentiful in the church. As it was explained to me by Pastor Al, this exchange was in no way hostile or confrontational. Still, it would seem that these young women raised an issue that is important for the church membership and (all-male) Elders Board to consider. As Pastor Al describes, "Right now . . . our Elders are going on a retreat and we are really talking about women's roles in the church. Just to really try to understand what the Bible says. So it's something that we're still trying to understand with the broader perspective, particularly as culture changes. We're trying to examine our own views to make sure they are biblically correct; [to make sure] that we haven't formed boundaries that might be too narrow or even too broad."

Al explains that the retreat for the church's male leaders will be guided by a careful study of scripture: "Paul says to Timothy, he says outright, "I do not think it is right for a woman to exercise authority over a man." What in the world did he mean by that? That's what we're going to explore. First of all, what did he mean by that? Second of all, if we can agree about what he meant, then what are the roles that women can have in a church that doesn't violate what Paul was saying there? And typically, those issues have to do with [such questions as]: Can a woman be pastor? Can a woman be an elder? Can she be a deacon or a deaconess? And then, on and on it goes. Can she teach a Sunday school class? If she can, what age [can the male students be]? That sort of thing. And that's what we're trying to figure out. What does it mean to exercise spiritual authority?"

Pastor Al acknowledges the influence of broader evangelical debates over women's access to church pastorship in framing the topics to be considered on the Elders Board retreat. He says that one "very well-respected evangelical" whose tape church leaders are currently circulating "says that the only spiritual authority is the elder-teacher role in the church. And that's the only role he would find objectionable for a woman. But he says that they can teach in mixed groups and all that." He continues: "But then on the other hand, you've got some [evangelicals] that say that a woman can't do anything. She can't even teach boys that are elementary school age. That's the other extreme. So, that's what we're looking at."

Pastor Al acknowledges that the resolution to this dilemma must be grounded in both theology (i.e., biblical injunctions) and practicality (i.e., maintaining member allegiance and congregational growth). On the theological side, Al says that the elders will "be very biblical about this" and will aim to "figure out what the Word really does say about it and get beyond our cultural norms. . . . It comes down to [this]: there is a God and He has spoken; He has spoken clearly. So we have got to figure out what did He say clearly about this issue? And we don't know yet. We're trying to figure that out. . . . And there are other factors involved."

Turning to more practical considerations, Al concedes that "other factors" will be discussed at the men's retreat on women's roles at Parkview, including "honestly, mere pragmatism. And that is to say that there are certain traditionalists that will never change. So you kind of say, 'Well, what rocks the boat the least?' There is also the issue that's real in the Bible about Christian liberty. We might even have the liberty to go way beyond what we have traditionally done, but perhaps it's not best for the body. For the sake of peace, we might refrain. So that's a real issue as well."

The weight of tradition would seem to dictate against women serving as pastors at Parkview any time in the near future. Members currently affiliated with the congregation joined Parkview aware that the church was led by an all-male pastorship. Parkview would risk losing congregants—perhaps in significant numbers—if it were to take an abrupt about-face concerning its tradition of patriarchal leadership. The formidable tradition of pastoral patriarchy in this congregation is manifested not merely as a social convention or organizational tradition; male leadership is embedded within its material culture.

At Parkview, the pulpit area is located front and center in the chapel. The area surrounding the pulpit is well-lit so that the preacher is easily visible to all churchgoers as he delivers his Sunday sermon. However, such visibility was initially purchased at the price of pastoral discomfort. Parkview pastors found themselves uncomfortably warm, at times even perspiring, when preaching under the hot glare of these pulpit lights. To solve this problem, the church installed unobtrusive air conditioning vents in the floor surrounding the pulpit. However, an unintended consequence of this architectural modification became apparent soon after the floor vents were installed. Women singing special musical numbers from behind the pulpit found their dresses rising into the air whenever the pulpit floor vents were activated by the chapel air conditioning system. Female soloists now discreetly hold down the sides of their dresses—standard attire for Parkview women—while singing from the pulpit. Although the all-male leadership at Parkview never intended for women to be excluded from the pulpit altogether, pastoral patriarchy has nevertheless become embedded within the church's fabric.

While it would be unwise to overstate the potentially minor changes likely to accompany the elders retreat, these occurrences provide evidence that Parkview produces gender on a number of distinct organizational levels—

through both its family ministry programs and its pastoral structure. Indeed, these organizational-level gender processes are closely intertwined. It is likely that Parkview pastors' general willingness to defend mutual submission within the home will enable this church to retain an all-male leadership within the church. Such an organizational strategy would be well suited to a church whose members hold quite heterogeneous views concerning questions of authority and submission.

The Dynamics of Wifely Submission among Parkview Spouses

When asked what the biblical term "submission" means to them, many of the spouses I interviewed drew on the discourse of wifely submission to articulate their views. Despite the caveats frequently offered in the course of these defenses of wifely submission, it was the wife's submission to the husband to which these respondents made reference.

Patriarchy Qualified: The Rhetorical Reinvention of Wifely Submission and Husband-Headship

Veronica Murray, a twenty-year-old woman married for just under six months to Philip, provides an explanation of wifely submission that is quite common among such respondents. Her commentary is laced with equally common qualifications. Veronica offers the following account: "Basically, I think in a Christian sense [submission] would be [concerned with] the role of the woman to not always buck horns with the man and fight his," she pauses momentarily, "not really his authority, because he doesn't have authority over me—but [not] to fight his lead in the marriage. Philip feels like such a man when I say, 'How do you want to do this?' Do you know what I'm saying? He feels big. It definitely helps [men] when they know that they have someone to protect. It puts a lot of responsibility on them, but it makes them act better. So I guess that is how I would define submission. It's not just, 'Whatever you say honey, beat me.' That's not at all what I'm saying. [Rather, it is] just not to buck horns always and constantly be fighting or nagging. You let him do this. If you want to talk about something, you can talk about it. But not continuously." Veronica, of course, is quite young and is in the early stages of her marriage with Philip. Nevertheless, several of the older, more experienced wives also embrace this concept of wifely submission.

Women who embrace this concept of wifely submission face two thorny dilemmas concerning the actual practice of submission. First, how can the submissive wife retain her sense of self-worth in a cultural climate that privileges expressive individualism and sometimes likens subordinate evangelical women to doormats? Second, how is the wife within a marriage predicated on her submission to her husband's authority to avoid becoming resentful of his authority or envious of his power? Concerning the doormat problem, many pro–wifely-submission women I interviewed acknowledge that their views no longer enjoy widespread cultural acceptance outside of evangelical circles but take pride in being different from women in the American mainstream. Regarding the issue of power envy, even the wife who spoke in the most glowing terms about the benefits of wifely submission— less pressure and responsibility for her—concedes that it "is not always pleasant." Taken together, these dilemmas are engaged through an array of innovative strategies employed by female proponents of wifely submission. In the interest of conciseness and coherence, I will distill three solutions to these problems from Veronica's account.

One method wives can use to overcome both the power envy and doormat problems is rhetorical in nature. Along with other women who embrace wifely submission, Veronica attempts to deconstruct the hierarchy implied by the term "submission." As she notes, Philip takes the "lead" in their marriage, but he does not exercise "authority over" her. For many Parkview women, terms such as these draw important distinctions between a wife's obligation to fall in line under an autocratic ruler and her choice to follow his benevolent leadership. Being trampled under foot (much like a doormat) is rejected in favor of "choosing" to submit. Such distinctions were particularly prominent among the younger wives within this group, suggesting once again that recent feminist critiques of the patriarchal family have challenged the hegemony of evangelical discourses concerning husband-headship and wifely submission. In this way, the patriarchal family has been problematized enough to require extensive explanations and myriad qualifications.

Second, while Veronica accepts the principle of hierarchy implied within the term submission, she does not believe that women are inferior because they submit to their husbands' leadership. In fact, Veronica's account suggests just the reverse. Interestingly, Veronica argues that it is the deficiencies in men rather than the inferiority of women that makes wifely submission the key to marital success. She justifies her submission to Philip based on what men—not women—apparently lack. She says: "Philip feels like such a man when I say, 'How do you want to do this?' . . . He feels big. It definitely helps [men] when they know that they have someone to protect. It puts a lot of responsibility on them, but it makes them act better."

This conceptualization is quite similar to Angela's depiction of the soft male ego that so desperately needs to be built up by wifely submission. Other women also commented on this apparent benefit of wifely submission. One wife I interviewed described how her mother's self-conscious—even strategic—submission operated within her parents' relationship. This wife said that her commitment to wifely submission came from "my mother always . . . talking about how you need to submit to your husband. I know that I'm a lot like my mother in that my mother's personality is a lot stronger than my father's. She is a lot more opinionated than he is. And yet, she is always deferring to him and always saying, 'Well, I don't like this or that. But your father thinks we should do this. And he needs to feel like he is the man, he's the leader, he's the head of our family. And to do that, I have to go his way.' " Far from being passive doormats, many of these women portray themselves as active strategists who have generously decided to defer to husbands whose fragile egos could not withstand the onslaught of women's overt assertiveness.

In a more practical sense, Veronica and many other spouses who defend wifely submission argue that this conceptualization does not rule out negotiation, discussion, or even genuine compromise. Although Veronica clearly relinquishes final-say power to Philip—you don't "buck horns always," you "let him do this"—she says that discussion is certainly part of the process. Other wives—and husbands, too—were careful to make this point as well. Even among the most avid proponents of wifely submission at Parkview, spouse-to-spouse discussions are considered not just an option, but the only proper place from which to begin the decision-making process within the home.

What about the self-proclaimed patriarchs in such families? Many husbands who embrace wifely submission are confronted with a dilemma different from that faced by their wives. Specifically, how can husbands defend the merits of wifely submission in the face of feminism without seeming like chauvinistic, insensitive, and outmoded patriarchs? Husbands to whom I spoke employ two strategies to overcome this dilemma. When husbands—both young and old—speak of wifely submission, they are typically quick to add either that all individuals (including husbands) must submit to authority of some sort or another (thereby naturalizing authority relations), or that a husband must love his wife to such an extent that he will neither act selfishly nor abuse his authority (thus placing boundaries around the exercise of headship).

Husbands who employ the first strategy to defend the legitimacy of wifely submission are not arguing for mutual submission. According to them, the husband within a marriage is not to submit to his wife per se. But these respondents do point out that husbands are expected to be submissive to other authority figures in life (e.g., bosses, church leaders, elders, and the ultimate authority figure—God). Thus, wives are technically not alone in their submission. One fifty-year-old husband, George, explains the importance of submission both outside of and within his marital relationship in just this way. Though he admits to having had some previous problems submitting to authority figures outside the home, George has largely overcome that difficulty. He extols the benefits of submission broadly understood and of wifely submission more specifically. George's wife, Madeline, was equally laudatory of his authority and her submission.

George says that submission "is like a military term. 'To line up under' is the way I understand it. And I fortunately had four years in the Air Force, which was very good for me. One of the things that I learned was the chain of command and the authority structure that God has put in place. It has helped me a lot, because in my early years I was having lots of problems with my wife's father, with my boss at work, and other things. It was simple rebellion. I had to learn to respect the positions even though I may not respect the personality." George concedes that submitting to duly appointed authorities remains difficult, but he is reassured by his experience with this principle and his faith in a God of order. "I still have problems with it, but not like I used to. I have seen in my own life the benefit of submitting to those authority positions, and letting God work through them. You know, if I am fighting them, on the one hand I am not thinking clearly. And secondly, I am not hearing what God is saying through these people. So, in the same sense, what I see in my wife's submission to me is that she sees me as God's authority and the responsible person here. And [she sees] that I am accountable to God.

In that sense, she can trust God to work through me. If I stumble and make a mistake, she can trust God to fix it."

Other men who defend wifely submission employ a second strategy to do so in the face of feminist critiques of patriarchal authority. These men focus more specifically on the internal dynamics of the marital relationship rather than pointing to the cascading levels of authority relations outside of the family. Husbands who discuss wifely submission in this way relativize its significance by describing at length how husbands are scripturally commanded to love their wives. In some cases, these men's emphasis on the reciprocity between wifely submission and a husband's loving headship edges toward the idea of mutual submission (though they did not use this term). One of these husbands, Kent Houston, describes this perspective.

Kent has just finished explaining to me how he failed to solicit input from Carole on a major business decision he faced recently—namely, moving his business office to a new location. Kent says he regretted his oversight when Carole brought this gaffe to his attention and subsequently sought her forgiveness. He gives the following description of submission: "Well, submission of a woman to a man, as I say, is very much the same as the submission of the church to Jesus Christ. And as Christ loves the church, so does the husband love his wife—if it's a good marriage, that is. And so, yes, she is submissive. He is considered the head of the household. He is considered the head of the family. And she, as such, is submissive. But submissive in love. And he is head of the household, but in love. In other words, he may be head of the household, but he loves his wife. And he does, you know, take her into account and listen to her better than I did," says Kent, laughing. Now looking me squarely in the eye, he says with a smile, "That's why I got in deep trouble."

"And when you say she is submissive in love, what do you mean exactly by that?"

"Well, she submits to her husband, I think, because she loves him. Because she trusts him. Because she knows that the decisions he's making are good for both of them. And I think this is the same way that the church responds to Jesus Christ. The church loves Christ, and is submissive because they know he's right. Because they know he's on the right track."

Kent continues by describing how these principles have operated within his own marital relationship with Carole. "I think submission, for the most part, has been my wife's role. She has been submissive. There are isolated instances when I have to be submissive. Because I have to be humble. And likewise she has to be humble at times. I have got to realize that, you know, that I am not always right. I am not perfect by any means. Neither one of us are. And so, sometimes you have to be humble, submissive to the other to understand and to really contemplate where the other is coming from. What their thoughts are. What their innermost feelings are. But, basically, submission is the role of the wife."

Delimited Submission: The Practical Contradictions Underlying Domestic Patriarchy

Remarkably, among the spouses who embrace this concept of wifely submission and reserve final-say rights for the husband, a preponderance could not recall an instance in which this marital chain of command had to be put into play. This pattern is crucial because, at its most basic level, the teeth of patriarchal power would be found in the practice of male domination within these homes. Yet it would seem that many interviewed couples are committed to wifely submission only in principle. In actual practice, these spouses rarely need to rely on this principle. One couple who touted the merits of male family leadership opted not to purchase drapes for their new home because they could not agree on what type to buy or how much money to spend. This same couple had recently purchased their home in a semi-rural/semi-urban area because one spouse preferred rural living and the other preferred a more urbanized milieu.

Such stories of compromise and negotiation abound in accounts collected from these couples. In practice, many of these pro–wifely-submission couples are able to come to some understanding that adequately addresses the interests of both the husband and the wife. Otherwise, they typically postpone the decision. Therefore, the husband in these marriages is often understood by both parties to be the leader of the family. Yet his leadership generally entailed not making decisions, but leading the family in a spiritual sense (e.g., initiating devotional activities such as family prayer; ensuring that the family attends Sunday services on a regular basis). The incisive distinction classical sociologist Max Weber draws between *authority* and *power* is instructive in this regard. Weber (1954a: 294) defined authority as the recognized right to rule—a right deemed legitimate by all parties even if it is never wielded against those subject to it. By contrast, Weber conceptualized power as the practical ability to achieve desired ends even in the face of others' resistance: "In general, we understand by 'power' the chance of a man or a number of men to realize their own will in a communal action even against the resistance of others who are participating in the action" (1954b: 180). For the most part, Parkview husbands wish to be recognized as leaders in their family (authority) without coercing their preferences on other family members (power). The symbolic authority enjoyed by many Parkview husbands has real-world effects, inasmuch as it neutralizes the need for these men to prove their headship through coercive patriarchal decision making (see Bartkowski, Wilcox, and Ellison 2000; Gallagher and Smith 1999).

Despite this pervasive nod toward men's symbolic household authority, a handful of Parkview couples could and did recount instances in which the wife actually submitted to her husband in some fashion. Two intriguing patterns emerge from my discussions with these couples. The first pattern concerns the reversibility of power relations within these marriages. The second, mentioned particularly by the wives, concerns the gift-giving economy that made the decision to submit not just a matter of principle but a practically worthwhile endeavor as well.

The first pattern—the reversibility of marital power relations in patriarchal families—is illustrated by Kent and Carole Houston's recent disagreement over his failure to consult her about moving his business office from its current locale to a new location. Borrowing from the gender lore of secular Judaism concerning the centrality of a mother's happiness to satisfactory domestic relations, Kent recounts how a resolution was achieved with Carole following his failure to solicit her input on his business decision: "Carole was very bitter. Just felt she was closed out. Just shut out of anything that was going on in my life. I say in my life—in my business life. And I could see that she was very bitter, very cold toward me. And of course, this doesn't make me happy. I could see that she wasn't happy. There's an old Jewish saying, 'If mama ain't happy, then ain't nobody happy.'" Laughing momentarily, Kent gathers himself and continues: "But anyway, I told her. I said, 'I know that you're unhappy. And in order for us to get our marriage back on track, we have to talk. And we have to talk in such a way that we're not screaming at one another; [that] we're not talking in anger; and [that instead] we're talking with level heads and open hearts.' And I said, 'We have to go through this thing. I have to find out what hurts you the most. And maybe [there is] something I can do, something can happen that will, you know, take away the hurt and bring us back together.' "

"And was that able to happen, in general, do you think?"

"Pretty much. Pretty much," replies Kent, smiling. Now leaning toward me and speaking in hushed tones, he offers the epilogue, "Still have to watch my p's and q's."

Within other contexts, wifely submission was viewed as a gift rather than an obligation or a duty. This form of quid-pro-quo submission operates very much like what Arlie Hochschild (1989) has identified as the marital economy of gratitude evidenced in American families writ large (see also Smith 2000). The case of Veronica and Philip Murray mentioned above is instructive. Concerning the issue of wifely submission, Veronica both talks the talk and walks the walk. A very able and gifted student, Veronica relinquished a full-tuition scholarship at a top-notch state university so that she could accompany her husband in his move across the country to finish his professional schooling in Texas. When I ask her during our interview what role, if any, submission plays in her marital relationship, she describes this chain of events as tears well up in her eyes. Philip, too, readily recognized this act of submission on Veronica's part. Reining in her sadness, Veronica explains to me and apparently reminds herself: "We've worked through that [decision for me to give up the scholarship and move here to Texas]. It was very hard. It is still hard. But I have to realize that my time is going to come. Next semester I'm going to be back in school, and eventually I'm not going to have to work. I'll be able to do what I want to do . . . so it will all work out. . . . We have an outside business and [Philip] knows that I want to quit my job. He knows how much that account has got to have in it before I can quit my job."

Thus, Veronica's act of submission to Philip has entailed painful sacrifices. Her school plans have been delayed. Veronica no longer enjoys the independent support of a scholarship that she herself earned. And she is currently working at an unsatisfying job when she would rather be in school. Yet, by both of their accounts, Philip deeply appreciates these sacrifices— and not simply through his rhetoric of gratitude. In the end, this couple has agreed that Philip will *work* (literally and figuratively) to alleviate the pain produced by Veronica's submission. How? Philip is charged with earning and saving enough money—over and above his full-time graduate school course load and assistantship—to enable Veronica to quit her job and go back to school shortly. In such cases, submission on the part of a traditional wife is interlaced with various types of quid pro quo exchanges.

The Dynamics of Mutual Submission among Parkview Spouses

Whereas some of the spouses at Parkview subscribe to wifely submission, others align themselves more closely with the discourse of mutual submission. And, not unlike gender relations within the patriarchal households described above, these seemingly egalitarian marriages are laden with internal points of contradiction. Couples who tout the merits of mutual submission simultaneously conform to and deviate from biblical feminist defenses of marital egalitarianism.

The Paradox of Mutual Submission: Male Leadership in Egalitarian Families

When asked about her views on the biblical concept of submission, one wife in her late forties, Rose Lehman, clearly situates her views within the discourse of mutual submission: "Well, first of all, my understanding of what those passages in Ephesians say is that [husbands and wives] are mutually submissive. So, I am to submit to him, but he also is to submit to me. Again, I think it just goes back to that teamwork thing. We are mutually submissive to each other. But submission to me is not—" Rose pauses, choosing her words, and then continues. "I mean, that [word] gets negative [reactions]. When people say 'submit,' it's like, 'Ugh, that's terrible.' I don't think it is. I don't think it is at all. I think being willing to sacrifice what you want for the people around you is a very noble thing. . . . That's strength. It's not weakness. You know, a lot of people don't see it that way. But I think it's mutual. I think we are to submit to each other, is my understanding of it. That's the way it's always been taught when they teach it in church. That's what we've been taught. It's mutual submission to each other." Rose proceeds to form an equilateral triangle with her thumbs and forefingers to illustrate her view of a good Christian marriage. Not unlike the triangular metaphor invoked by egalitarian evangelical commentators, she envisions Christ at the top and the two spouses—equal teammates—at the base corners.

Rose and her husband Jake seem largely in agreement on this issue. Early in my interview with him, Jake describes the most important components of a Christian marriage. His response resonates with the egalitarian sensibilities of his wife: "The most important component [of a Christian marriage] would be both partners understanding who the boss is. The boss being Christ. And having a servant's heart towards each other. I'd have to say—and, at least, I believe that Rose believes this too—that we both feel like in our married life that we are both trying to live up to the standards of a higher authority."

To underscore his point, Jake counterposes their convictions to evangelical Christians who do not share such an egalitarian view of marriage: "We see a lot of fundamental Christians where their concept is the husband has the iron fist." Jake pounds his fist on the table to illustrate this style of authority, and then continues. "What he says goes, and everybody else follows behind him. But biblically, I don't think that's necessarily true. You see leadership as being a servant-leader. And that is a task that we share. We have different roles of course. But I think the whole servant-leader role is something that we both share. So I would say that the primary focus [of a Christian marriage] is on who the higher authority is. . . . It helps when we do problem-solving. When there is conflict, as there is always going to be in marriage, it kind of gives us a referee in a sense. . . . Christ."

Jake, then, articulates a unique understanding of servant-leadership in that he does not occupy that position alone. Although evangelical advice authors use that term in a gendered fashion (the husband is the servant-leader), Jake construes both himself and his wife as servant-leaders in their family.

During the course of our conversation, however, Jake's point of emphasis seems to change somewhat concerning this issue of domestic power. When asked minutes later about his understanding of the term "submission," Jake becomes more equivocal—melding the language of mutual submission with references to a patriarchal family structure: "The obvious answer for submission is that you either give in or follow one's authority, someone else's authority. And I guess what I would submit is that to me the willingness of Rose to accept my leadership in some area basically puts the greater burden on me to lead properly. And the Bible also talks about husbands submit to your wives and wives to your husbands."

Having offered this malleable definition of submission, Jake proceeds to outline the conditions under which Rose's submission to his leadership would not be warranted: "At least in our family, I see this submission as being almost an earned right. If I was being completely unbiblical in the way that I was attempting to lead the family, I would expect Rose not to submit to me because there is a higher authority that she submits to. And if I am wrong in that area, then I need to be confronted about it. And so, yes, I think that she has a responsibility to submit to my leadership as long as it's deserved and it's the proper spiritual leading. If it's not, then I think that she also has a responsibility to say so. So blind submission I don't see as being biblical. And again, it's a two-way street. Husbands are to submit too. So I would say, at least in our marriage, that the whole idea of submission is one of responsibility on my part and, I think, one of discernment on her part."

"Responsibility on your part?"

"Responsibility to be a spiritual leader and to have well thought out, well planned decisions. Doing things [like] putting others first in our family. And if I get off on some weird tangent, then I don't necessarily see that her responsibility would be to submit to that." Like Pastors Bill and Al, then, Jake reserves the right to call himself the leader of his family even as he embraces mutual submission. And, like Pastor Stephen, he sees male family leadership as an earned right that must be exercised in a responsible, selfless fashion.

How can such equivocation be explained? Such contradictory rhetoric from husband-advocates of mutual submission seems to serve two purposes. First, this symbolic nod to the husband's family leadership distinguishes these men from non-evangelical, secular, and feminist proponents of democratic family relations. Given the polarized character of debates over family power within American society at large (Hunter 1991) and within American evangelicalism itself (Bartkowski 1997, 1999, 2000), these men probably do not wish to seem *too egalitarian*. Evangelical Protestantism is very much about being different—being in but not of the world, being saved amid the unsaved. These men could be construed as deviating from their evangelical convictions—by lacking any sense of distinctiveness from mainstream American culture—if they were knee-jerk egalitarians.

Second, these men live within a religious congregation (Parkview) where gender traditionalism and the patriarchal family retain much popularity. Many spouses at Parkview maintain a commitment to a patriarchal family in which a wife is ostensibly called to submit to her husband. Rhetorical nuance (mutual submission undergirded by male family leadership) enables husbands like Jake to build bridges between their own egalitarian sensibilities and the more traditional-patriarchal commitments of fellow congregants. What about the notion that the biblical term submission is a military word literally meaning "to line up under?" Most spouses committed to mutual submission generally do not interpret the word this way, while others with more traditional sensibilities are free to do so.

For Rose and Jake, these definitions of submission as mutual servanthood are highly congruent with their life circumstances. Jake has just recently started his own business. Inasmuch as start-up businesses often take time to draw a client base, Rose's paid employment as a college instructor and professional consultant is instrumental in making possible Jake's entrepreneurial venture. Both Jake and Rose work approximately fifty hours per week, though Jake takes advantage of the flexibility permitted by his self-employment, often arranging his schedule around that of their two children (one a preteen and the other a teenager). More often than not, he makes breakfast for them and takes them to school; this and other parenting duties they attend to jointly.

A Leader Is as a Leader Does: Marriage, Gender Practice, and Men's Friendships

Subjective contradictions, such as those outlined for Jake Lehman above, are only one type of gender paradox that emerges from within families that embrace the concept of mutual submission. Another type of contradiction endemic to such families pertains to a husband-wife disparity concerning the precise definition of submission. Gender relations in the Weiss household—wife Heather and husband Ben—are characterized by just such a contradiction.

Heather and Ben are in much the same position, structurally speaking, as Rose and Jake Lehman. Like Rose and Jake, both Heather and Ben work for pay full-time, about fifty hours each week. And like Jake, Ben has recently started his own business. Ben, too, is relying upon the financial provision of his wife, Heather, to see them through the formative years of his self-employment.

Rose and Heather, good friends by dint of their involvement at the church and their similar life circumstances, are largely in agreement concerning this issue of submission. Echoing the themes raised by Rose, Heather Weiss explains that submission means "to come alongside someone. And in that, to me, when I think of somebody coming alongside—whether it's to encourage you or to hold you accountable—I don't see that as a dominating type of submission. There's someone there because they want what's best for you."

"And what role, if any, does submission play in your marital relationship?" I ask.

"I just don't submit," Heather responds, laughing. "No. You know, I guess I should also say that I think that it's such a two-way thing. If I was married to someone who told me I had to do certain things, I would not be very submissive under the definition of what most people see as submission. You know, I see my husband as the most encouraging person in all of life. Somebody who, whether it's work-related or home, as a general rule does anything possible to help me to excel and to do better. . . . But I see [submission] more as walking alongside than I see it as beneath or in any way under him."

Ben Weiss's definition of this term differs strikingly from that embraced by his friend, Jake Lehman, and—most notably—from the definition offered by his own wife. Ben has had no formal theological training, but relies on lessons learned in informal Bible study courses he took in college under the tutelage of a rigorous Bible instructor. Ben draws upon this theological training to describe his interpretation of biblical references to submission. Ben explains: "Submission is a Greek word, *hupotasso*. It means literally 'to arrange yourself in an orderly manner under.' I studied this scripture one time because I was in a Bible study and it was given to me by a guy who was leading the Bible study. . . . And one of my passages that I needed to study was a Peter passage that has to do with the husband-wife relationship. . . . Essentially what it says is, 'Husbands, love your wives as Christ loved the church.' That was the man's admonition. And it said for wives to submit themselves to their husbands. And if you study the context of that, submission has to do with arranging yourself in an orderly manner under your husband."

It is somewhat perplexing that Ben and Jake are such close friends. Ben (a proponent of wifely submission) and Jake (an advocate of mutual submission) would seem to be at virtually opposite ends of an ideological continuum—not exactly the best recipe for an enduring, meaningful friendship.

How, then, do these men worship together and maintain a close friendship with such apparently discordant views? More importantly, how are these ideological differences managed between Ben (who embraces wifely submission) and his wife, Heather (who subscribes to mutual submission)?

Gender practices—which often contradict gender ideals—hold the key to understanding this nexus of intimate relationships. Despite the points of ideological divergence described above, Jake and Ben's household practices are strikingly similar—egalitarian. When asked what role submission plays in his marital relationship with Heather, Ben's practical commitment to mutual submission is boldly evidenced: "In the broad Christian sense, we often submit to one another because we love each other." By way of illustration, Ben adds that marital reciprocity applies even to the sexual component of his relationship with Heather where, he says, "mutual submission" would apply "if my wife has a sexual need or if I have a sexual need."

Ben Weiss and Jake Lehman are similar in another way as well. Like Jake, Ben's practical commitment to mutual submission is flanked by his understanding of himself as the family's leader. Here again, though, this leadership is bounded by eminently practical factors—including Ben's deep respect for the needs and interests of other family members. A real servant-leader in practice (if not in stated ideology), Ben leads his fellow family members in a manner that is consistent with their interests rather than his own: "Though I think I am the spiritual leader in our home, I am not the kind of guy who sits down and says, 'OK, everybody, we're going to have a little Bible study now.' My leadership style is more as we're going, you know, here's my opportunity to teach on some spiritual issue. There are times when I wish I was more of a corporate leader. I am really more of a one-on-one leader in that respect. I guess maybe it's most every father's dream to be able to kind of command the attention of his troops so to speak. If I tended to do that, it would be like, 'Sure, Dad. Ha ha.' "

Ben admits to experiencing "some discomfort" because his desire to be the "corporate leader" is inhibited by practical family circumstances that really do not permit him to do so: "There are some people out there that I admire [who] can get together and do—what am I thinking? Oh, the Advent candle. I look at [families that do] that and think, 'That would be kind of neat to pull that off.' But the way we work as a family, it's kind of like, 'You want me to light the candle and talk about religion when Monday Night Football is on?' I mean I can just hear my fifteen-year-old saying that. I guess we have never been a big ritual people with a family devotion time on Monday nights or Sundays before church. We have never been ritual people. So, that's probably got something to do with it."

Following up, I inquire of Ben: "So that's just kind of where it stands, and you're comfortable with that?"

"I guess," Ben replies. "I confess that we don't do enough planning together. And maybe this is an area where I have not planned to bring the family together corporately as the spiritual leader of the family that I have said that I am supposed to be. So, probably a lack of planning. And usually those kinds of plans would be talked over with my wife. It's not just something I am just going to go off and do by myself and make everybody march to my drum. I wouldn't do that." Consequently, although Ben is quite envious of fathers who can "command the troops," he recognizes the serious costs that would accompany the imposition of such an authoritarian family structure, at least in his and Heather's home. Wifely submission in word ultimately gives way to mutual submission in deed.

Eight

Labor of Love?

*Financial Provision, Housework, and
Child Care in Parkview Families*

Evangelical family discourse is ideologically fragmented concerning the relationship between gender and domestic labor. If we define domestic labor in broad terms to include financial provision as well as the division of domestic chores and childcare responsibilities, the dominant discourse within contemporary evangelicalism supports husband-providership and wifely domesticity. By contrast, dissident evangelical commentators argue that separate spheres are restrictive for spouses, inhibit the development of marital intimacy, and are not supported by a correct reading of the Bible. In contrast to dominant indictments of two-career couples, these equality-minded commentators contend that financial provision, domestic chores, and childcare responsibilities should be shared equally.

Where on these discursive continua do families at Parkview locate themselves ideologically? And to what extent do these couples' household practices conform to or depart from their stated ideological commitments? Consistent with the concepts of family adaptive strategies and "doing gender," I now explore the negotiation of domestic labor among four evangelical families at different stages of domestic life, including younger and older couples, and a family with no children alongside three families with children of various ages. I catalog the life experiences of these four different types of households to illuminate the diverse ways in which cultural and congregational resources can be used to face the exigencies of evangelical marriages at different stages in a family's life course.

Future So Bright? A Working Wife and Helpmate Husband

Married for fifteen months and without children, Dan and Amy Humphreys are each thirty years old and are highly active members at Parkview. Both have been longtime Christians—Dan for over fifteen years and Amy for over twenty. They are both currently employed. Dan works at home at two different part-time jobs, one of which is as a fundraising consultant.

When asked about Parkview's core message concerning a man's primary roles and responsibilities in the home, Dan articulates his agreement with the views he has heard expressed at the church: "Materially, that it's I would think clearly the man's role to be the primary breadwinner through life. And as far as taking care of kids, that's mixed. Obviously women are more capable of taking care of kids in certain ways than men are. I mean, physiologically and things. But those are shared responsibilities. And yet I think a mother is more of a nurturer than the husband. But if the husband isn't filling the gap in other areas to let the woman have the freedom to nurture the kids and still have her own free time to decompress from that and other things, then he's not fulfilling his role. . . . [He needs to] be the point of financial and physical stability for the family." In this way, Dan's views about a man's family responsibilities are quite clearly situated within the dominant evangelical discourse of husband providership.[1] He also considers these responsibilities to be consonant with the spiritual leadership that husbands should offer to their families.

What about the wife's primary domestic responsibilities? Here again, Dan invokes themes from the dominant evangelical discourse of wifely domesticity. He says that the church teaches, and he agrees, that a wife should be "a helpmate to her husband. . . . Her primary role would be to be a support and encouragement to her husband." As for the specific allocation of domestic chores, however, he seems a bit more suspicious of dominant discursive conceptualizations: "When you break it up into cooking and cleaning, I think those can go both ways. [A wife's primary role is] not to take care of the house. But I see it as to be a help. I mean, God created Eve to be a helpmate for Adam." Doubling back a bit on his initial response, Dan concludes that being "a help" to her husband "usually comes through [a wife] taking care of the home and creating a place where the man can have a home—where he doesn't have to worry about that, so he can go worry about making money and providing in other areas."

Amy agrees with Dan's views on these matters. In fact, she speaks in much more practical terms about her convictions on these issues. Amy is currently employed in a marketing job at which she works forty hours per week. She anticipated remaining employed after getting married. With this idea in mind, Amy spent ten months on a job search after they arrived in their current city of residence. Amy does not seem displeased with her current job per se, but she is somewhat dissatisfied with the employment situation in her family. As a thirty-year-old woman who wants several children, Amy would like begin that phase of their life in the not too distant future. "I am thirty and I want to have three kids," Amy says, "and I have got to get started soon." Laughter follows her remark, but this is a matter both Amy and Dan treat quite seriously. Amy would like to raise their children full-time, and Dan is fully supportive of that arrangement in principle. Both Dan and Amy value having been raised by mothers who were not employed outside the home. However, Dan's current income alone is not sufficient to support that arrangement in the Humphreys household. As it turns out, Dan's employment is seasonal, and his job as a fundraising consultant is commission-based.

In point of fact, Amy is the primary financial provider—"the major bread-winner," as Dan puts it—in their household. And, according to both of them, this situation has generated considerable stress in their marriage. As someone who conducted an extensive job search, Amy is sympathetic toward Dan's employment difficulties, which she describes as "circumstances that were out of his control." Yet she also finds herself frustrated about her work-load within their family. "I felt like I found myself in the situation that was the opposite of what I wanted," she says. "And I was just frustrated because I felt like I was going to work every day, and I was doing the cooking, the cleaning, and paying the bills and everything. And because he didn't have a full-time job, I felt like I was doing more than he was, I guess."

Amy and Dan have enlisted several coping strategies to resolve these stressful circumstances and unrealized desires. For one, they discuss these issues and they pray about them. Amy comments: "As far as trying to resolve it, I think I just said, 'This situation has got to change because we both know that it's not the way things should be.'" Amy admits to being pretty angry during one recent discussion, because "I feel like I had to be the motivator for him to work, and I didn't like being in that role." When confronted with her feelings, Amy says that Dan's response was "even-keeled" and "calm." Laughing nervously, she remarks: "It's usually just me ranting and raving. And he doesn't say anything. Then we pray about it. We usually always pray about it, and that helps calm my nerves. Prayer is the key to resolving anything."

In addition, Dan seeks to relieve some of the pressure brought about by Amy's double role via his additional domestic chore contributions—at least to the extent that he feels able to do so. By both of their accounts, Dan is an inept cook and is not a reliable purchaser of basic household goods such as food and sundries. He therefore spends just over thirty minutes per week on these household tasks combined, in contrast to Amy's total of nine hours cooking and shopping weekly.

This theme was a common refrain among many interviewed wives. The received wisdom among many of my female respondents portrayed husbands as simply incompetent or highly unreliable where certain tasks were concerned, often centering on those chores that are most time-consuming. Examples of such wives' misgivings include some husbands' apparent inability to sort the laundry correctly prior to washing clothes, as well as several husbands' seeming untrustworthiness in purchasing healthy and satisfying foods. The dominant discourse of wifely domesticity is truly hegemonic in such homes. Hegemony entails not only the dominance of a set of ideals, but a particular type of dominance that is sustained through commonsensical, taken-for-granted assumptions about the seemingly natural character of social relations. It is assumed that husbands are simply incapable of performing or even learning to perform many of the household tasks at which their wives show such proficiency.

Amy and Dan's relationship was no exception to this pattern, with the former overseeing most of the shopping, cooking, and laundry—arguably the most time-intensive tasks in any home. Among these tasks alone, Amy's total labor contribution of eleven hours compares with Dan's one-hour total investment. Since Amy and Dan live in an apartment, the most time-consuming of the typical husband's tasks—namely, yardwork and household maintenance—were nonexistent.

Both Dan and Amy recognize that keeping the checkbook balanced is not his forte. Amy pays the bills and keeps financial records, estimated to take about two hours per week, because she is more "organized" and "detail-oriented." Amy recounts the following incidents: "We have all our money in one checkbook. Whenever he writes a check, he just takes the checkbook but doesn't ever write down the amount. So he used to come home and tell me verbally, 'Oh, by the way, I wrote a check for so-and-so dollars and cents,' expecting that I would remember it. Well, that's a little bit much for me. So now, we've got this system where he's got to write it down when he comes home. But sometimes he forgets. And sometimes the checkbook doesn't balance. Our bank account sometimes goes under the minimum and we pay these finance charges. So that's caused conflict because I think, 'If I'd been doing it, this would have been avoided.' But he didn't let me know about such-and-such, and now we're paying bank charges."

The resolution to this dilemma, according to Dan, is to "be responsive" to Amy's financial record-keeping system. His remarks suggest that both of them hold some power and responsibility where this matter is concerned: "If she's responsible for the finances, then I need to submit to her way of doing the finances. So, I put her in charge. Then she says, 'If you don't put this note down, I'm going to kill you.' Then I need to put the note down. She tells me what I need to do, and I work towards fulfilling that."

Dan's main task contribution, consequently, comes in the form of chores that he feels capable of completing: washing the bathtub as needed, and washing the dishes and performing post-meal cleanup chores. Regarding the former, Amy hates cleaning the bathtub and Dan has agreed to do it upon her request. Consequently, he spends about forty minutes per week cleaning house (cleaning the bathtub, it would seem) in contrast to Amy's three hours cleaning house. As for washing the dishes, Dan admits to being motivated by the obviousness of the task before them, as well as by a mixture of guilt and sympathy. When asked about the rationale for dividing household chores in this fashion, Dan replies: "The chores have been divided the way they have mostly because I'm pretty lazy and Amy is a very organized and detail-oriented person. She hates scrubbing the tub, so she says, 'Dan, you've got to be able to scrub the tub because I hate doing that.' I say, 'OK, I don't mind. That's pretty easy to do.' And I do the dishes because, I don't know, that's real tangible. I mean, what am I going to do after I eat? Sit down and read a book or watch TV while she's cleaning up? And I just couldn't. I couldn't take that, because I care too much for my wife."

"Why couldn't you take that?"

"She does too much. And [washing dishes is] something that's every day. It's visible. With the bills, they're not there every day. It takes thinking ahead, organizing. But every day there is this pile of dishes, and I'll just watch her. She'll be in there slaving away. That's something I can do and I ought to do, because it just doesn't feel right for me to be doing nothing while she's doing something that's so obvious. And yet you could say that about the other things, I guess. But that's—" Dan pauses momentarily, then boldly announces, "Yeah, I do the dishes because it's the least I can do." He laughs. "And I enjoy it too. I have grown to like that. It's automatic. She does them and it's like, 'Get out of the kitchen. That's my job.' Because it's one of the few things I can do where, if she wants to, she can just sit down and relax or something. Yeah, that's why that happens. And the reason I don't do more of the others is that she's more organized. You know, I'll fold laundry and things. On Saturday, we do a couple loads, and I'll help out with that. But she's the one that takes the initiative to say, 'Now it's time that the laundry gets done.' And I'll fold clothes and things. I'll put them away. Again, that's just because we're here and it's to be done. Why shouldn't I help it with it? But she is more proactive in that."

Thus, Dan considers himself responsible for washing the dishes—it is one way that he can contribute, and it is glaring enough that it does not require much forethought. Amy appreciates his dishwashing contribution, commenting on the fact that "he has voluntarily taken it up" and concluding that he is "a great husband" for his thoughtfulness on this issue. Still, it is somewhat unclear as to what extent washing dishes actually is Dan's job. When surveyed about their household practices, Dan reported that he had spent three and a half hours washing the dishes the previous week; Amy reported spending four hours at this same task during that week. When all tasks are taken into consideration within the Humphreys household, Dan reports spending just under six hours per week on all domestic chores whereas Amy reports investing twenty hours per week toward household tasks.

By way of comparison, only four other husbands invest less time toward all household chores combined, two of whom are employed for over sixty hours per week and one of whom combines full-time paid employment with full-time graduate school. The husband with the smallest investment toward household chores (four hours total per week) reports working the most hours for pay (sixty-eight hours per week). This husband, however, is not an executive in some greedy law firm or high-powered business enterprise; rather, he is one of the hard-working pastors at Parkview E-Free. His wife—whom he describes as highly "detail-oriented" and, consequently, the "task manager" in their home—was in the process of becoming employed again. He conceded that the division of labor in their family, which currently is not compounded in complexity by children, would have to change with her shift back to the paid work force. To that end, he apologized to his wife profusely over the phone following our interview; our conversation, he said, had "convicted" him of his "sin of neglect" toward their domestic task arrangement. On that note, several pastors at the church forthrightly acknowledged the contradiction in working for a pro-family organization that makes such serious inroads into the time they would otherwise like to spend with their own families.

For their part, Dan and Amy hold out hope that this is a time of transition for them. After all, they are still newly married, Dan continues to seek out various employment alternatives, and they care very deeply for one another. As Dan explains, "for Amy and I, we truly believe that God led us to be married. We look at the circumstances leading up to our marriage and [conclude that] God desires us to be together. If it's hard, He's allowed that to happen to improve our characters." Dan takes solace in "the knowledge that God has created our marriage, that we are now one, that that's His design and His plan, and that that's the best for us ultimately because it is His desire" that we be together.

Moreover, Dan seems to believe—and Amy concurs—that these job-related difficulties can be put behind them with some careful planning. As to what could be done to improve their family life, Dan strikes a note of optimism while explicitly acknowledging that Amy's tenacity will be instrumental in moving them toward their collective goal: "The most glaring [area for improvement] would be for me to get a more stable employment situation. I have been at this commission thing for a long time, and it's not—" Dan pauses momentarily, then continues. "I'd rather just have an office job where I go in and get paid, and I know what I'm doing. . . . I've been looking for different things, and continue to pray that God would." Dan reflects, "I don't know if it's more energy, or if I would find a job that would provide adequately. And that's what I would like to see definitely in the next year. Where I could say, 'Well, Amy, we can start a family and not worry about how we're going to prepare for it financially.' I guess nobody is ever ready for kids across the board. And financially, that's just one of those things. But I think that would do a lot to put our roles where they ought to be and where we both want them to be."

Now taking a somber tone, Dan admits, "I'm really lazy, and that's by way of confession. I am not pursuing that as hard as I ought, I think, to improve our life. This is something we talk about, and again Amy takes more initiative on it than I do. That would help give us more of a direction for our life. You know, what's our five-year, what's our ten-year plan? I think that over Christmas, we'll go on vacation and we probably need to sit down and evaluate that. I think that we feel like there is a purpose to what we're doing. It's bigger than day to day, [but] I'm not very goal-oriented. And Amy is more that way. I think if I can get to know God a little bit better, and just get through the day. . . ." Dan concludes, "I am very easily satisfied. Not that Amy isn't. But I think I should get my role as a breadwinner nailed down better and have a more defined purpose for our lives." Despite the challenges of the present, Dan and Amy hope that with some careful planning their future together can be quite bright indeed.

Make Room for Daddy: Husband-Providership and the Coparenting Predicament

In at least two respects, Brian and Patti Erickson's life resembles that of Dan and Amy Humphreys. Both couples are quite involved at Parkview, not only in attending services virtually every week but also in volunteering in various church groups. Also, these couples are about the same age: Dan and Amy are thirty years old, while Brian and Patti are each twenty-eight. Yet there ends the similarity between these two families. Brian and Patti have been married for almost five years, compared with Dan and Amy's fifteen-month-old marriage. More importantly, Brian and Patti are in the midst of a very different phase of their marital relationship: they have a

fifteen-month-old daughter, Shelby, and as I interview them they are expecting their second child. Moreover, Brian and Patti are a single-income family.
As a computer consultant, Brian earns a salary substantial enough for them
to live comfortably—though not lavishly—on his income alone. Patti, a stay-
at-home mother, enjoys raising their daughter full-time even as she readily
acknowledges the challenges associated with her decision to do so.

When asked about Parkview's teachings concerning a Christian man's
family responsibilities, Brian responds, "Well, I have never heard them say
that the man is the only one that should be the breadwinner." He then proceeds to talk about a husband's leadership in the family, which "doesn't
mean that he is in a more important place . . . the man as a leader needs to
be a servant. . . . [Husbands] lead by serving." When I then inquired about
any discernible messages concerning a Christian wife's family roles and
responsibilities at Parkview, Brian is again careful and measured in his
response: "She's a helpmate to her husband. I guess she would be like the
cornerstone of the family. She really is the one that holds the family together.
It's hard. Discernible messages? We will do studies of books, and we'll talk
about women of the Bible. Probably the messages that come out about
women are messages that [Pastor] Al will try to apply from the scriptures. I
don't know that I could boil it down to one or two bullet points or messages,
other than [that she is] the helpmate to the husband."

Brian expresses his agreement with the church's perspective—to the
extent that Parkview articulates a particular message—on these issues. He
proceeds to explain why he thinks it is important that a husband acts as the
family's leader and a wife acts as her husband's helpmate. Brian's response
mixes general statements on this issue with biblical references and illustrations from his own family relationships: "One, I think it's natural. It suits both
the husband and the wife to their best strengths. I think the man excels more
in the leadership role of the family. And the woman excels in taking care of
the family, being a part of the family. I feel like the church is pretty careful,
because we have a lot of women in our church who work [outside the home].
I don't think that's frowned upon at all. [Yet, at the same time,] I feel like we
place a high importance on the mother-wife role in the home and how important it is. There are things my wife does that I just can't do. I see it with our
daughter, [Shelby, in the way that] she reacts to my wife. Patti has a lot of
strong points that I just don't have."

"Anything come to mind in particular?"

"I think her gentleness and tender spirit with Shelby. That would be one element. The other obvious conclusion you'd say is that it's biblical. It's a biblical model. You see it with Adam and Eve. Eve being the helpmate. And you don't see that as an unhealthy thing. They were very good together. So I think it's very important that you not skew the model. I think it gets skewed a lot, because it's not handled correctly. It can be mistreated for sure."

"Mistreated?"

"It can be abused. I think the man can hold it over the wife."

"And you had mentioned that your daughter responds to your wife's tenderness and gentleness. How would you characterize your qualities then?"

"Well, I think it would be the same but not to that extent. She has a real deep rapport with Shelby. Part of that is because she is at home right now." Turning then to his own contributions to Shelby's development, Brian says, "I would say leadership. I am trying to set an example for her. The contrast would be, especially as she gets older, teaching her how a man should treat a woman by her mother and by herself. Things my wife definitely won't be able to do."

Patti is similarly careful in discussing the way that responsibilities have been allocated within their home. In stark contrast to what might be expected of a stay-at-home evangelical mother and quite contrary to the notion of enforced domesticity, Patti defends their distinctive family roles and responsibilities as a personal choice. This type of response was quite common among other wives—and, for that matter, husbands—that I interviewed. "Roles" were often equated with legalism and rigidity, and were even likened by one respondent to "boxes" in which husbands and wives can unfortunately become trapped. Using the word "decision" repeatedly while referring to household roles, Patti indicates that she does not think that all families should fall in line and emulate the arrangement that seems to work so well for her and Brian. This is not to say that she is without an opinion on the matter of family roles, though, because she most definitely has strong feelings on the subject. Yet the forcefulness of her opinions is tempered both by her rhetoric of choice and by her Christian desire not to "pass judgment" on others without "walk[ing] in their shoes."

Patti acknowledges that "obviously we have chosen for me to be at home. Therefore I do think that there is a definite need to be at home, and I think it should be more likely the mother or whatever." However, Patti wrestles with an optimal degree of tolerance regarding dual-earner families with preschool-age children. "I can't speak for anyone else. We have made our own decisions, and I have a definite opinion. But I really feel like I am accountable for my own child. Everyone can make their decisions as well. I am not going out and condemn[ing] them. There are plenty of people in our neighborhood who are out there working. And I am not going to say that their children are going to end up in prison or become horrible derelicts. . . . We have had to have an opinion. Not everything is OK, [which is often] the opinion that you use to float around with. We've had to come down and actually say, 'What do we believe in for our own personal family, with what happens within these four walls?' "

Patti thus carves out subjective space within evangelical discourse for a dual commitment on this hot-button issue of stay-at-home mothering. On the one hand, she is personally committed to stay-at-home mothering—not even so much stay-at-home parenting, as indicated by her stating forthrightly that "I think it should be more likely the mother" who stays at home. Yet, on the other hand, she evinces a definite respect for a plurality of role-choices within families. Her assertion that day care itself does not produce "horrible derelicts" compares strikingly with James Dobson's vivid exemplars of children who apparently did not get enough adult parental supervision as youngsters—Lee Harvey Oswald and Charles Manson. Thus, while Patti "holds dearly" her beliefs about the propriety of stay-at-home motherhood for her family, she quickly adds that she "wouldn't get in anybody's face about [her] beliefs because people are responsible for their own children."

Patti admits to some degree of difficulty in sustaining these divergent views. The tension between tolerance and judgment on this issue is particularly difficult to sustain in the face of those who glorify stay-at-home mothering. As a stay-at-home mother, Patti is well aware that her choice to be a full-time mom is replete with vicissitudes not faced by dual-earner couples who have considerably more disposable income than she and Brian do. Patti is angered by people who say "You are so lucky to be at home. I wish I could be at home" as she watches "them tool off in new cars." But, here again, Patti's Christian convictions lead her to believe that it is "not right" for her "to judge them"—a most difficult task as she sees her husband "driving around in his thirteen-year-old car." In the end, Patti says that her family has "been very blessed. So I count it [as] a privilege, I guess, for me to be able to be home." Laughing, she concludes, "There are days where I would like to get in someone's face and say, 'I have an opinion on this!' Just because I think it's a give and take. There are things that are easier about being away from the home and not having that responsibility twenty-four hours a day. Like when you get sick, you can take a sick day. But there are also things that are harder [about being an employed mother]. I can't imagine carrying two loads. I can be singleminded this way."

In some respects, household tasks and childcare responsibilities in the Erickson household are broken down along traditional lines. As for household chores, Brian attends to outdoor tasks, household maintenance, and auto upkeep for about ten hours per week, while Patti spends no time on such tasks; and Patti spends approximately twelve hours per week washing dishes, cleaning house, and grocery shopping compared with Brian's three hours. But this seemingly traditional task allocation is not based on the essentialist notions of instrumental masculinity and service-oriented femininity evidenced within the dominant evangelical discourse on this topic.

When asked why the domestic tasks are divided this way in their household, Patti and Brian both speak of fairness (broadly understood, given their distinctive family responsibilities); individual preferences or talents; and particular personal needs. Both feel that the household responsibilities are apportioned fairly, with Patti adding that "at this point, [staying home] is my job." She says that she wants to be "pulling [her] weight" in the family. Patti concludes that since Brian is "going off to work and working hard from eight to five, I need to be accomplishing some things here so that when he comes home we can have family time." As for Brian, he explains that he likes to do yard work, particularly gardening; Patti, on the other hand, suffers from debilitating pollen allergies that place definite limits on her ability to perform such tasks. Brian is oftentimes capable of fixing the cars himself, and wishes to save the expense of paying someone else to perform automobile maintenance.

Fairness in the sense of split-down-the-middle equality, however, is not the guiding principle in Brian and Patti's division of household chores, nor is it for most of the couples to whom I spoke. Many couples I interviewed view such equalized arrangements as coercive and stifling. Still, Patti and Brian do share a considerable number of responsibilities within the home. Each spends time paying bills and keeping financial records (about an hour weekly for each), performing laundry-related detail (four hours for Patti, two hours for Brian), and preparing meals (four hours each).

More importantly, there is a mutual desire within this home to have both Patti and Brian quite involved in parenting Shelby. Brian, for example, is solely responsible for bathing Shelby nightly; Patti says she has bathed her daughter about two or three times in the fifteen months since they have had her. The goal, as Patti explains it, can be summarized as follows: "I perceive anything [concerning Shelby] that occurs during the time that Brian is at work as being mine. And then the rest I will make sure that he is aware that we are splitting it fifty-fifty." As indicated by Patti, this goal is still just that— an unachieved aim—because she "has to make sure that [Brian] is aware that we are splitting it fifty-fifty." Thus, beyond this bathing issue, task parity where parenting responsibilities are concerned has been a bit elusive. Why? Brian typically spends about sixty hours per week working at his job and, like many full-time-plus employed spouses, he is often at work from early in the morning into the early evening hours. Sixty-hour work weeks, about five twelve-hour days, require nothing less. Consequently, when he is home, Brian is frequently unaware of what needs to be done regarding their daughter's welfare. According to Patti, "He doesn't see [some of the things that need to be done for Shelby]. Like if she is talking in the morning, he is less likely to be the one that gets out of bed and [that] goes and gets her instinctively. But we have worked on that."

Patti illustrates how she and Brian are jointly trying to resolve these issues prior to the arrival of their second child: "Again, just by virtue of me spending the most time with her, I am more aware of something that has to be done and I am more likely to have to ask. I talk about this with a lot of my friends on the block who stay at home. You don't usually hear the husband say, 'Honey, can you watch the kids? I am going to get a haircut.' He'll say, 'I am going to get a haircut Saturday morning.' Whereas I have to ask."

Interestingly, Patti sees Brian's aversion to proactive coparenting partly as her "own fault." She admits, "I have set it up that way. . . . We have tried to work on this lately, where he's had time with her. Like an entire Saturday. If you are not with them around the clock, how do you know what to do? When I ask him to get her dressed for church, and if it ends up that I have to come in there to show him where the socks are, well I would rather just go ahead and take care of it myself. Well that's wrong on my part, because nothing has changed for the future. Whereas if I leave them alone for a whole day, he figures out what she likes, doesn't like, those things. I have the advantage of knowing her inside and out much better than he does. Which can be both a joy and a pain."

For her part, Patti is attempting make genuine coparenting less elusive by becoming "better able to communicate and also to let go. Not to be controlling like, 'No, no, no. She never wears that outfit,' or 'She hates bananas.' Who knows? She may eat them for him. So, that's where I think that I have to be a better communicator." Her struggle continues, however, because of the natural tendency for childcare investments to become gendered over time. Using the nursing of their child as an example, she says, "Can't say that anybody else could feed her in the middle of the night. So that naturally evolved that I was the one waking up. And from that—well, she slept through the night very early—I was the one to get up and take care of her first thing in the morning."

Patti and Brian, however, are also striving to reorganize this early-morning child care task. As Patti explains it, "with me being more tired—expecting the second child, and also I have terrible allergies and can't take any [medication] being pregnant—I am a zombie in the morning. So Brian is more likely to say, 'Can I go get her? Get her up out of bed and get her diaper on?' Those things, while I am still kicking into gear. As opposed to me thinking that I was the only one who could do it. Or that I had to do it." Thus, like Dan and Amy Humphreys, Patti and Brian Erickson conclude that where they face difficulties concerning domestic labor, they do so together.

Coprovider, Homemaker, and Mother:
A Wife's Triple Burden

Ben and Heather Weiss, who were introduced in chapter 7, are similar to the Humphreys in their general labor force commitments—like Dan and Amy, Ben and Heather are a dual-earner couple. Ben, an architect who has recently become self-employed, invests about fifty hours per week in his business. Heather, a trained nurse and clinical director, works about forty-five hours outside the home herself. More consistent with the life circumstances of Patti and Brian Erickson, however, the Weisses have children in their household. Their children are considerably older than fifteen-month-old

Shelby Erickson, however, and the Weisses are at a different stage of their marriage than either of the two couples described above. The Weisses' two sons are teenagers and their daughter is almost ten years old. Both Ben and Heather, who met and became teenage sweethearts more than twenty years ago, are in their early forties.

When asked about the church's teachings concerning a Christian husband and wife's family roles, Ben Weiss responds: "I have never heard anyone say at E-Free, 'This is what a man ought to do. This is what a woman ought to be doing.' I don't think they make an issue out of 'roles' for men and women in the church or in the home at E-Free. . . . Since we have been at E-Free in five years, I don't think I have heard them outline what they think a man's or a woman's role are."

"Do you think that's intentional?" I ask.

"Not necessarily," he replies. "I think that if the scripture is dealing with it as Al is preaching through passages, then he will deal with what the Scripture is saying. So if I were to give you an answer, I would have to reflect on what those scriptures are and tell you what I think [Pastor] Al would say, or tell [you] what I think." Like both husbands described above, Ben then proceeds to discuss spiritual leadership within the home, which, it turns out, does not necessarily entail specific domestic labor responsibilities.

Heather sees the situation in somewhat—though not completely—different terms. Like her husband Ben, Heather Weiss does mention a husband's spiritual leadership being emphasized at E-Free; yet, as an employed mother of three children, she does sense a general orientation at Parkview toward wives being considered homemakers. She began working full-time soon after their family arrived in this Texas city. She acknowledges that Al, the pastor at Parkview, "has not preached much" on the specific topic of women's family roles, but concludes: "I am sure they probably support the woman as pretty much the homemaker. . . . I am sure, [if they] had a choice, they would choose that a woman be at home versus working." For Heather, this potential source of tension between the church's teachings and her life circumstances is not a serious point of friction. She has "never heard anything taught at E-Free that makes [her] feel" uneasy about being an employed mother.

Yet Parkview is not necessarily insulated from generalized evangelical support for wifely domesticity. Therefore, as an evangelical Christian,

Heather grapples with issues related to her family role and her identity as a woman, mother, and coprovider. She explains: "When [some evangelicals] see a woman that works full-time in a Christian family, I often wonder if they see them as 'liberal' or [as someone who] lives in a family that has chosen that." Heather locates the source of anxiety over being a working mother partly within herself and partly within evangelical culture at large: "I think that [it] is my own convictions [that sometimes make me uneasy about working outside the home]. Being a Christian pretty much all of my adult life, I have just been through umpteen studies—be it women's Bible studies or small group studies. And a lot of the teachings that you hear address women in the home. So I think, personally, I have to constantly wrestle with where I need to be. And [wrestle with] guilt feelings [such as] 'Should I not be working full-time?' "

Heather admits that her feelings of guilt become most acute when "things begin to be unsettled at home. Whatever it is. You know, when I have a kid that's struggling with a subject in school, I constantly question, 'Would they not be doing that if I weren't a full-time working mom?' " Heather says that Ben is "so supportive" and performs "a lot" of household chores, concluding: "You know, we have three well-adjusted kids right now who like where they are. So I try to remember that, and that me staying at home might not make any difference on what one of our kids might make on a test."

Apart from just focusing on the positive aspects of their family situation, Heather also has another strategy for resolving her recurrent anxiety about working full-time outside the home. Regardless of the fact that she is, in a very practical sense, a coprovider in her family, Heather believes that the homemaker label—the dominant designation of evangelical wifehood—falls to her in their family: "You know, I still carry that role. I definitely see myself as the homemaker versus Ben. . . . You know, typically in a Christian marriage, the female's role is—if there are kids—nurturing the kids as well as being a homemaker. You know, that takes time."

Time indeed. Few people could argue with Heather's self-designation as homemaker upon examining her practical contribution to the domestic task load in her home. In addition to her full-time employment (forty-five hours per week), she invests about the same amount of time toward household chores (more than forty-three hours weekly). Among Heather's most time-consuming tasks are preparing meals (more than twelve hours weekly);

washing, ironing, and mending (ten hours weekly); cleaning house (seven hours weekly); and washing dishes and cleaning up after meals (six hours weekly). Heather would seem to have two full-time jobs. Ben does not invest as much time toward household chores as Heather, and unlike her, he is not considered the family's homemaker. He dedicates just over twenty-eight hours per week to household chores. Heather is quite thankful for all that Ben does around the house. Is her gratitude misplaced? That would seem to depend on the baseline of comparison used in such an evaluation. Even after accounting for the five-hour difference in their paid work weeks (Ben's fifty to Heather's forty-five hours), she spends an extra ten hours per week—or about an extra twenty-two full days per year—performing household chores.

Yet, in dedicating more than twenty-eight hours per week to domestic tasks, Ben is quite involved in housework relative to other evangelical husbands in this study. Taken as a whole, the husbands in this study contribute an average of thirteen hours toward domestic chores—a figure that is less than half of Ben's domestic-task contribution. Moreover, Ben's domestic chore investments for a typical week are fairly spread out, and break down as follows: six hours driving other family members to work, school, or some other activity ("chauffeuring," as Ben puts it); four hours preparing meals and four hours washing dishes; five hours on outdoor tasks/household maintenance; three hours paying bills; two hours each on cleaning house, shopping for groceries or household goods, and auto maintenance; and thirty minutes washing, ironing, or mending clothes. Only two other husbands in this study report investing more hours toward domestic tasks than does Ben—Jake Lehman (the other self-employed husband whose entrepreneurial efforts are being supported largely by his wife's income) and a full-time student who is being supported through school by his working wife (this latter couple has no children).

When asked why the household chores are divided in this fashion, Ben and Heather offer various rationales. For Ben, the division of chores is predicated largely on personal preference and natural ability. Ben enjoys yard work and even does some landscaping. Ben explains: "Let's use this scenario. . . . Heather probably is not physically strong enough to start our lawn mower. So how is she going to mow? And that's just one of the things. So there is some physical strength involved in some of the things that I do outside. Obviously, there are women who mow yards. But the mowers we happen to have, I guarantee you, she could not start. Her little, bony arms won't do it. And also, I am horrible at sewing. If I go to sew something, then it looks like, you know, there are threads sticking out everywhere. So, we're gifted a little bit I guess in some ways versus other ways, and we tend to use those strong suits."

For Heather's part, she attributes task allocation largely to "the environment you grew up in. I mean, I pretty much saw my mom do" these same chores. She also suggests that personal preference plays a part: "I don't like dirty bathrooms and I don't think they bother Ben." It would seem, however, that there is a connection between the values and role-modeling with which a person is raised on the one hand and their task preferences and "natural" abilities on the other. Echoing the common refrain among interviewed wives, Heather contends, "I am not sure that I would want Ben loose in the grocery store too much. . . . He buys lots of junk food." Laughing, she qualifies her overstatement. "No, he buys pretty healthy food. [But] I am not sure we could make meals out of the things he would buy."

References to gender difference do not figure into Ben and Heather's accounts of their day-to-day parenting responsibilities. By all estimates, they share quite evenly a vast assortment of parenting responsibilities (e.g., parent-child leisure activities, playing or working on projects, helping with reading or homework). Heather is well aware of the baseline-of-comparison issue for domestic contributions where childcare responsibilities are concerned. She observantly notes that the standards of parenting adequacy for fathers are considerably lower than those for mothers. "I just think that probably your general American adult or general family person perceives that the mom would spend more time with the kids than the dad. And, you know, that's just based on years of our society, and that moms are more nurturing than dads. Not in our family," says Heather, laughing.

Heather is proud of Ben's paternal involvement and is comforted by the fact that her working outside the home has probably contributed to the warm father-child relationships in the Weiss home: "It's interesting, the amount of time you perceive that [fathers] should spend [with their children] versus what you perceive you should as a mom. It's different. I think Ben is just right. He spends a lot of time in comparison to some men. And to me, that's one of the positive things that is brought out by a wife that works. He works half a day on Fridays, because I don't have help with the kids on Monday or Friday. So I take off early Monday and he takes off early Friday. Then we have help those other days. So, no, I think he's right on track there."[2]

What does the future hold for Heather and Ben Weiss? They both hope that, ultimately, Heather will not need to work in order for them to make ends meet. When asked what she thinks could be done to improve her family life, Heather responds without hesitation: "Probably the first thing I would do is I would not work full time."

"And how would that improve things, do you think?" I ask.

"Some of my tension is based upon time constraints," she replies. "Be it having meals prepared. Be it laundry or whatever. You know, there are some things where it's just not organizing or preparing for things. Just happening in a haphazard way causes tension. . . . Whether it's having three kids that are hungry at six o'clock or whatever. That's probably the first change that I would make. I don't know that I would ever quit completely. But I would probably go to three or four days a week."

"And what do you find most rewarding about work that you would never quit completely?"

"I like being out," Heather replies. "I like a lot of things about being out and around. I enjoy the other people. It's challenging. It's rewarding to do a good job and to be recognized for that."

For his part, Ben would like Heather to have the choice to work outside the home, to be a stay-at-home mother, or to combine those roles as she sees fit. He greatly appreciates Heather's financial and emotional support as he gets his business off the ground. Yet, notwithstanding Parkview's pastoral silence on this issue, Ben's personal opinions on the matter are clearly reflective of the dominant family discourse of husband-providership within contemporary evangelical Protestantism. He sees financial provision in his family, at least, as falling under the rubric of spiritual leadership incumbent upon him. Once again, equality per se is not the guiding principle here. In Ben's estimation, he should provide his wife, Heather, with the choice to work or not, whereas he "does not feel like [he is] supposed to have a choice in that matter." Ben concludes, "I feel like it is my spiritual leadership obligation to financially provide. It's not important for me [to have a choice in that]. I don't feel that struggle of wishing I had more time off. That's no big deal for me. But, for Heather, I wish I could give her the choice."

Working the Margins: Civic Engagement
and the Shackles of Wifely Domesticity

Unlike the Weisses and the Ericksons, Kent and Carole Houston—both in their early seventies—have no children currently living in their household. Married to one another for more than fifty years, Kent and Carole have two grown nonresident children, and so are at a very different life-stage than the Humphreys, the Ericksons, or the Weisses.

Kent was raised in a Methodist home where his mother emphasized to him and his siblings the importance of religious instruction and the centrality of the Bible to Christian living. Carole was raised as a Southern Baptist. Though Kent and Carole were on-and-off churchgoers for much of their married life, it was not until seven years ago that their religious convictions were renewed. After friends invited them to a prominent local Bible church, Kent and Carole decided to become members of that church. While at that particular congregation, River's Bend Bible Church, Kent had a conversion experience. Kent explains: "We had gone to River's Bend one Sunday and we were sitting there and, I don't know, it was just a very strong urging from within me that said, 'This is where you belong. You need to sink your roots.' And I turned to Carole and I said, 'Hon, I think we need to join this church and I think we need to become involved in this church. We need to be a part of this church.' She agreed, so we did. And this I think is basically when I openly professed and pursued Christianity."

After a time, the worship services and music at River's Bend became more contemporary in style. Raised as a Southern Baptist, Carole expressed her displeasure with this turn of events and began to attend Parkview for the more traditional worship style offered there. As she describes it, "I just don't like Christian rock. It just doesn't appeal to me. Kent didn't want to leave. But I said, 'I just can't. It's not the way. I am angry by the time the pastor at River's Bend comes up to preach. I am really irritated. And I don't think this is the sort of thing to do in church. It's not good for me.' So I changed and went to E-Free." Following a period during which Kent and Carole attended separate churches, Kent—who embraces the notion of wifely submission and considers himself the head of the household—decided that they needed to be united in their church membership. Yet, rather than ask Carole to resume attending the church of his choice, he joined her at Parkview. This was not an easy decision for Kent, as he describes: "My relationship with a number of the people at River's Bend was very good. . . . And also I was involved in the Missions Committee at River's Bend. . . . Elgin [the congregation's missions pastor] and I got to be pretty well acquainted. . . . He was one of the main reasons why I was very reluctant to leave River's Bend. But I sat down and talked to Elgin about it. I just opened my heart to him and told him that I wasn't leaving because I was mad at anybody. I loved that church. . . . But I just explained to him that Carole felt uneasy about the music situation and she wanted a change; and that I felt like we ought to go to the same church." This principle of give-and-take has been a recurrent theme within Kent and Carole's relationship.

Kent is quite clear that providership is incumbent upon a family's husband and that child-rearing is primarily the wife's responsibility. The wife in a marriage, according to Kent, "usually . . . is the helper . . . the mate . . . the mother of the children. She is the primary teacher of the children, particularly in their tender years. In infancy and early childhood, I think the mother's role is ever, ever so important." Yet, Kent is not thoroughly wedded to this notion of husband-providership and wifely domesticity. Moving away from mothering per se and speaking more directly about household chores, Kent suggests: "Oh, you know, keeping house, cooking, this sort of thing— I guess that's primarily a woman's responsibility. But it can be a man's responsibility too. It just kind of depends on how things work out." Similarly, where husband-providership is concerned, Kent takes some effort to explain that every rule must have some room for exceptions or "extremes" where husband-providership "might not work. In other words, you have some men who do not have the innate capabilities, maybe, to make a good living. Their role might be better served in the, you might say, the role that the woman ordinarily takes. It might be better for him to be the housekeeper, the cook, the child-raiser, this sort of thing. If the woman is one who has great capabilities, who has the proper innate abilities to be, you might say, the breadwinner. And I don't know. For her to be the breadwinner, that doesn't necessarily say that she's the head of the household. A man can still be the head of the household even though he may not be the breadwinner."

This nuanced understanding of spousal roles stems in part from practical circumstances that have figured into Kent and Carole's long marital relationship. Like so many other women she knew, Carole spent several years in the post–World War II era supporting Kent's educational endeavors with her paid employment. Indeed, Carole spent considerably more time in paid employment than many of her friends and acquaintances. Kent had obtained an engineering degree only to find that engineering was not what he wanted to do with his life. He decided instead on a career path to which he felt better suited—medicine. With the support of Carole's employment, Kent dove headlong into the many years of additional schooling required by this professional change of course.

Kent and Carole had a young son, Greg, while Carole worked full-time and Kent was pursuing his medical degree. Not only the breadwinner but also the primary parent, Carole recounts the childcare dilemmas she faced and how she sought to resolve them. Initially, she tried putting Greg in a day-care center while she was at work and Kent was at school. Her son was not at all fond of that arrangement, and she takes a dim view toward day-care centers even to this day: "I don't think [day-care centers] are good. . . . Although Greg had to be taken care of [this way] when I worked when he was quite young . . . it didn't work for me because he didn't like it. And, of course, [because] he was unhappy, I was unhappy."

Her resolution to this dilemma was found in a different arrangement—in-home child care. Carole explains, "I got a woman who had a little girl just about his age. And she would come pick Greg up every morning and take him. She kept him until I got off from work." Although Greg initially had misgivings about this arrangement, it worked out quite well in the end. "It was really funny," Carole says, smiling as she recalls the circumstances under which her son's—and, by extension, her own—caregiver anxieties were thankfully relieved. "Greg wasn't sure he was going to like [the woman charged with supervising him]. But she came up to get him in a convertible, and he waved me goodbye happily. . . . He never had another thought about it."

Carole remained employed partly to support Kent's shifting occupational aspirations. She laughs, "I thought I was married to a perennial college student. He began to look like it." Yet, at the same time, she explains that supporting one's husband financially while he was in school "was just one of those things that one did. You know, this was post–World War II. And most of the wives had to work when their husbands came back and went back to school [because] they had been taken out of school to be in the service. So, it was sort of the thing that most of us did. Most of us who had been in college went to work so that our husbands could finish school with the thought of the husband being the breadwinner. . . . It was just a routine thing one did."

Supporting Kent's extended education, however, was not the only reason that Carole worked. She also found her paid job incredibly satisfying. Yet, in the last year of Kent's degree program, the couple decided to have another child. Carole recalls, "When I had my second child, we decided I was not getting any younger. You know, now people have [children] at forty, but I was thirty-three. And we thought that if I didn't have another child, we probably would never have one." With the launching of his medical practice and the promise of his steady income, Kent thought it best that Carole stay home and raise their new daughter full-time. They no longer needed her income, in contrast to the preceding decade when their young son was growing up and Kent's schooling prevented him from providing for them financially.

Carole found herself in a double bind. In principle, she agreed with Kent that ideally she should become a full-time mother. Moreover, partly due to her Southern Baptist heritage, Carole felt committed to the notion that a wife should be responsive to her husband's stated needs. Kent had asked her to stay home and raise their daughter, and she felt some obligation to honor his request. Carole asserts: "I do think that a wife should really give in to her husband's requests." Carole places a strong emphasis on this last word, as if to distinguish it from "orders" or "demands." She continues: "If he feels strongly enough to ask you to do [something], you should do it. And it's not always easy, because a modern woman does not want to be tied down to those rules. And when you are educated and intelligent, it's very hard."

The bind for Carole was precisely this. Carole herself was an educated, intelligent, modern woman. Carole's commitments in principle to full-time mothering and wifely responsiveness conflicted with her desire to remain employed at a job she found very satisfying. Carole recounts forthrightly her feelings about her secretarial job with the superintendent of a large city school district: "it was very hard for me to quit working. . . . I enjoyed it. I enjoyed being out and seeing people and being with people. And the appreciation they had of me. You miss [that appreciation], you know, when you quit working. . . . I thoroughly enjoyed [it]. I was an art major, [and] I would have never gotten a job as an artist. So, I really enjoyed my work." Her conflicted feelings notwithstanding, Carole acceded to Kent's request and to her own principled convictions about the importance of stay-at-home mothering. But that is hardly the end of their story.

As Carole moved out of the work force, Kent began pouring virtually all of his time and energy into building his medical practice. Both of them express some regrets about that period in their lives. Carole was largely on her own in raising their children. Kent stepped in as needed to mete out discipline in response to some of the more serious infractions on the part of the children. But for the most part, Kent was not around. Kent still harbors deep misgivings about his minimal contribution to parenting at that time in his life: "I guess my lack of involvement in child care and parental responsibilities [was] partly because I felt so inadequate at it. I felt like I didn't know how to handle my kids. And neither did Carole. But she learned, and I was kind of standoffish. . . . I put my professional endeavors ahead of my family. And that's wrong, even in school. Your family still comes first. . . . I didn't spend anywhere near as much time with my kids as I should have."

Carole, on the other hand, did what she could to attend to her domestic and child-rearing responsibilities without giving up out-of-home pursuits altogether. The answer to her double bind was found in changing her notion of what constituted work. Carole, who had misgivings about relinquishing her paid job outside the home altogether, shifted her attention to a different sort of work—volunteer work in civic organizations. And, given the way she attacked the tasks that lay before her, her volunteer involvement was work indeed. Even to this day, she is a docent at a local art museum; she volunteers at a popular botanical garden; she remains quite involved with a local shelter for homeless adolescent girls; and, as someone who has just inherited a sizable amount of money from a now deceased friend, she is in the process of setting up a scholarship fund for underprivileged students who otherwise would not have the opportunity to attend college.

Volunteer work gave Carole a life of her own outside the family and helped her to remain balanced and well-rounded, much the same way that paid work now does for many wives. Yet Carole is careful not to glorify her life or her extensive volunteer pursuits. Like many present-day employed wives, her husband's career-mindedness forced her to sacrifice and struggle in order to balance her out-of-home commitments with her domestic responsibilities. Today, she says that a Christian husband "must be devoted to his wife, and put her above everything but God. . . . It's one of my hardships in marriage. Because Kent has gone to school. And I had to sort out a lot myself while he was in school because he studied so much. And then when he started into his career, it was the same way. He had to work all the time.

He put, more or less, his career before his family. Which is very typical, I think, of most men. And if you're going to be good in his line of work," she concludes, "you make a very poor husband in a way. That's an adjustment that I had to make."

As a means of coping with Kent's career-mindedness, Carole initially found her herself "hoping eventually that he would have more time." When she realized that this was probably a vain hope, she "just started doing volunteer work. And I have worked very hard." Carole in fact concedes that Kent "would have been happier if I would have been working at a job because I wouldn't have been quite so spread out. Because I did work very hard. I probably overdid it." Still, Carole sought to achieve a balance between her homemaking and volunteering commitment. "I was always home in the evening, the afternoon. I didn't let it interfere with that part of my life. And then when my daughter got in school—she went to a private school—I quit doing anything for two years because she got out of school at one o'clock. I couldn't go do things in the morning and go to a luncheon, or play bridge, which I liked to do. And I just quit doing everything for two years so I could pick her up at school."

Kent and Carole's life today is considerably different and much less harried than in the years when they were raising their children. Now well established in his career, Kent is able to work fewer hours. Carole, still an active volunteer, has cut back on her commitments in recent years. Now that their circumstances are less time-restrictive, Kent and Carole take some time off from their various commitments to do some traveling together. A few years ago, they decided to take an extended trip. Kent favored a visit to Alaska, wanting to visit the "pristine country" there "before it gets totally defiled." Yet, as a self-described "tightwad," Kent was a bit dismayed by the price of booking them on a tour of Alaska. Carole wished to travel to England. As Kent describes it, Carole was "not particularly enthralled about going to Alaska." They went to England. Kent recounts the experience: "I wasn't just jumping up and down or thrilled to death about going to England. But it had a lot of things. We saw a lot of things and did a lot of things that were very nice. . . . It wasn't a bad trip for me. It just was not my first choice. But it was her first. And I think she thoroughly enjoyed it. And because she enjoyed it, I did too."

Conclusion

Refashioning Evangelical Families for the Twenty-First Century

Godly Marriages in a Millennial Age

This volume began by calling attention to previous studies that, taken together, provide contradictory findings about gender and family relations within the evangelical religious subculture. While many studies have suggested that evangelicals are the most vocal defenders of traditional gender and family arrangements, recent inquiries—focused for the most part on conservative Protestant women—have called attention to the nuances that mark this subculture. I have sought to extend this research by examining how evangelical husbands and wives negotiate gender in tandem with one another and in the context of their congregational commitments.

Culture War or Civil War? The Significance of Ideological Debates among Evangelical Elites

The substantive portion of this study began by examining the contours of gender and family discourse promulgated by evangelical luminaries (part 2). First, whereas some conservative Protestant family advice authors contend that men and women are essentially different from one another, others argue for a more androgynous conceptualization of gender. This gender difference–gender sameness debate is not adequately conceptualized as a simple dichotomy, however, because evangelical authors who argue for gender difference disagree about the extent to which gender blending is desirable or possible. Radical essentialists—who are outspoken opponents of feminism, gay rights, and social engineering—are quite critical of virtually any perceived melding of masculine characteristics with their feminine counterparts. Moderate essentialists, by contrast, contend that men and women are characterized by predispositional but mutable differences. Essentialism remains the dominant discourse within evangelicalism, and the attention that continues to be commanded by commentators such as James Dobson, Tim and Beverly LaHaye, and Elisabeth Elliot suggests some measure of sustained dominance. Yet, increasingly forceful criticisms from biblical feminists and other sameness-minded commentators, combined with the splintering of the essentialist camp into radical and moderate factions, indicates that the dominance of this discourse is eroding among evangelical elites.

A second point of discursive debate among evangelical elites centers on divergent prescriptions about the exercise of family power. The dominant evangelical discourse supports a patriarchal family. Previously, this family model was predicated on the rhetoric of husband-headship and wifely submission. But recent years have witnessed a shift in elite support toward a neopatriarchal family model in which husbands are now urged to become servant-leaders within the home. This transformation of patriarchal discourse among conservative Protestant elites can be traced, in part, to evangelical feminist critiques of male household authority. The oppositional discourse of family power promulgated by biblical feminists and equality-minded evangelicals is predicated on the concept of mutual submission. Within the context of this discourse, evangelical feminists and moderate essentialists enjoin the husband and the wife to share domestic decision-making authority equally.

Finally, divergent advice concerning the allocation of household responsibilities (i.e., financial provision, housework, and child care) highlights the complex and contested state of evangelical gender and family discourse. Conservative Protestant purveyors of a husband-breadwinner/wife-homemaker family model are engaged in a rancorous debate with equality-minded evangelicals who recommend domestic task sharing and ungendered coparenting. The rise of dual-earner families and the corresponding increased reliance on out-of-home child care are among the issues that continue to be debated by these authors. Although this particular debate is still dominated by traditionalist advocates of a separate spheres ideology, the hegemony of this discourse has been partly undermined by the massive influx of wives and mothers into the paid labor force. Because biblical inerrancy is the defining characteristic of contemporary evangelicalism, each of these debates can be traced to the divergent scriptural interpretations articulated by rival coteries of family commentators.

The extensive analysis of evangelical family advice manuals undertaken in part 2 of this book suggests that further modification of Hunter's culture wars thesis is in order. This thesis construes elite evangelicals as the vanguard proponents of orthodoxy who are fighting to protect the legitimacy of the traditional family in a post-traditional world. Recent critical scholarship on the culture wars thesis has highlighted the ways in which quotidian culture—specifically, the attitudes and practices of non-elite religious adherents—does not conform to tidy typologies such as orthodox versus progressive (see, e.g., Becker 1997; Smith 1998; R. Williams 1997; Woodberry and Smith 1998). My study echoes this criticism about the real-world limitations of the culture wars thesis, but I also suggest that the notion of rhetorical polarization among orthodox-evangelical versus progressive-mainline/secular elites is overstated. A careful reading of conservative Protestant family advice manuals reveals no consensus about gender and family relations even among elite evangelicals. To be sure, several of the most popular authors in the evangelical family advice genre (e.g., James Dobson) are ardent defenders of the traditional nuclear family. In this way, elite evangelical family discourse remains somewhat beholden to the orthodox defense of a traditional (actually, late Victorian bourgeois) family. Yet the perspective of these authors is hotly disputed by progressivist evangelicals—biblical feminists and equality-minded religious conservatives.

Unfortunately, the culture wars thesis does not provide social researchers with a language for understanding the intense controversy—and the resulting ideological changes such as discursive shifts from wifely submission/husband-headship to mutual submission/servant-leadership)—generated by such internecine discursive conflicts.[1] Moreover, the culture wars thesis does not effectively explain how a shared evangelical commitment to biblical inerrancy (an orthodox form of moral authority) can produce such radically divergent gender and family discourses among conservative religious luminaries. If there is a culture war over the family in the United States at large, it clearly coexists with a civil war being waged within conservative Protestantism by leading evangelical family commentators.

The discursive civil war raging among evangelical elites is quite functional for this religious subculture. Such ideological diversity would seem, in principle at least, to permit evangelical spouses greater latitude in negotiating their gender identities and managing the vagaries of everyday life. Consider this issue from the perspective of an evangelical husband or wife perusing his/her local Christian bookstore. If the unabashed rhetoric of gender difference articulated by James Dobson and Beverly LaHaye does not mesh with this evangelical spouse's particular sensibilities or life experiences, surely this consumer of elite evangelical culture can find an acceptable alternative in Gary Smalley's tracts on sensitized masculinity or evangelical feminists' defense of androgyny. The ideological diffuseness that marks this heterogeneous advice literature is, of course, bounded by the shared moral values to which all evangelicals are beholden—most notably, a pervasive commitment to the authoritativeness of the Bible. Consequently, contemporary evangelical advice on family life carefully balances the breadth of ideological diversity with an uncompromising commitment to foundational (i.e., biblical) values.

Given the sheer breadth of ideological diversity within this religious subculture, it is difficult to imagine that evangelicals are oppressed or constrained by having at their disposal such wide-ranging gender ideals. The diverse array of conservative Protestant family discourses surveyed in part 2 of this study point to the ongoing emergence of new cultural tools in the ideological repertoire of American evangelicalism. These tools enable contemporary evangelicals to negotiate their subcultural distinctiveness from mainstream American values (Smith 1998) and contribute to the ongoing vitality of conservative religious definitions of family (Wilcox and Bartkowski 1999). In the end, perhaps elite commentators outside this religious subculture (who, quite tellingly, have not produced as expansive a marriage self-help literature) have something to learn from conservative religious elites about how to engage in reflexive, values-based civic discourse (see Lakoff 1996; Sandel 1996). Rather than throwing out the old for the new, elite evangelical culture provides conservative Protestant couples with an ever-widening array of discourses (traditional, progressive, and innumerable permutations) through which these spouses can fashion gender identities and marital relationships that are at once anchored and dynamic.

Religion, Marital Dynamics, and Social Context: Tandem Gender Negotiations among Evangelical Couples

In part 3 of this volume I examined the everyday negotiation of gender and family relations among evangelical couples at the Parkview Evangelical Free Church—a prominent, affluent, and largely white conservative Protestant congregation in Texas. Using participant-observation, in-depth interview, and primary survey data, I explored the contours of gender relations within this church and several of its families. Three key findings—respectively paralleling my interest in issues of gender difference, family power, and domestic task allocation—emerged from this portion of the study.

First, essentialist rhetoric figures prominently into the construction of gender within this congregation. However, the general commitment to masculine-feminine difference among the pastors and members of this church is typically peppered with caveats of various types. Such caveats allow members of Parkview to retain their commitment to the generic rule of gender difference while accounting for the numerous exceptions to this rule. Such exceptions include, for example, the Parkview wives who have strong personalities and heterogeneous life experiences that contradict dominant evangelical conceptualizations of delicate and vulnerable femininity. Couples in this congregation have cultivated nuanced gender identities that, given the plethora of subcultural gender discourses at their avail (radical essentialism, moderate essentialism, and androgyny), enable them to move about deftly within parameters that are in but not of the world. Because the ideas produced through these heterogeneous discourses construct a life-world that is both orderly ("men and women are different") and complex ("women are meek, but I am not"), they provide Parkview couples with a vast cultural repertoire through which to craft gender identities that are flexible yet rooted in meaningful values systems.

Second, these spouses creatively reconstruct evangelical discourses of submission and family power. The innovative negotiation of family power was particularly intriguing in light of the overtly patriarchal structure of this church. All of the pastors, elders, and Sunday school teachers at Parkview are men. Yet there is a terribly complex relationship between this congregation's patriarchal structure on the one hand, and its culturally defined ideologies of family power on the other. Some family ministers endorsed wifely submission; others defended the merits of mutual submission; and one prominent women's leader at the church evinced support for both of these perspectives during her popular Bible study courses. How could the pastors and teachers at this congregation function effectively together while holding such seemingly disparate views? The answer to this question resides in the dynamic definitions of submission—wifely submission here, mutual submission there—that circulate among the leaders of this church.

Similar patterns surfaced in my interviews with spouses at Parkview: some couples endorsed the principle of wifely submission and others embraced the ideal of mutual submission. Among the husbands and wives, as well as within Sunday school classes, the most common references on this topic construed submission as the wife's responsibility. Yet, the dominance of this ideology gave way in myriad instances to questions about the actual meaning and practical significance of this term. In-depth interviews with couples about the significance of submission within their marriages indicated that even in the most traditional households family power is often a site for struggle and negotiation. And, in an effort not to appear too egalitarian, many proponents of mutual submission are careful to underscore the importance of spousal role differentiation in their lives.

Finally, I examined how select couples from this church negotiated the competing discourses of domestic labor within contemporary evangelicalism. Rather than examine the processes underlying financial provision, housework, and child care seriatim, I analyzed how all of these dimensions of family labor were negotiated within four households situated at various points in their domestic life courses. Gender relations within these families were refashioned to address complex domestic exigencies by the creative utilization of resources from the evangelical cultural repertoire. Some husbands, for example, envisioned themselves as the family provider despite the indeterminacy of their own career paths and a reliance on their wives' income. Among the wives discussed in this chapter, a stay-at-home mother eloquently described both the vicissitudes and rewards of full-time motherhood; others struggled to balance their familial responsibilities with different types of extradomestic commitments (e.g., paid labor force participation, extensive civic engagement) as well as previous experiences and future aspirations.

This portion of my study, then, sought to underscore the importance of examining evangelical marriages as tandem negotiations in which many different types of social relations converge: elite and pastoral idealizations of Christian family life; a husband or wife's present life circumstances and unrealized desires in interaction with those of a spouse and other family members; and the broad social forces (historical moment, class privilege) that shape family life. While the overall focus of my analysis is clearly informed by the now sizable literature on the social bases of identity negotiation, it is noteworthy that previous studies of evangelical gender relations have generally ignored the complex couple dynamics—i.e., a husband's and wife's tandem negotiation of gender identity, family power, and domestic labor—that emerge within the context of conservative Protestant marriages. Examining husbands' and wives' family experiences in concert is crucial because the everyday circumstances in which home sharing, relationship building, and parenting become meaningful are negotiated in relation to one another—as well as in light of a family's social and historical location—rather than in isolation.

Within the middle-class and upper-middle-class evangelical marriages examined here, class privilege intersects with religious convictions to influence the manner in which Parkview couples negotiate gender.[2] In one sense, many of these women's and men's class-specific experiences (advanced education, professional careers) have encouraged them to question dominant evangelical conceptualizations of innate feminine responsiveness to masculine initiation. Anne Carson's critique of biological legitimations of gender difference in light of her professional training as a registered nurse provides a rich illustration of class privilege acting to subvert gender traditionalism. And where issues of family power are concerned, many of the couples in this study—even those who embrace domestic patriarchy—express serious reservations about unqualified defenses of wifely submission. These spouses have been exposed to feminist critiques of sexism through their educational pursuits and see women exercise authority quite competently in professional settings. Consequently, many Parkview spouses evince gender sensibilities that are somewhat progressive in character—a fact not unrelated to their class-specific social experiences.

At the same time, class privilege has enabled many of these couples to implement quite traditional notions of husband-providership and wifely domesticity in their own homes. A preponderance of married women at Parkview actually had the opportunity—or anticipated having the choice—to leave the labor force in order to take on primary parenting responsibilities within their households. And many married men within this congregation worked in well-paying professions in which husband-providership complemented by wifely domesticity could still sustain the family's ownership of a spacious home in a relatively affluent neighborhood. Such forms of economic privilege are not without their own quandaries; yet, they are dilemmas faced by those in privileged circumstances. The point here is that contextual factors other than religious convictions per se influence the negotiation of gender and family relations among these couples. To be sure, social class does not determine how such negotiations will play out in particular homes among Parkview couples; however, the pervasiveness of economic privilege at this church provides couples who have divergent gender ideologies (traditionalist versus egalitarian) with common ground of another sort—namely, the value-tensions and domestic dilemmas associated with middle-class evangelical family life.

Parkview as a Church for All Seasons: Authority, Compassion, and Congregational Dexterity

Finally, my case study of congregational dynamics at the Parkview Evangelical Free Church highlights the institutionalized resources that evangelical faith communities can utilize to engage in effective family ministry. By oscillating between evangelical gender discourses of traditionalism and progressivism, leaders and members within Parkview walk the fine line between two competing moral imperatives—authority on the one hand, and compassion on the other. Becker (1997, 1999) suggests that religious leadership within congregations is likely to be perceived as effective when it balances these two moral logics—authority (that is, institutionalized hierarchies, codified scriptural interpretations, unwavering ethical strictures) and compassion (namely, religious imperatives for caring, fellowship, and forgiveness). When Parkview leaders and members endorse a patriarchal family structure via the rhetoric of husband-headship and male family leadership, they are practicing an ethic of authority. This particular manifestation of an authority-based moral logic uses family traditionalism to produce a sense of congregational character and integrity in the face of a (secular, liberal) world that is perceived to have yielded shamelessly to a homogenizing form of gender egalitarianism. As with many of the congregations Becker studied, the moral logic of authority institutionalized at Parkview becomes a means of producing a collective congregational identity that is boldly demarcated from its surrounding milieu. At the same time, however, Parkview's commitment to authority is tempered by a congregational ethic of compassion evidenced within its ministry to families. This ethic of compassion is evidenced through frequent pastoral endorsements of mutual submission within the home, and through leaders' prescriptions enjoining the husband to love his family in such a self-sacrificing way that he would give up his life for his wife.

Taking a cue from Becker's research on the institutionalized negotiation of congregational conflict, the key to understanding Parkview's family ministry lies in not examining these moral logics in isolation from one another. Rather, authority and compassion are produced through local pastoral discourse, congregational structures, and everyday practices that hold these two moral orientations toward gender relations in an ongoing productive tension. This productive tension is manifested among a pastoral team that, taken as a whole, can appeal to congregants and prospective members who have traditional sensibilities (husband-headship/wifely submission) or egalitarian leanings (mutual submission).

In many cases, both authority and compassion are affirmed simultaneously within a single sermon, Bible study, or marriage counseling forum at Parkview. To revisit briefly the site of the women's Bible study discussed in chapters 6 and 7, the gendered imagery Angela Butler used to liken the male ego to a leaky balloon invokes moral logics that gravitate deftly between themes of authority and compassion. On the one hand, images of the leaky male ego overtly challenge the legitimacy of male authority by implying that the essence of manhood is weakness and deficiency—literally defining the male ego by its holes.[3] Men's egos are so deficient, Angela says, that they need to be "built up" by continuous compliments from their wives. Wifely compassion is manifested here by a woman's proactive use of compliments to plug the holes in her husband's ego. Within the context of this ministerial metaphor, it is difficult to disentangle notions of compassion and authority. If the wife is in charge of shoring up her husband's leaky ego, is she not exercising a form of authority in doing so? On the other hand, however, this same leaky male ego imagery affirms patriarchal authority in the domestic realm: because men have such weak egos, they need wives who will submit willingly—indeed, compassionately—to a husband's decision-making authority in the home. When defined in this way, wifely compassion can be understood as consonant with feminine acquiescence and passivity.

It is through such ambiguous gendered metaphors that Parkview produces a dexterous congregational culture that is at once authority-minded and caring. Parkview's congregational dexterity is a valuable resource for an organization that seeks to remain responsive to the changing landscape of American evangelicalism writ large and to the conservative Protestant families whose allegiance it hopes to win and sustain. Rich, multilayered pastoral narratives, along with a (formal) all-male pastorship complemented by (informal) female leaders in family ministry, are means by which Parkview can meet the needs of a fast-growing membership that is itself characterized by ideological heterogeneity and diverse family arrangements. Given recent research suggesting that the gender and family attitudes of evangelicals are more internally heterogeneous than those of mainline religious adherents (Gay, Ellison, and Powers 1996), what better way to minister to a heterogeneous religious subculture than to be a church for all seasons where contested issues like gender roles and family relations are concerned?

It is, however, crucial to understand that the dexterous definitions of Christian marriage that circulate at Parkview and among its families are situated within—and steadied by—a congregational structure that is itself unabashedly patriarchal. At this congregation in which only men can act as pastors, elders, and Sunday school teachers, the family ministry focus on men's domestic compassion (mutual submission, servant-leadership) seems to be purchased at the price of women's congregational authority. Consequently, the twin moral imperatives of compassion and authority are not always and everywhere open to a wide latitude of negotiation at Parkview. Rather, the formal authority structure of this church is more stolid and bounded than the gender definitions within its family ministry program and the everyday household practices of its members. Domestic egalitarianism is made possible by congregational patriarchy.

This study, then, adds to a growing scholarly literature on conservative Protestant gender relations and family life. To date, scholarship in this area has focused largely on the social experiences of evangelical women or, more recently, individual husbands and wives interviewed as stand-alone respondents. While acknowledging the many significant contributions of previous inquiries into conservative Protestant family life, I have sought to enrich this research literature by examining how the gender identities of evangelical husbands and wives are negotiated in tandem. Moreover, my goal has been to locate these couples' gender negotiations within a multilayered social context—domestic arrangements within such households, congregational dynamics at their local church, and the shifting discourses of family life promulgated by elite evangelicals. It is, in the last instance, a vast network of social relationships that gives meaning to these spouses' most private and personal experiences of their selves, marriages, families, and religious convictions. To that end, I hope that the stories I have recounted here will foster an enriched and more holistic understanding of evangelical family life.

Appendix A: Textual Analysis Methodology

Given the centrality of evangelical advice manuals to my analysis of conservative Protestant gender and family discourse, the methods I employed to select and analyze these primary source documents bear some elaboration.

Selection of Advice Manuals

In general, three criteria guided the selection of texts utilized in this analysis. First, many of the analyzed texts are best-selling manuals. Several of these manuals boast from half a million to more than one million copies sold or in print (e.g., Cooper 1974; Dobson 1991; LaHaye 1968; Smalley 1988a, 1988b), while others claim smaller but nonetheless impressive sales figures (e.g., Elliot 1976; Gabriel 1993; LaHaye 1976). The popularity of these volumes can also be gauged by reprintings, the release of new editions, and publishers' awards. Many of the manuals included in my sample have been reprinted several times, have been re-released as revised and expanded editions, or have won formal accolades (e.g., "Book of the Year" or "Critics' Choice" awards) from evangelical publishers' associations (e.g., Bilezikian 1985; Christenson 1970; Cooper 1974; Gabriel 1993; Scanzoni and Hardesty 1992; Swindoll 1991; Van Leeuwen 1990).

Second, the preponderance of gender and family manuals in my sample were written by prominent evangelical gender and family commentators who are highly visible within conservative Protestantism at large. Among the most prominent are James Dobson, president and founder of Focus on the Family; Tim and Beverly LaHaye, cofounder of the Moral Majority and Concerned Women for America, respectively; Gary Smalley, president of Today's Family and a speaker for Promise Keepers, a popular evangelical men's movement; E. Glenn Wagner, vice president of Promise Keepers; Fred and Florence Littauer, cofounders of CLASS (Christian Leaders, Authors, and Speakers Seminar); and prominent evangelical feminists such as Letha Scanzoni and Nancy Hardesty (author of the biblical feminist manifesto *All We Can Be*), Rebecca Merill Groothuis (former editor for InterVarsity Christian Fellowship), and Anne Bowen Follis (who has lectured widely and appeared on television talk shows).

Finally, beyond sales claims and author prominence, I have also sought to generate a sample of popular advice manuals that reflects the ideological and temporal diversity evident in contemporary conservative Protestant gender and family discourse. To this end, I have sought to sample manuals written by both men and women, advancing divergent prescriptions for family life, and published at various points in time (ranging roughly from the late 1960s to the mid-1990s).

Analysis of Advice Manuals

Each of the manuals was analyzed for (1) the advice it offered pertaining to family life, (2) the rhetorical devices utilized to mediate such advice (e.g., direct injunctions, personal vignettes, narratives of families known by the author), and (3) the various rationales (i.e., scriptural, anecdotal, scientific) used to legitimate the author's recommendations. The manuals were then reanalyzed to refine the coding scheme in two significant ways. First, I reread manuals to account for themes that emerged at some point during the initial stage of analysis, thereby insuring that all manuals in the sample were read with the same set of interpretive frames in mind. Second, by reanalyzing the manuals I was able to highlight the rhetorical contradictions within individual advice manuals and the discursive shifts within multivolume bodies of work written by particular authors.

Apart from the theoretical merits of examining these manuals, the value in carefully examining the advice proffered therein is twofold. First, and most obviously, these manuals contain valuable prima facie data about the contours of conservative Protestant gender and family discourse. While no set of advice manuals could be said to capture the nuances or permutations of a discourse as complex as that found in evangelical Protestantism, the diversity of this sample allows me to move beyond offering a simple snapshot of these discursive disputes at one point in time. Instead, because I have read and carefully analyzed well over fifty of these advice manuals (the majority of which are cited directly in this study), I can trace recent historical trends and chart discursive innovations in this advice literature over the course of the last several decades.

A second advantage provided by these primary source documents concerns the theological legitimations the authors employ to justify their rhetorical claims and prescriptions for family living. Evangelical Christianity is defined largely by its commitment to biblical inerrancy. These authors spare neither ink nor paper where scriptural rationales for their family advice are concerned. Consequently, this portion of the study not only seeks to describe what leading religious conservatives believe about evangelical Christian gender and family relations, but also illuminates how they justify these convictions—that is, why they believe what they believe. And because the textual data analyzed here are rhetorical constructions intended to persuade evangelical men and women to live proper Christian lives, they provide highly detailed descriptions of what these authors perceive to be God's plan for family living. While it can hardly be said that mine is the definitive interpretation of these texts, I have taken great pains to represent as fairly as possible the positions of these various commentators.

Appendix B: Participant-Observation and In-Depth Interview Methodologies

The data for this portion of the study were collected at a prominent evangelical church in Texas from December 1995 to March 1997. I refer pseudonymously to this church as the Parkview Evangelical Free Church (or Parkview, for short). Parkview is a fast-growing, fairly new church in a large Texas city. The membership rolls of this church registered about five hundred persons during the early portion of my fieldwork, with Sunday service attendance estimated at about eight hundred. However, since that time, increases in membership and in attendance at Sunday services have been substantial enough to prompt both the addition of another set of Sunday services and the search for a new building to accommodate the larger numbers. During 1997 alone, for example, the church added 150 new members (a 30 percent increase over the 1995 membership rolls). Sunday services during the latter part of this same year typically attracted fifteen hundred churchgoers in total (a 90 percent increase over 1995 estimates).

Participant-Observation and In-Depth
Interview Procedures: Data Collection and Analyses

Over the course of approximately two years, I observed and interacted with leaders and members of this church in a variety of forums (weekly services, Sunday school classes, and Bible studies, as well as informal conversations and in-depth interviews typically conducted at the homes of consenting couples from the congregation). The majority of my observational data from the church were collected in 1996, though I have remained in contact with some individuals in this congregation into 1999. The preponderance of my forty-six in-depth interviews with twenty-three married couples were conducted in the latter part of 1996, after I became familiar with the organizational dynamics of this church and cultivated a rapport with its leaders and members. My participant-observation research was conducted at the Parkview Evangelical Free Church, and not in the homes of this congregation's families. Interviews were typically conducted in couples' homes. On one occasion I attended a women's Bible study that took place in the home of a prominent member. I gathered field data from the men's ministry program headed by Parkview's pastor through my attendance at fourteen of these noontime men's gatherings. The analyses presented in this study could have been complemented by more extensive data-gathering in the homes of these various evangelical families (see, e.g., Stacey 1990). However, as a sole investigator with limited funds, labor power, and time to conduct this study, I opted not to do so.

I interviewed husbands and wives separately, with the typical interview lasting about ninety minutes. The participation of interview respondents was typically solicited through my attendance at various Sunday school classes, called Adult Bible Fellowships in this church. When I was not attending services (which I did on twenty-four occasions), I could be found in one of five Adult Bible Fellowships offered for married couples at different life stages—classes for (1) engaged and newly married couples [seven observations]; (2) couples married for a few years, typically without children [eight observations]; (3) couples married for several years with preschool or grade-school–aged children [fifteen observations]; (4) married couples with teenage children [nine observations]; and (5) older married couples, typically with grown (nonresident) children [eight observations]. I also attended four sessions of Parkview's class for newcomers to the church, and five sessions of a Sunday school class for single adults. With the exception of these last two classes, the boundaries demarcating Adult Bible Fellowships from one another were somewhat porous, so that members could select an Adult Bible Fellowship as much on personal preference or friendship networks as on stage of life. In this rapidly growing church, these classes were typically well attended (generally thirty or more members could be found in attendance). Carefully and discreetly, I took handwritten fieldnotes when conducting participant-observation research at these worship services, Sunday school classes, Bible studies, and "praise and worship" singing sessions. Because Parkview audiotapes the pastor's Sunday morning sermon, I transcribed and analyzed selected sermons during the period of my research. Given the scope of this monograph (i.e., analyses of advice manuals, participant-observation, and interview data), I draw on these materials only in as much detail as space permits.

Typically, respondents volunteered to be interviewed after I had visited their Sunday school class several times. I also attempted to select interviewees at various life-course stages and with diverse family arrangements to insure some degree of diversity in my sample of respondents. All in-depth interviews were conducted using a semistructured format. Semistructured interviews provide all respondents with the opportunity to address the same set of questions but also permit probing to ascertain more detail concerning issues raised during the course of any one interview. My fieldnotes and interview transcripts were analyzed using three interpretive frameworks: (1) a theory-generated coding scheme, based on the theoretical framework articulated in chapter 1; (2) an emergent themes technique to capture other issues that surfaced apart from those highlighted by the theoretical frame; and (3) narrative analyses, including stories of marital conflict, housework dynamics, and childcare issues as articulated by pastors and spouses. My in-depth interview questionnaire is reproduced at the end of this appendix.

Interview Respondent Survey: Characteristics of Interview Sample

Each in-depth interview was accompanied by a respondent survey (not displayed here, but available on request) designed to ascertain demographic characteristics, as well as additional information on my respondents' family attitudes and household practices. Many of these survey questions about family attitudes and household practices were culled from various sociological surveys (i.e., the National Survey of Families and Households, the General Social Survey, and the Oklahoma City Survey). I use this data as contextual information. Completed interview respondent surveys were coded, entered into a data analysis program, and analyzed.

Consistent with the generally well-educated membership in this church, the forty-six husbands and wives I interviewed—all of whom are identified by pseudonyms—had attained high levels of education. Men averaged 18.09 years of education (range = 16 to 23), equivalent to a master's degree; women averaged 16.22 years of education (range = 13 to 20), the equivalent of a bachelor's degree. Although this sample of pastors and members was not randomly selected from the congregation, my ethnographic observations give me no reason to believe that their educational attainment differs markedly from that of the church membership at large. Along with such educational capital, many members of this congregation are economically privileged. Again, using my nonrandom sample of interview respondents as a guide, the typical couple reported a household income of between fifty and sixty thousand dollars annually. Nearly half of the twenty-three couples interviewed (twelve couples, based on husbands' responses) reported annual household incomes of over sixty thousand dollars. Several of the less economically well off couples I interviewed were young and included at least one member in school pursuing a professional degree.

Because I wished to study the religious bases of gender negotiation within these families, I restricted my sample of interview respondents to members whose identities as evangelical Christians were highly salient to them. All of my respondents were either members of Parkview or, if relatively new to the church, intending to become members in the very near future. The typical couple attended services every week. On average, respondents reported having been evangelical Christians for 21.57 years. Men reported praying an average of four times per day and reading the Bible four times weekly; women reported praying three times per day and reading the Bible an average of five times per week. (In actuality, these figures on prayer frequency are underestimates; many respondents chose not to try to tally the brief, informal, and private prayers in which they often engage.)

In keeping with the conservative Protestant commitment to the authority of the Bible, these respondents are clearly evangelical in theological orientation as well. All of my respondents reported holding the Bible in very high esteem. When surveyed about their scriptural convictions, all respondents either strongly agreed (85 percent) or agreed (15 percent) with the statement, "The Bible is God's word and everything happened or will happen exactly as it says." Not one respondent indicated ambivalence or disagreement with this question in the interview respondent survey. Most of my respondents were also quite inclined to agree with the statement, "The Bible is the answer to all important human problems." Among those spouses interviewed, 63 percent strongly agreed with this statement, while 28 percent agreed with it. Also, when surveyed about the relative importance of (1) the Bible; (2) family and friends; (3) the teachings of your church; and (4) your own personal judgment, these spouses on average rated the Bible as their most important decision-making resource. On a scale with 1 signaling "not very important" and 5 indicating "very important," husbands (mean = 4.78) and wives (mean = 4.96) alike indicated the overriding importance biblical directives exerted on their life decisions.

Given the otherwise homogeneous nature of this congregation and my interview sample—generally affluent, well-educated, Anglo (all but one respondent was white), and theologically conservative—I sought sampling diversity in other areas. To understand how gender is negotiated within different family contexts, I interviewed both younger and older couples, as well as both recently married spouses and older "veterans" of marriage. Therefore, age of respondents ranged from 20 to 74 (overall mean age = 36.17); in addition, my respondents had been married to their current spouse anywhere from 3.5 months to 53 years (mean length of marriage = 11.72 years). The vast majority of my respondents were first-time spouses in their current marriage; only two couples (four respondents total) reported having been in previous marriages. In each case, those prior marriages had ended in divorce. I also interviewed (1) couples with no children (nine couples total, with one expecting their first child at the time of the interview); (2) spouses with resident children of varying ages (thirteen couples); and (3) couples with grown nonresident children (two couples). Questions pertaining to children were tailored appropriately to each of these couples.

Finally, I interviewed both dual-earner and single-income couples. In the end, I spoke to twelve dual-earner couples and eleven single-income families; of the latter, all were husband-provider/wife-homemaker couples. As might be expected among such well-educated respondents, the vast majority of dual-earner couples consisted of both spouses being employed in professional, full-time occupations (husbands averaged 47 work hours per week, while employed wives averaged 41 hours of paid work weekly). Several of the dual-earner couples I interviewed had children; however, the majority of two-income families consisted of young husbands and wives who did not yet have children but hoped to at some point in the future.

In-Depth Interview Questionnaire (investigator-administered)

Religious Involvement

1. To begin, tell me a bit about your religious background. When and why did you become a Christian? [Probe, if needed:] If there was a particular event or personal experience which prompted your conversion, could you describe it for me?

2. What are the beliefs or convictions that are most important to you as a Christian?

3. Why do you attend Parkview? What attracted you to Parkview?

Christian Marriage and Family Life

4. What do you think are the most important components of a Christian marriage?

5. What does Parkview teach about a Christian man's proper roles and primary responsibilities in the family? Do you agree or disagree with these views? Explain.

6. What does Parkview teach about a Christian woman's proper role and primary responsibilities in the family? Do you agree or disagree with these views? Explain.

5b/6b. [If respondent noted differences:] Why do you think men's and women's family roles should be allocated as you have described?

7. Couples sometimes face difficulties of one kind or another during the course of their marriage. At times, these difficulties may even generate disagreements. Think of a recent disagreement you have had with your spouse. What was the disagreement about and how did you attempt to resolve it?

8. Various passages in the Bible stress the importance of submission in Christian married life.

    (a) Could you explain to me what the term submission means to you?

    (b) What role, if any, does submission play in your marital relationship?

Housework and Child Care

9. [For couples with no children, pose as "If you had a son/daughter . . ."]
    What do you think are the most important lessons that can be communicated to your son about becoming a man?
    What do you think are the most important lessons that can be communicated to your daughter about becoming a woman?

10. In most homes, there are a number of household tasks that need to be

completed by someone in the family on a fairly regular basis. Consider those tasks that are your primary responsibility and those for which your spouse is primarily responsible.

(a) In general, which tasks are your responsibility?

(b) Which chores are your spouse's responsibility?

(c) Is there any particular reason that household chores have been divided this way?

(d) How do you feel about the division of chores in your household? Do you think it's fair?

(e) Does the division of household chores ever produce conflict in your marriage? If so, describe. (E.g. What chores? Under what conditions?)

11. [If no children presently living in household, pose as "*If* or *when* you had children . . ."] In families with children, there are numerous child-related activities and parental responsibilities which also arise.

(a1) What do you perceive to be your childcare or parental responsibilities?

(a2) What are your spouse's childcare or parental responsibilities?

(a3) Is there any particular reason that the childcare or parental responsibilities have been divided this way?

(b1) How do you feel about the amount of time that you get to spend with your child(ren)? Would you like it to be more, less, or the same as it is?

(b2) How do you feel about the amount of time that your spouse spends with the child(ren)? Would you like him/her to spend more, less, or about the same amount of time with the child(ren)?

(c) Does the amount of time either of you spend with the child(ren), or the type of childcare responsibilities each of you have, ever produce disagreements between the two of you? If so, explain.

(E.g., What are they about? Do they get resolved? How?)

Family Life Improvement

12. What do you think could be done to improve your family life? What could be done to improve the lives of families in America generally?

Notes

One Evangelical Family Life and America's Culture Wars

1. I use the terms "evangelical" and "conservative Protestant" interchangeably for stylistic convenience, aware that there are scholars who draw distinctions between these two terms. I sometimes use the term "Christian" to refer to the husbands, wives, and families depicted in this study. Although this last term is sociologically inaccurate, it is the label my subjects most often use to identify themselves.

2. The terms "evangelical Protestants" and "evangelicals" account for forty-eight separate references in the index of *Culture Wars*, while "fundamentalism" and "fundamentalist Protestantism" are referenced twenty-two times. Moreover, prominent conservative Protestant organizations (e.g., Focus on the Family, Concerned Women for America) as well as leading evangelicals (e.g., James Dobson, Jerry Falwell, Tim LaHaye) figure prominently in Hunter's analysis of religious conservatives who advocate traditional family values.

3. The power of such pejorative depictions of fundamentalism is underscored by the domain expansion of this term within periodicals positioned on the left of the political spectrum such as *The Nation*. Indeed, the term "fundamentalism" is now used quite broadly to impugn "ideologically oriented" political programs that have no relationship whatsoever to religious conservatism (Schwenninger 1998; see also *The Nation* 1998).

4. My understanding of discourse as a series of culturally embedded conversations is generally consistent with poststructuralist theory (Fairclough 1995; Macdonell 1986; Terdiman 1985), such as that evidenced in the work of Foucault (1972, 1978. See also Frank 1992; McNay 1994). However, I am receptive to the work of critical scholars—feminists among them—who have sought to redress the way theories of discourse reduce virtually all forms of social interaction and subjective experience to linguistic determination (see Connell 1995; de Lauretis 1986,

1987; Eagleton 1996; Flax 1992; Henriques et al. 1984; Hollway 1984, 1995; Lupton and Barclay 1997; Mahoney and Yngvesson 1992). As should be clear from a careful reading of parts 2 and 3 of this volume, I believe that both discursive and extradiscursive (Hollway 1995) elements of social experience merit scholarly investigation.

Two   Evangelical Families in Historical Perspective

1. Various scholars have called attention to the individualistic theological convictions (when compared with Anglicanism), the emotional worship styles, and the populist base of support for early American evangelicalism; however, an emphasis on individualism within these early religious communities was nevertheless overlaid by collectivist orientations (see, e.g., Boles 1972; Flynt 1981; McLoughlin 1968). A close reading of evangelical statements of faith (Soper 1994: 39) reveals that individualistic sensibilities stand alongside collectivist sentiments. As evidenced here, these competing orientations are still manifested in evangelical gender discourse, conservative Protestant organizations, and the everyday family practices of Christian spouses.
2. Hunter (1983: 24) argues that evangelicalism had become the "unquestionably predominant" form of American Protestantism by the middle of the nineteenth century. The hegemony of mid-nineteenth-century evangelicalism altered not only this religion's commitment to egalitarian gender relations, but its view of slavery as well. Wayne Flynt (1981: 24–25) traces such ideological transformations to the gentrification and growing affluence of evangelicals by the mid–nineteenth century.
3. Not all reform-minded evangelicals supported women's entrance into the public sphere during the late nineteenth and the early twentieth century. Many Social Gospel evangelicals generally embraced a progressivist political agenda even while they evinced strong support for the Victorian separate spheres ideology (Fishburn 1981).

Three   Discourses of Masculinity, Femininity, and Sexuality

1. Following other gender scholars, I use the term "essentialist" as a shorthand reference to describe the convictions of groups or individuals who subscribe to the belief that gender differences are categorical, innate, and resistant to change. The term itself is derived from the belief that there are distinctive masculine and feminine "essences" that strongly impact men's and women's ostensibly divergent modes of thinking, feeling, and acting. The essentialist evangelical commentators examined here use both theological and nontheological arguments (e.g., references to biological science or psychology) to justify their position. In the end, however, evangelical essentialists give primary weight to the notion that God intentionally ordained gender difference for the good of men, women, and families. The historical emergence of essentialism and the various rationales enlisted to support it are treated more thoroughly in the work of Sandra Bem (1994) than I am able to review here.

2. Such recommendations for wifely sexual restraint notwithstanding, at least one prominent author committed to essentialist ideals expresses anxiety that wives might act too sexually passive. Concerned that inhibited women may be unable to gratify their husbands' sexual desires, Linda Dillow (1986) admonishes her female readers to "be aggressive" sexually, and provides a whole chapter of innovative techniques for wives to apply in the bedroom (as well as in many other rooms of the married couple's house!). Dillow (1986: 194–195) asserts that "most husbands long for their wives to be more aggressive. A husband wants to know his wife longs for him just as he longs for her. . . . Ask God to show you some clever things you can do to make your marriage a love affair. Be willing, however, to put aside any inhibitions."

Five   Separate Spheres or Domestic Task Sharing?

1. More so than any of these authors, Larry Crabb points out that essential gender differences can be manifested in various types of domestic-task allocation. Such advice, however, is rife with contradiction. On the one hand, Crabb (1991: 158) argues that "the spheres of a man's and woman's responsibilities, though overlapping considerably, are in some measure distinguishable." Overlaid upon this argument for separate spheres, however, is Crabb's antipathy for the "legalistic" enactment of "tightly defined" marital roles and domestic responsibilities (1991: 208–209). Most other authors cited here are much less ambiguous concerning these issues.

Introduction to Part III   Tandem Gender Negotiation among Evangelical Spouses

1. These same themes are articulated in articles 1, 4, 5, 6, and 8 of the Evangelical Free Church of America Statement of Faith (see Hanson 1990).

Eight   Labor of Love?

1. Dan Humphreys's views about husband-providership are not shared by all husbands I interviewed from the church, a point that is illustrated by other families featured within this same chapter. Disagreement about the church's stance toward husband-providership may hinge partly on what exactly constitutes "official" church teachings. Some respondents seem to restrict the category of church teachings to pastoral messages from the pulpit; others seem to view church teachings through a broader rubric that includes Sunday school class teachings. Overlaid upon this issue, it must be remembered that women cannot serve as pastors at Parkview. Inasmuch as the pastorship is a professional career, women are denied access to this career path at Parkview.
2. Interestingly, Heather refers to getting help with the children both in the first person singular ("I don't have help with the kids on Monday or Friday") and in the collective form ("we have help those other days").

Conclusion   Refashioning Evangelical
Families for the Twenty-First Century

1. In a similar fashion, the strictness thesis (Iannaccone 1994) that currently enjoys popularity among sociologists of religion leaves largely untheorized the ongoing process of cultural production, as well as the seminal issues of cultural diversity and conflict, within contemporary evangelicalism (see Smith 1998; see also Woodberry and Smith 1998 for insightful critiques). Conservative religions, according to this logic, impose rather stringent "costs" on their members, thereby minimizing the participation of "free riders" who would otherwise dilute the "strength" of social bonds within such churches. The findings presented in Part 2 of this study suggest that conservative Protestant strictness concerning family issues is collectively negotiated through the ever-growing genre of best-selling evangelical family advice manuals—which themselves contain many different prescriptions for domestic life, all founded in inerrant readings of the Bible. The ideological diversity found in this genre is likely one key to the growth of a *generic, panconservative Christianity* (Wagner 1990, 1997) that can be remolded to fit different congregational and domestic contexts for a heterogeneous religious subculture. Space limitations do not allow me to provide a more thoroughgoing assessment of the empirical costs and benefits associated with the strictness thesis.
2. Consequently, there is every reason to believe that the gender processes detailed in this study take on a qualitatively different character within other social contexts—for example, within working-class conservative Protestant churches and families (see Rose 1990; Stacey 1990), within African-American evangelical congregations (see Gilkes 1985), and within conservative Protestant families living outside North America (Brusco 1995). It is therefore important to remain mindful that the men and women at Parkview represent a specific type of evangelical— well-educated, economically privileged, and located squarely within the American professional class. In light of evidence that points to the growth of evangelicalism among the American middle class, my study investigates gender processes and family practices among a burgeoning subpopulation within conservative Protestantism.
3. From a psychoanalytic perspective, the "leaky balloon" characterization of the male ego could be seen as a feminized ego. Some scholars have highlighted the fact that leakiness can serve as a gendered metaphor. These researchers point to cultural imagery that stigmatizes women's leaky (i.e., menstruating, lactating) bodies as insurgent, undisciplined, and lacking containment (Grosz 1994; Lupton and Barclay 1997).

References

Acker, Joan. 1990. "Hierarchies, Jobs, Bodies: A Theory of Gendered Organizations." *Gender & Society* 4:139–158.

———. 1992a. "Gendered Institutions: From Sex Roles to Gendered Institutions." *Contemporary Sociology* 21:565–569.

———. 1992b. "Gendering Organizational Theory." In *Gendering Organizational Theory,* ed. Albert J. Mills and Peta Tancred, 248–260. London: Sage.

Ammerman, Nancy T. 1987. *Bible Believers: Fundamentalists in the Modern World.* New Brunswick, N.J.: Rutgers University Press.

———. 1997. *Congregation and Community.* New Brunswick, N.J.: Rutgers University Press.

Balswick, Jack, and June Balswick. 1995. *The Dual-Earner Marriage: The Elaborate Balancing Act.* Grand Rapids, Mich.: Fleming H. Revell.

Bartkowski, John P. 1995. "Spare the Rod . . . or Spare the Child? Divergent Perspectives on Conservative Protestant Child Discipline." *Review of Religious Research* 37: 97–116.

———. 1996. "Beyond Biblical Literalism and Inerrancy: Conservative Protestants and the Hermeneutic Interpretation of Scripture." *Sociology of Religion* 57: 259–272.

———. 1997. "Debating Patriarchy: Discursive Disputes over Spousal Authority among Evangelical Family Commentators." *Journal for the Scientific Study of Religion* 36: 393–410.

———. 1999. "Godly Masculinities Require Gender and Power." In *Standing on the Promises: The Promise Keepers and the Revival of Manhood,* ed. Dane Claussen, 121–130. Cleveland, Ohio: Pilgrim Press.

———. 2000. "Breaking Walls, Raising Fences: Masculinity, Intimacy, and Accountability among the Promise Keepers." *Sociology of Religion* 61: 33–53.

Bartkowski, John P., and Helen A. Regis. 2001. "Religious Civility, Civil Society, and

Charitable Choice: Faith-Based Poverty Relief in the Post-Welfare Era." In *Faith, Morality, and Civil Society,* ed. Dale McConkey and Peter Lawler. Lanham, Md.: Lexington.

Bartkowski, John P., and W. Bradford Wilcox. 2000. "Conservative Protestant Child Discipline: The Case of Parental Yelling." *Social Forces* 79: 265–290.

Bartkowski, John P., W. Bradford Wilcox, and Christopher G. Ellison. 2000. "Charting the Paradoxes of Evangelical Family Life: Gender and Parenting in Conservative Protestant Households." *Family Ministry* 14: 9–21.

Bartkowski, John P., and Xiaohe Xu. 2000. "Distant Patriarchs or Expressive Dads? The Discourse and Practice of Fathering in Conservative Protestant Families." *The Sociological Quarterly* 41: 465–485.

Becker, Penny Edgell. 1997. "What is Right? What is Caring? Moral Logics in Local Religious Life." In *Contemporary American Religion: An Ethnographic Reader,* ed. Penny Edgell Becker and Nancy L. Eiesland, 121–145. Walnut Creek, Calif.: AltaMira Press.

———. 1999. *Congregations in Conflict: Cultural Models of Local Religious Life.* New York: Cambridge University Press.

Bem, Sandra Lipsitz. 1994. *The Lenses of Gender: Transforming the Debate on Sexual Inequality.* New Haven, Conn.: Yale University Press.

Bendroth, Margaret L. 1984. "The Search for 'Women's Role' in American Evangelicalism, 1930–1980." In *Evangelicalism and Modern America,* ed. George Marsden, 122–134. Grand Rapids, Mich.: William B. Eerdmans Publishing.

———. 1993. *Fundamentalism and Gender: 1875 to the Present.* New Haven, Conn.: Yale University Press.

Berger, Brigitte, and Peter L. Berger. 1983. *The War over the Family: Capturing the Middle Ground.* New York: Anchor Books.

Bilezikian, Gilbert. 1985. *Beyond Sex Roles: What the Bible Says about a Woman's Place in Church and Family.* 2d ed. Grand Rapids, Mich.: Baker Books.

Blain, Jenny. 1994. "Discourses of Agency and Domestic Labor." *Journal of Family Issues* 15: 515–549.

Blanche, Giselle S., and Rae R. Newton. 1995. "Protestant Fundamentalists and Sex Role Attitudes, 1977–1993." Paper presented at the annual meetings of the American Sociological Association.

Blumberg, Rae Lesser, and Marion Tolbert Coleman. 1989. "A Theoretical Look at the Gender Balance of Power in the American Couple." *Journal of Family Issues* 10: 225–250.

Boles, John B. 1972. *The Great Revival, 1787–1805.* Lexington: University of Kentucky Press.

Boone, Kathleen C. 1989. *The Bible Tells Them So: The Discourse of Protestant Fundamentalism.* Albany, N.Y.: SUNY Press.

Brasher, Brenda. 1998. *Godly Women: Fundamentalism and Female Power.* New Brunswick, N.J.: Rutgers University Press.

Brown, Karen McCarthy. 1994. "Fundamentalism and the Control of Women." In *Fundamentalism and Gender,* ed. John Stratton Hawley, 175–201. New York: Oxford University Press.

Brusco, Elizabeth E. 1995. *The Reformation of Machismo: Evangelical Conversion and Gender in Colombia.* Austin: University of Texas Press.

Burkett, Larry. 1995. *Women Leaving the Workplace: How to Make the Transition from Work to Home.* Chicago: Moody Press.

Butler, Judith. 1990. *Gender Trouble: Feminism and Subversion of Identity.* New York: Routledge.

Chodorow, Nancy J. 1994. *Femininities, Masculinities, Sexualities.* Lexington: University Press of Kentucky.

Christenson, Larry. 1970. *The Christian Family.* Minneapolis, Minn.: Bethany House.

Cohen, Susan, and Fainsod Katzenstein. 1988. "The War over the Family is Not over the Family." In *Feminism, Children, and the New Families,* ed. Sanford M. Dornbusch and Myra H. Strober, 25–46. New York: The Guilford Press.

Cole, Edwin Louis. 1982. *Maximized Manhood.* Springdale, Pa.: Whitaker House.

Connell, R. W. 1987. *Gender and Power: Society, the Person, and Sexual Politics.* Stanford, Calif.: Stanford University Press.

———. 1990. "The State, Gender, and Sexual Politics: Theory and Appraisal." *Theory and Society* 19: 507–544.

———. 1995. *Masculinities: Knowledge, Power, and Social Change.* Cambridge, Mass.: Polity Press.

Conover, Pamela J., and Virginia Gray. 1983. *Feminism and the New Right: Conflict over the American Family.* New York: Praeger.

Cooper, Darien. 1974. *You Can Be the Wife of a Happy Husband.* Wheaton, Ill.: Victor Books.

Crabb, Larry. 1991. *Men and Women: Enjoying the Difference.* Grand Rapids, Mich.: Zondervan.

Davis, Kathy. 1995. *Reshaping the Female Body: The Dilemma of Cosmetic Surgery.* New York: Routledge.

———, ed. 1997. *Embodied Practices: Feminist Perspectives on the Body.* London: Sage.

Davis, Nancy J., and Robert V. Robinson. 1996. "Religious Orthodoxy in American Society: The Myth of a Monolithic Camp." *Journal for the Scientific Study of Religion* 35: 229–245.

DeBerg, Betty A. 1990. *Ungodly Women: Gender the First Wave of American Fundamentalism.* Minneapolis, Minn.: Fortress Press.

de Lauretis, Teresa. 1986. "Feminist Studies/Critical Studies: Issues, Terms, and Contexts." In *Feminist Studies/Critical Studies,* ed. Teresa de Lauretis, 1–19. Bloomington: Indiana University Press.

———. 1987. *Technologies of Gender.* Bloomington: Indiana University Press.

Denzin, Norman K. 1993. "Sexuality and Gender: An Interactionist/Poststructural Reading." In *Theory on Gender/Feminism on Theory,* ed. Paula England, 199–221. New York: Aldine de Gruyter.

Dillow, Linda. 1986. *Creative Counterpart.* Nashville, Tenn.: Thomas Nelson.

Dobson, James. 1975. *What Wives Wish Their Husbands Knew about Women.* Wheaton, Ill.: Tyndale House.

———. 1982. *Doctor Dobson Answers Your Questions.* Wheaton, Ill.: Tyndale House.

————. 1991. *Straight Talk: What Men Need to Know, What Women Should Understand.* Revised and expanded edition. Dallas, Tex.: Word.

Durham, Martin. 1985. "Family, Morality, and the New Right." *Parliamentary Affairs* 38: 180–191.

Eagleton, Terry. 1996. *The Illusions of Postmodernism.* Cambridge, Mass.: Blackwell.

Eisenstein, Zillah R. 1982. "The Sexual Politics of the New Right: Understanding the 'Crisis of Liberalism' for the 1980s." *Signs* 7: 567–588.

Elliot, Elizabeth. 1976. *Let Me Be a Woman.* Wheaton, Ill.: Tyndale House.

————. 1981. *The Mark of a Man.* Grand Rapids, Mich.: Fleming H. Revell.

————. 1991. "The Essence of Femininity." In *Recovering Biblical Manhood and Womanhood: A Response to Evangelical Feminism,* ed. John Piper and Wayne Grudem, 394–399. Wheaton, Ill.: Crossway.

Ellison, Christopher G., and John P. Bartkowski. 2001. "Conservative Protestantism and the Division of Household Labor among Married Couples." *Journal of Family Issues* (in press).

Epstein, Cynthia Fuchs. 1988. *Deceptive Distinctions: Sex, Gender, and the Social Order.* New Haven, Conn.: Yale University Press.

Fairclough, Norman. 1995. *Critical Discourse Analysis: The Critical Study of Language.* New York: Longman.

Faludi, Susan. 1991. *Backlash: The Undeclared War against American Women.* New York: Anchor.

Falwell, Jerry. 1980. *Listen, America!* New York: Bantam.

Farrar, Steve. 1990. *Point Man: How a Man Can Lead His Family.* Portland, Ore.: Multnomah.

Feher, Shoshanah. 1997. "Managing Strain, Contradictions, and Fluidity: Messianic Judaism and the Negotiation of a Religio-Ethnic Identity." In *Contemporary American Religion: An Ethnographic Reader,* ed. Penny Edgell Becker and Nancy L. Eiesland, 25–49. Walnut Creek, Calif.: AltaMira Press.

Fishburn, Janet Forsythe. 1981. *The Fatherhood of God and the Victorian Family: The Social Gospel in America.* Philadelphia: Fortress Press.

Flax, Jane. 1992. "Beyond Equality: Gender, Justice, and Difference." In *Beyond Equality and Difference,* ed. Gisela Bock and Susan James, 193–210. London: Routledge.

Flynt, Wayne. 1981. "One in the Spirit, Many in the Flesh: Southern Evangelicals." In *Varieties of Southern Evangelicalism,* ed. David Edwin Harrell Jr., 23–44. Macon, Ga.: Mercer University Press.

Follis, Anne Bowen. 1981. *"I'm Not a Women's Libber, But . . ." and Other Confessions of a Christian Feminist.* Nashville, Tenn.: Abingdon.

Foucault, Michel. 1972. *The Archaeology of Knowledge & The Discourse on Language.* New York: Pantheon.

————. 1978. *History of Sexuality, vol. 1: An Introduction.* New York: Pantheon.

————. 1985. *The Use of Pleasure: Vol. 2 of the History of Sexuality.* New York: Pantheon.

Fowler, Robert Booth. 1986. "The Feminist and Antifeminist Debate within Evangelical Protestantism." *Women and Politics* 5: 7–39.

Fraker, Anne T., and Larry C. Spears, eds. 1996. *Seeker and Servant: Reflections on Religious Leadership.* San Francisco: Jossey-Bass.

Frank, Manfred. 1992. "On Foucault's Concept of Discourse." In *Michel Foucault: Philosopher,* 99–116. New York: Routledge.

French, Marilyn. 1993. *The War against Women.* New York: Ballantine.

Frick, Don M., and Larry C. Spears, eds. 1996. *On Becoming a Servant-Leader: The Private Writings of Robert K. Greenleaf.* San Francisco: Jossey-Bass.

Friedman, Jean E. 1985. *The Enclosed Garden: Women and Community in the Evangelical South, 1830–1900.* Chapel Hill: University of North Carolina Press.

Gabriel, Ginger. 1993. *Being a Woman of God.* Revised and expanded edition. Nashville, Tenn.: Thomas Nelson.

Gallagher, Sally K., and Christian Smith. 1999. "Symbolic Traditionalism and Pragmatic Egalitarianism: Contemporary Evangelicals, Families, and Gender." *Gender & Society* 13: 211–233.

Gay, David A., Christopher G. Ellison, and Daniel A. Powers. 1996. "In Search of Denominational Subcultures: Religious Affiliation and 'Pro-Family' Issues Revisited." *Review of Religious Research* 38: 3–17.

Getz, Gene A. 1974. *The Measure of a Man.* Ventura, Calif.: Regal Books.

———. 1977. *The Measure of a Woman.* Ventura, Calif.: Regal Books.

Gilkes, Cheryl Townsend. 1985. " 'Together and in Harness': Women's Traditions in the Sanctified Church." *Signs* 10: 678–699.

Grasmick, Harold G., Linda P. Wilcox, and Sharon K. Bird. 1990. "The Effects of Religious Fundamentalism and Religiosity on Preference for Traditional Family Norms." *Sociological Inquiry* 60: 352–369.

Green, John C., James L. Guth, Corwin E. Smidt, and Lyman A. Kellstedt, eds. 1996. *Religion and the Culture Wars: Dispatches from the Front.* Lanham, Md.: Rowman & Littlefield.

Griffith, R. Marie. 1997. *God's Daughters: Evangelical Women and the Power of Submission.* Berkeley: University of California Press.

Groothuis, Rebecca Merrill. 1994. *Women Caught in the Conflict: The Culture War between Traditionalism and Feminism.* Grand Rapids, Mich.: Baker Books.

Grosz, Elizabeth. 1994. *Volatile Bodies: Toward a Corporeal Feminism.* Bloomington: Indiana University Press.

Gundry, Patricia. 1977. *Woman Be Free! Free to Be God's Woman.* Grand Rapids, Mich.: Zondervan.

———. 1980. *Heirs Together: Mutual Submission in Marriage.* Grand Rapids, Mich.: Zondervan.

Hanson, Calvin B. 1990. *What It Means to Be Free.* Minneapolis, Minn.: Free Church Publications.

Hardacre, Helen. 1993. "The Impact of Fundamentalisms on Women, the Family, and Interpersonal Relations." In *Fundamentalisms and Society: Science, the Family, and Education,* ed. Martin E. Marty and R. Scott Appleby, 129–150. Chicago: University of Chicago Press.

Hardesty, Nancy A. 1984. *Women Called to Witness: Evangelical Feminism in the 19th Century.* Nashville, Tenn.: Abingdon Press.

Hassey, Janette. 1986. *No Time for Silence: Evangelical Women in Public Ministry around the Turn of the Century.* Grand Rapids, Mich.: Academie Books.

Henriques, Julian, Wendy Hollway, Cathy Urwin, Couze Venn, and Valerie Walkerdine, eds. 1984. *Changing the Subject: Psychology, Social Regulation, and Subjectivity.* London: Methuen.

Hertel, Bradley R., and Michael Hughes. 1987. "Religious Affiliation, Attendance, and Support for 'Pro-Family' Issues in the U.S." *Social Forces* 65: 858–882.

Hochschild, Arlie, with Anne Machung. 1989. *The Second Shift: Working Parents and the Revolution at Home.* New York: Viking.

Hollway, Wendy. 1984. "Gender Difference and the Production of Subjectivity." In *Changing the Subject: Psychology, Social Regulation and Subjectivity,* ed. Julian Henriques, Wendy Hollway, Cathy Urwin, Couze Venn, and Valerie Walkerdine, 227–263. London: Methuen.

———. 1995. "Feminist Discourses and Women's Heterosexual Desire." In *Feminism and Discourse: Psychological Perspectives,* ed. Sue Wilkinson and Celia Kitzinger, 86–105. London: Sage.

Hunter, James Davison. 1983. *American Evangelicalism: Conservative Religion and the Quandary of Modernity.* New Brunswick, N.J.: Rutgers University Press.

———. 1987. *Evangelicals: The Coming Generation.* Chicago: University of Chicago Press.

———. 1991. *Culture Wars: The Struggle to Define America.* New York: Basic Books.

Iannaccone, Lawrence R. 1994. "Why Strict Churches are Strong." *American Journal of Sociology* 99: 1180–1211.

Ingersoll, Julie J. 1995. "Which Tradition, Which Values? 'Traditional Family Values' in American Protestant Fundamentalism." *Contention* 4: 91–103.

Juster, Susan. 1994. *Disorderly Women: Sexual Politics and Evangelicalism in Revolutionary New England.* Ithaca, N.Y.: Cornell University Press.

Klatch, Rebecca. 1988. "Coalition and Conflict among Women of the New Right." *Signs* 13: 671–694.

Kniss, Fred. 1997. *Disquiet in the Land: Cultural Conflict in Mennonite Communities.* New Brunswick, N.J.: Rutgers University Press.

Komter, Aafke. 1989. "Hidden Power in Marriage." *Gender & Society* 3: 187–216.

Kranichfeld, Marion L. 1987. "Rethinking Family Power." *Journal of Family Issues* 8: 42–56.

LaHaye, Beverly. 1976. *The Spirit-Controlled Woman.* Eugene, Ore.: Harvest House.

LaHaye, Tim. 1968. *How to Be Happy Though Married.* Wheaton, Ill.: Tyndale House.

———. 1977. *Understanding the Male Temperament.* Grand Rapids, Mich.: Fleming H. Revell.

Lakoff, George. 1996. *Moral Politics: What Conservatives Know that Liberals Don't.* Chicago: University of Chicago Press.

Lewis, Robert, and William Hendricks. 1991. *Rocking the Roles: Building a Win-Win Marriage.* Colorado Springs, Colo.: NavPress.

Lienesch, Michael. 1993. *Redeeming America: Piety and Politics in the New Christian Right.* Chapel Hill: University of North Carolina Press.

Linamen, Karen Scalf, and Linda Holland. 1993. *Working Women, Workable Lives: Creative Solutions for Managing Home and Career.* Wheaton, Ill.: Harold Shaw Publishers.

Littauer, Florence. 1994. *Wake Up Women! Submission Doesn't Mean Stupidity.* Dallas, Tex.: Word.

Littauer, Fred. 1994. *Wake Up Men! Headship Doesn't Mean Lordship.* Dallas, Tex.: Word.

Lorber, Judith. 1994. *Paradoxes of Gender.* New Haven, Conn.: Yale University Press.

Lupton, Deborah, and Lesley Barclay. 1997. *Constructing Fatherhood: Discourses and Experiences.* Thousand Oaks, Calif.: Sage.

Macdonell, Diane. 1986. *Theories of Discourse: An Introduction.* New York: Basil Blackwell.

Mahoney, Maureen A., and Barbara Yngvesson. 1992. "The Construction of Subjectivity and the Paradox of Resistance: Reintegrating Feminist Anthropology and Psychology." *Signs* 18: 44–73.

Manning, Christel. 1999. *God Gave Us the Right: Conservative Catholic, Evangelical Protestant, and Orthodox Jewish Women Grapple with Feminism.* New Brunswick, N.J.: Rutgers University Press.

Mason, Mike. 1985. *The Mystery of Marriage: As Iron Sharpens Iron.* Portland, Ore.: Multnomah.

McDannell, Colleen. 1986. *The Christian Home in Victorian America, 1840–1900.* Bloomington: Indiana University Press.

McLoughlin, William G., ed. 1968. *The American Evangelicals, 1800–1900: An Anthology.* New York: Harper & Row.

McNamara, Patrick H. 1985a. "Conservative Christian Families and Their Moral World: Some Reflections for Sociologists." *Sociological Analysis* 46: 93–99.

———. 1985b. "The New Christian Right's View of the Family and Its Social Science Critics: A Study in Differing Presuppositions." *Journal of Marriage and the Family* 47: 449–458.

McNay, Lois. 1994. *Foucault: A Critical Introduction.* New York: Continuum.

Moen, Phyllis, and Elaine Wethington. 1992. "The Concept of Family Adaptive Strategies." *Annual Review of Sociology* 18: 233–251.

Mollenkott, Virginia R. 1983. *The Divine Feminine: Biblical Imagery of God as Female.* New York: Crossroad.

The Nation. 1998. "Bombast on Baghdad." March 2.

Oliver, Gary J. 1993. *Real Men Have Feelings Too.* Chicago: Moody Press.

Orum, Anthony M., Joe R. Feagin, and Gideon Sjoberg. 1991. "Introduction: The Nature of the Case Study." In *A Case for the Case Study,* ed. Joe R. Feagin, Anthony M. Orum, and Gideon Sjoberg, 1–26. Chapel Hill: University of North Carolina Press.

Peek, Charles W., George D. Lowe, and L. Susan Williams. 1991. "Gender and God's Word: Another Look at Religious Fundamentalism and Sexism." *Social Forces* 69: 1205–1221.

Pevey, Carolyn, Christine L. Williams, and Christopher G. Ellison. 1996. "Male God Imagery and Female Submission: Lessons from a Southern Baptist Ladies' Bible Class." *Qualitative Sociology* 19: 173–193.

Piper, John, and Wayne Grudem, eds. 1991. *Recovering Biblical Manhood and Womanhood: A Response to Evangelical Feminism.* Wheaton, Ill.: Crossway.

Pocock, J.G.A. 1984. "Verbalizing a Political Act: Toward a Politics of Speech." In *Language and Politics,* ed. Michael J. Shapiro, 25–43. Oxford: Basil Blackwell.

Pride, Mary. 1985. *The Way Home: Beyond Feminism, Back to Reality.* Westchester, Ill.: Crossway Books.

Quebedeaux, Richard. 1974. *The Young Evangelicals: Revolution in Orthodoxy.* New York: Harper & Row.

Rose, Susan D. 1987. "Women Warriors: The Negotiation of Gender in a Charismatic Community." *Sociological Analysis* 48: 245–258.

———. 1990. "Gender, Education, and the New Christian Right." In *In Gods We Trust,* ed. Thomas Robbins and Dick Anthony, 99–117. New Brunswick, N.J.: Transaction.

Sandel, Michael J. 1996. *Democracy's Discontent: America in Search of a Public Philosophy.* Cambridge, Mass.: Belknap Press of Harvard University Press.

Scanzoni, John. 1983. *Shaping Tomorrow's Family: Theory and Policy for the 21st Century.* Beverly Hills, Calif.: Sage.

Scanzoni, John, and William Marsiglio. 1993. "New Action Theory and Contemporary Families." *Journal of Family Issues* 14: 105–132.

Scanzoni, Letha Dawson, and Nancy A. Hardesty. 1992. *All We're Meant to Be: Biblical Feminism for Today,* 3d ed., revised. Grand Rapids, Mich.: William B. Eerdmans Publishing Company.

Schwenninger, Sherle R. 1998. "Clinton's World Order." *The Nation,* February 16.

Siddons, Philip. 1980. *Speaking Out for Women—A Biblical View.* Valley Forge, Pa.: Judson Press.

Smalley, Gary. 1988a. *If Only He Knew: Understanding Your Wife.* Grand Rapids, Mich.: Zondervan.

———. 1988b. *For Better or For Best: Understanding Your Husband.* Grand Rapids, Mich.: Zondervan.

———. 1994. "Five Secrets of a Happy Marriage." In *Seven Promises of a Promise Keeper,* 105–113. Colorado Springs, Colo.: Focus on the Family.

Smith, Christian. 1998. *American Evangelicalism: Embattled and Thriving.* Chicago: University of Chicago Press.

———. 2000. *Christian America? What Evangelicals Really Want.* Berkeley: University of California Press.

Soper, J. Christopher. 1994. *Evangelical Christianity in the United States and Great Britain: Religious Beliefs, Political Choices.* London: Macmillan.

Stacey, Judith. 1990. *Brave New Families.* New York: Basic Books.

Stacey, Judith, and Susan E. Gerard. 1990. "'We Are Not Doormats': The Influence of Feminism on Contemporary Evangelicals in the United States." In *Uncertain Terms: Negotiating Gender in American Culture,* ed. Faye Ginsberg and Anna L. Tsing, 98–117. Boston: Beacon Press.

Stocks, Janet. 1997. "To Stay or to Leave? Organizational Legitimacy in the Struggle for Change among Evangelical Feminists." In *Contemporary American Religion: An*

Ethnographic Reader, ed. Penny Edgell Becker and Nancy L. Eiesland, 99–119. Walnut Creek, Calif.: AltaMira Press.

Swindoll, Chuck. 1991. *The Strong Family.* Portland, Ore.: Multnomah.

Terdiman, Richard. 1985. *Discourse/Counter-Discourse: The Theory and Practice of Symbolic Resistance in Nineteenth-Century France.* Ithaca, N.Y.: Cornell University Press.

Thorne, Barrie, and Marilyn Yalom, eds. 1982. *Rethinking the Family: Some Feminist Questions.* New York: Longman.

Van Leeuwen, Mary Stewart. 1990. *Gender and Grace: Love, Work, Parenting in a Changing World.* Downers Grove, Ill.: InterVarsity.

Wagner, E. Glenn, with Dietrich Gruen. 1994. *Strategies for a Successful Marriage: A Study Guide for Men.* Colorado Springs, Colo.: NavPress.

Wagner, Melinda Bollar. 1990. *God's Schools: Choice and Compromise in American Society.* New Brunswick, N.J.: Rutgers University Press.

———. 1997. "Generic Conservative Christianity: The Demise of Denominationalism in Christian Schools." *Journal for the Scientific Study of Religion* 36: 13–24.

Weber, Max. 1954a. "The Social Psychology of the World Religions." In *From Max Weber: Essays in Sociology,* ed. H. H. Gerth and C. Wright Mills, 267–301. New York: Oxford University Press.

———. 1954b. "Class, Status, Party." In *From Max Weber: Essays in Sociology,* ed. H. H. Gerth and C. Wright Mills, 180–195. New York: Oxford University Press.

Weber, Stu. 1993. *Tender Warrior: God's Intention for a Man.* Portland, Ore.: Multnomah.

West, Candace, and Sarah Fenstermaker. 1993. "Power, Inequality, and the Accomplishment of Gender: An Ethnomethodological View." In *Theory on Gender/ Feminism on Theory,* ed. Paula England, 151–174. New York: Aldine de Gruyter.

———. 1995. "Doing Difference." *Gender & Society* 9: 8–37.

West, Candace, and Don H. Zimmerman. 1987. "Doing Gender." *Gender & Society* 1: 125–151.

Wilcox, Clyde. 1987. "Religious Attitudes and Anti-Feminism: An Analysis of the Ohio Moral Majority." *Women and Politics* 7: 59–77.

———. 1989. "Feminism and Anti-Feminism among Evangelical Women." *The Western Political Quarterly* 42: 147–160.

Wilcox, Clyde, and Ted G. Jelen. 1991. "The Effects of Employment and Religion on Women's Feminist Attitudes." *The International Journal for the Psychology of Religion* 1: 161–171.

Wilcox, W. Bradford, and John P. Bartkowski. 1999. "The Evangelical Family Paradox: Conservative Rhetoric, Progressive Practice." *The Responsive Community* 9: 34–39.

Williams, Christine L. 1995. *Still a Man's World: Men Who Do "Women's Work."* Berkeley: University of California Press.

Williams, Patricia J. 1997. "Fate and Fundamentalism." *The Nation,* December 1.

Williams, Rhys H., ed. 1997. *Culture Wars in American Politics: Critical Reviews of a Popular Myth.* New York: Aldine de Gruyter.

Woodberry, Robert D., and Christian S. Smith. 1998. "Fundamentalism et al.: Conservative Protestants in America." *Annual Review of Sociology* 24:25–56.

Index

About the Author

John P. Bartkowski is an associate professor of sociology at Mississippi State University. His research examines the contribution of religious communities to cultural debates about family life and civil society.